04/

Muswell Press

Much More of this, Old Boy... ? Scenes from A Reporter's Life

Peter Paterson

Raised in an orphanage from the age of four to fourteen, Peter Paterson joined a small London weekly newspaper in 1948 at a salary of £1.25 a week before finding himself, entirely due to an ability to write shorthand, spending his national service on Field Marshal Montgomery's staff in London and Paris. Over nearly sixty years he has written for a wide range of papers and magazines, including the *Daily* and *Sunday Telegraph*, the *Spectator* and the *New Statesman*, as well as making documentaries for BBC Radio Four's World Tonight programme and presenting TV's What the Papers Say. His final twenty years in journalism were misspent as TV critic of the *Daily Mail*.

Much More of this Old Boy
Scenes from a Reporter's Life

Text Copyright Peter Paterson 2011
© Muswell Press Ltd 2011

First published in Great Britain February 2011
ISBN 978-0-9565575-3-7

A CIP record of this book is available from The British Library.

Book design by THIS IS Studio
Cover image: Nicholas Garland, *A Fool Who Guesses Right*
© 2011 Drawings by Nicholas Garland
Printed and bound by JF Print Ltd, Sparkford, Somerset

Muswell Press Ltd
www.muswell-press.co.uk

To all the reporters I have worked with,
friend and foe alike.

l to r: Ian Waller, Nicholas Garland, Richard Bennett, John Thompson

Much More of this, Old Boy... ?
Scenes from A Reporter's Life

SITTING on a gravestone in Highgate Cemetery, north London, one bright summer morning in 1955, I was awaiting the arrival of a Soviet admiral who was due to place a wreath on the grave of Karl Marx.

It was one of those brief moments of total ecstasy when everything appears to be going so well in life that one is subsumed by a feeling of extreme, almost ethereal, happiness.

As I sat there, disrespectfully smoking a cigarette on the resting place of some north London burgher, I was reflecting on my immense good fortune just ten years after leaving the orphanage where I had been brought up from the age of four, and with no influential connections or university degree, to find myself wandering freely around London and further afield, dependent only on a puppy dog enthusiasm and an ability to write shorthand, in a job that made me unassailably happy – and, it must be said, quite insufferably smug.

My farewell from Spurgeon's Orphan Homes, once I achieved the longed-for leaving age of fourteen, involved a meeting with Doctor Green, the superintendent, resplendent in mortarboard and gown, presenting me with a new suit of clothes, ten shillings, and a Bible. It was a bemusing little ceremony involving just the two of us, Dr Green determined to ensure that I went out into the world as a missionary for the Christian ethics he represented and I had been taught while I, eager to get away, scarcely listened to his well-meaning homily.

The suit, a brown single-breasted pinstripe, the ten bob, and even the Bible, alas, have all disappeared, the first quickly outgrown, the second spent in a flash, and the scriptures a casualty of one of several libraries I have built up and then lost in the course of a peripatetic life.

Along with these parting gifts I was told that I must be good, always observing the school motto, Sequimini Optima - Latin, not a subject on the orphanage's syllabus, for Follow the Best - and to bring pride on the institution that had for so long cared for me. Caring, of course, is a word of various subtleties, in this instance describing a system that practised such Victorian principles as never sparing the rod nor tangibly demonstrating much that could be interpreted as affection for its young charges. Hugs and good-night kisses were not allowed for by the system.

In the years that followed I came particularly to resent the school motto, which seemingly consigned those of us reared under its rubric to a role as subordinates, rather than – as I would romantically have preferred - leaders: put on the rack, however, I'd have to admit that this is more or less how, in my chosen trade, things turned out for me. I cannot claim to have risen right to the top, though I did for a while achieve the rank of assistant editor of the *New Statesman* magazine, with full editorial responsibility only when both the editor and deputy editor were away on holiday, or sick at the same time - i.e. rarely. And for one insanely happy month in the 1970s I edited a temporary international newspaper set up by the International Red

Cross on behalf of an assortment of non-governmental organisations lobbying a United Nations conference on trade and development in Nairobi. Unfortunately, most of my large volunteer staff succumbed to the lure of Kenya's safari parks and deserted their posts, leaving a tiny nucleus of three Britons and a Sri Lankan to get on with it. The high point for me was the arrival at the conference of a minister in the Soviet government: WHAT IS THIS MAN DOING HERE? was the headline we ran – for communist internationalism was not noted for strings-free aid to developing countries - causing the most tremendous rumpus among the delegates and the NGOs.

To picture the grand naval personage for whom I'd been hanging about in Highgate, when he finally arrived at Marx's tomb half an hour late, along with a substantial entourage from the Russian embassy, imagine the squat, rectangular and scowling figure of John Prescott, deputy prime minister of Britain half a century later, attired in full military uniform, his ample prow covered in medals. As for the regime the admiral represented, I'd already expunged the attractions of communism from my system, though I would have Marxist friends of various hues right up to, and beyond, the point when the Berlin Wall fell in 1989.

An additional reason for my light-heartedness was that I knew the admiral would rate no more than a dutiful paragraph or two telephoned over to the office of the national news agency that employed me as a reporter.

I had a wife and baby son at home, a three-bedroom suburban semi carrying a mortgage of £1,750, and a 1934 Austin Twelve with wire wheels, a luggage grid, and enough room in the back to hold a dance, all maintained on an income of £14 a week – plus the reportorial perk of (on a news agency, extremely modest) expenses.

Marriage, which I have appreciated sufficiently to sample three times since, provided comfort and security and an escape from a life lived in digs. Not that I saw a great deal of my newly-created family, for ambition being the most selfish of spurs, I welcomed every chance of an 'out of town' assignment, and my normal working hours often stretched from early morning to late at night. Sometimes they encompassed night shifts – I was at the office when my first child was born in the middle of the night, something, incidentally, that nobody thought the slightest bit odd in the 1950s when fathers, mercifully, were neither expected nor welcomed in the delivery room whatever the hour.

It's conceivable that my good luck in falling so easily into a calling that required no entrance exams and offered companionship, variety, and enormous fun, also had the effect of infantilising its practitioners, seduced by the feeling that life was not a doleful or serious business, but a constant lark. I certainly cannot remember, until I became a TV critic, among the loneliest of journalistic tasks, when it was not fun.

But the greatest and most long-lasting satisfaction I felt during my learner-driver years as a journalist lay in the close-up view I had of a truly golden age of British politics, a period I was privileged to witness so closely that I felt part of it, which in a sense I was, albeit an insignificant one. This was a time when fine oratory was still a requirement of politicians, when the differences between the parties seemed clear-cut and deep-seated – witnessing the debates on the abolition of the death penalty and the Suez crisis was enthralling - and more than 80% of the voters routinely went to the polls to elect a government. A contrast with today's idea of civic duty, which appears largely to consist of paying premium rates to cast votes over the telephone to choose between contestants in TV reality shows. We have turned our backs on the political class in disgust over their greed and apparent irrelevance, but in the unjustly scorned 1950s, even the young regarded politics as a thrilling and entirely free activity: today it bores most of them to death.

When I first crept on to the scene as a young, part-time parliamentary reporter, Winston Churchill had already made his 1951 comeback as prime minister following his landslide defeat in 1945. His post war downfall had been regarded at the time with astonishment, particularly by foreigners, who failed to factor in to the electorate's perceived act of ingratitude towards the great war leader the drag anchor effect of the social and economic policies the Tories had pursued during the pre-war years.

In line with the Conservative resurgence was the spectacle of an exhausted Labour Party, straight from its five-year transformation of Britain into a welfare state after 1945, falling into faction-fighting and a querulous state of unelectability that would leave them in the political wilderness for thirteen frustrating years.

I watched Churchill from the House of Commons press gallery, on the hustings, and one snowy night in his Woodford constituency when his son, Randolph, was so drunk he toppled off the edge of the platform from where his father was reaching the peroration of his address to his constituents: he calmly ignored the kerfuffle going on a couple of yards to his right as Randolph, cursing loudly, clambered back on to the platform.

My job for the news agency also meant reporting the courts at every level, including coroners' courts, and murder trials at provincial assizes and the Old Bailey. Attending the courts and the Commons made me conscious that I was part of a tradition stretching back to the note-taking clerk who reported the proceedings of the 'bloody assize' trials conducted by Judge Jeffreys in the reign of James II and Charles Dickens reporting parliament at a time when the right to reveal the day-to-day proceedings of the House to the voters had been won only a few decades earlier.

My employers, the *Exchange Telegraph*, were in competition with the much larger *Press Association* as well as the reporters of the three London evening newspapers, the *Star*, the News and the Standard, so my duties were sometimes akin to running in a bizarre type of relay race. I would write notes for anything between ten minutes and half an hour, before a colleague would take over, whereupon I would cede my place in the press box in court or my perch in the gallery of the Commons to him (always a him at that time) to phone over an account of my part of the story to the office. For trials or sensational inquests we employed a man called Charlie who would rent a telephone in a pub near the court or reserve a public telephone by the simple expedient of pocketing a key piece of the mechanism to prevent anyone else using it. On taking possession of our now-private phone we would immediately be put through to a copytaker at the agency operating a typewriter at greater speeds than can be achieved on today's computer keyboards.

It was in a phone box in the Commons' press gallery that I heard for the first time the weary cry emitted by a long succession of copytakers throughout my years as a reporter, addressed, I soon realised, not just to me but to everyone, regardless of rank and experience: one marvellous thing to be said for journalism is that, whatever your background, it is in almost every way egalitarian, summed up in the phrase that a reporter is only as good as his last story. I remember discussing the habitually discouraging voices of copytakers with James Cameron, the greatest foreign correspondent of his day, on how his own eminence failed to earn him immunity from this treatment, never mind how newsworthy the story he was dictating or wherever in the world he might be phoning from. After he, I, or any other reporter, had read over a few paragraphs, any slight pause in the narrative would invariably be met by a long sigh from the typist followed by the refrain, 'Much more of this, old boy?'

Over the course of decades of on-the-road reporting, until the arrival of laptops, mobiles and e-mail consigned copytakers to the fate of postillions and apothecaries, this agonised groan emitted by the bored, possibly even envious functionary sitting at his typewriter with headphones clamped to his ears and listening to an excited reporter dictating his story, never failed momentarily to lower one's own spirits. (Curiously, the call centres now employed by newspapers to handle the small amount of dictation traffic generated by reporters have not, I'm told, inherited the cry of the old copytakers.)

I soon found that routinely rubbing shoulders with the great and the good does not elevate reporters to their ranks, give or take the odd case of the glamorous girl reporter who subsequently marries the film star she was sent to interview. Most of the rich and the famous who exchange a few words with a journalist, or submit to a lengthy interview, haven't the least idea who they are when they meet again. An example was offered by the 16th Duke of Norfolk, hereditary Earl Marshal and organiser of Elizabeth II's Coronation in 1953. A veteran *Daily Express* reporter told me how he and his colleagues had worked surprisingly harmoniously with the famously aloof Duke during daily briefings on arrangements for the event, feeling that they were on quite matey terms by the time, to Norfolk's credit, it all passed off flawlessly. But when he greeted the aristocrat on the racecourse some months after the Coronation, the Duke looked at him with extreme distaste, muttering, 'Thank God, I don't have to talk to you people any more!'

Journalism, gradually, brought me an education, though once quite early on, feeling slightly left out in a discussion with colleagues and rivals boasting of their university careers, I feebly interjected that I had attended the university of life: Lew Gardner, an Oxbridge graduate who had moved from the communist *Daily Worker* to the right-wing *Sunday Express*, which in another age would have been Genghis Khan's favourite reading, looked at me pityingly and observed, 'Failed your degree, I presume?' I was not offended, simply wondering how come all of us were doing more or less the same job, whatever our educational background.

I would not contest that some of the circumstances of my childhood in Spurgeon's were uncomfortable, even shocking in the light of today's official attitudes towards childcare, but I have no intention of producing a 'misery memoir', but a report on how, in my recollection, things were.

Had I not been sent to Spurgeon's Orphan Home the entire course of my life would have been very different, and I would probably have found myself happy enough earning a living as a bus driver in rural Wales, as a taxi driver in London, or as a long-serving clerk, possibly promoted in due time to departmental under-manager status in some large company. So I have to confess that an element of shame and resentment towards the institution that raised me remained with me for many years, feelings I now realise to have been foolish, ungrateful, unfair, and snobbish: in fact, whatever the shortcomings embedded in the orphanage's Victorian child-care values, some of which were still shared by much of the rest of British society in the 1930s and 1940s, I belatedly realise I have a great deal to thank my carers for, whatever my feelings at the time.

To relate how I progressed scholastically, athletically and in terms of behaviour in my ten years at Spurgeon's I have to rely almost entirely on my own memory. Beyond the first year or so after I left the orphanage I have seldom met any of my schoolmates, so while thinking of writing this memoir I wrote to Spurgeon's (Spurgeon's Orphan Homes has now disappeared, but under the name of Spurgeon's Child Care, has become a religious charitable organisation devoted to the welfare of children in many parts of the world, while fashionably shortening its name simply to Spurgeons). I explained that I was seeking school reports, photographs - 'any information you possess about me, however sensitive – there's no-one else alive who could possibly be hurt or embarrassed by the circumstances that landed me at Spurgeon's, or anything I got up to in my time there'. The response was bleak, consisting only of one piece of evidence that I had ever even attended the orphanage, let alone spent so long in their charge.

It arrived as three smudgy photostat sheets apparently taken from two different registers, most of each page understandably blotted out to exclude any entry except the one referring to me. The first recorded that I had been 'accepted' on 24th July 1935, 'admitted' on 26th August 1935, and 'dismissed' on 1st September, 1945. A column headed 'certificates' gave my birth date, 4th February 1931, but those headed 'parents marriage' and 'death of father' were left blank.

The other document was from an 'Admissions' and 'Dismissions' register, repeating the dates of my arrival and departure from Spurgeon's. Admissions, however, contained columns for 'Father's Occupation' and 'Religious Profession', both entered as a handwritten 'Not Known'. And this was the sum total of information to be derived from a decade in their care, whether because records were lost or destroyed during the war, or apart from the barebones of date of admission and dismissal, never kept. It was clear that I would have to scratch my brains to recall what it was like to live for most of one's childhood in such an institution: Quick, thy tablets, Memory!

But all this was far from my thoughts as I preened myself in the cemetery sunshine and reflected on what a lucky fellow I was. For I was embarked on an occupation that was to give me more than I ever returned, enabling me to do more or less whatever I wanted in the appreciation of wine, women and, had I been the least bit musical, perhaps song as well. This memoir explains why, and how, I was brought up in an institution for orphaned, part-orphaned and illegitimate children, and follows my adventures in the reporting trade from the tiny local newspaper I joined almost by happenstance in 1948, experiencing life on a provincial newspaper, a news agency and national dailies, to working for the so-called 'intellectual' weeklies, freelancing, and broadcasting, until my retirement as TV critic for the *Daily Mail* fifty almost sixty years later.

Given the economic woes now afflicting great newspapers that in my time seemed as safe as the Bank of England was once thought to be, the waves of redundancies brought by recession and the slump in advertising, plus the new duties and responsibilities brought by the so-called blogosphere, I believe I laid down my pen at the right time.

Chapter 2

THE journey was not a comfortable one, and the swaying motion made me throw up over my new sailor suit as I clung to the pole with one hand and my Nan's skirt with the other. It was the first time I had ridden in a clanking, wooden-seated London tram.

Out on the pavement of the Clapham Road, Stockwell, Nan mopped me down, before we walked a few yards to a set of forbidding cast-iron gates bearing the intertwined initials SO, the cipher for Spurgeon's Orphan Homes, the institution, in its several locations, that was to be my home.

Inside, after checking in at a small gatehouse, we walked down a long stone corridor, its walls painted an impenetrable dark green below and a sickly mustard-yellow above. At the end of the corridor was a small scullery-like room smelling of carbolic and occupied by a large woman in a nurse's apron. I was too fascinated by her bare, brawny arms and her hair, jet black, straight, and cropped in a pudding basin style, to take in the muttered conversation she was having with my Nan.

Finally, I heard the nurse say, 'Don't worry, Mrs Hopkins, he'll be as happy as a sand boy in no time.' I didn't know what a sand boy was, or why he should stand as a symbol for happiness, but once the phrase was out, Nan turned to go.

As the door closed and her shoes click-clacked into the distance, the sheer enormity of what was happening finally struck me. I was being left behind with this strange and frightening woman, deserted by the person I loved and trusted most in the world, with hardly anything but a peck on the cheek in the way of a goodbye. I began to wail in protest. With Nan now out of earshot, the nurse brusquely picked me up, sat me in a shallow white sink and turned on the single tap.

As the cold water cascaded over my head I was stunned into silence by the insult. So this was what happened to sand boys.

Up to this point in my life – it was 26th August, 1935 and I was six months past my fourth birthday – I'd been an indulged and happy little boy, the darling of my Nan who was delighted to have acquired a baby of her own to look after when her own daughters (Alexandrina and Wilhelmina, more familiarly, Rene and Mina) had married and left home, each now with a child of their own.

I had been gifted to Nan by her niece, my mother, a Scots girl from a large Glasgow family whose wildness had resulted in her being farmed out and semi-adopted by a manager at the city's Singer Sewing Machine factory. In 1931, Katherine Paterson found herself unmarried and pregnant, an intolerable position in those harsher and more judgemental days, and she ran away to London, where at St Mary's Hospital, Paddington, she produced me, promptly handing me over to Aunt Enid, known as Enie.

A tiny woman, Aunt Enie was married to Ernest Hopkins, a painter of shop blinds who had served in the army throughout the Great War, subsequently joining the Black and Tans, a formation of ex-soldiers recruited to suppress rebellion in Ireland, and towards whom, correctly it would seem, history has not been kind.

Ernest's appearance was dominated by a bristling Kitchener moustache, and he spent his evenings reading from his collection of cowboy stories kept high on top of a cupboard behind his armchair. In a good mood, he would take me to the pub on fine Sunday mornings and buy me a lemonade and a bag of mixed peanuts and raisins while I waited, as children were required to do in those days, outside.

At other times his mood was very different. He would go to the pub on his own, returning late, drunk and violent. The Hopkins' eldest son, Vic, a widower who had re-married, lived next door with his large family, including his son, another Peter, who was my playmate. The pair of us would hide, terrified, under the living room table while a rampaging Ernest hurled dishes about, yelled at Nan, and finally spattered his Sunday lunch against the wall. Vic would be summoned through the gap in the fence between the houses to pacify his father.

No modern memoir can be regarded as complete without the author detailing the sexual abuses he suffered in childhood. But despite my subsequent sojourn at Spurgeon's and the reputation such places have acquired as playgrounds for paedophiles, the only abuse I ever encountered, before the inevitable arrival of self-abuse as the hormones kicked in years later, came from old Ernest.

I would not regard the incident as at all traumatic, only bemusing: indeed, I only remembered it many years afterwards, quite without the efforts of a recovered memory therapist. I must have been approaching four years old and Nan had gone downstairs to make tea while I hopped into their bed as I did on Sunday mornings. On this occasion, Ernest drew my hand under the bedclothes and placed it on his male member, inviting me, 'Feel my sausage'. How and why would he be hiding a sausage under his pyjamas, I wondered? Fortunately Nan returned just at that moment, angrily berating her husband and, whether deliberately or by accident, pouring a cup of hot tea over his crotch, forcing him to leap from the bed. I have wondered since whether this incident contributed to the decision to send me away to the orphanage.

I would also act as Nan's assistant dresser when she was getting ready in the morning. Despite the slightness of her tiny figure she invariably wore a corset over her vest, and it was my task to sit behind her on the bed and fasten the tiny, round, cloth-covered buttons into the loops running the length of the garment, which was manifestly designed more for warmth than for either fashion or passion. I was not to realise it, but I was unwittingly acquiring a skill that might have stood me in good stead in later life had not corsets been rendered redundant by the time I was in any position to take advantage of such knowledge.

Our house, No. 38 Berkeley (pronounced Burkley) Road, was in Manor Park, a working-class suburb on the outer edge of the East End of London that has now, I see, become predominately Asian in character. It was only a walk from common land called Wanstead Flats, the gateway to more affluent places like Woodford, the final constituency represented by Winston Churchill in his parliamentary career. Ernest and Nan rented the redbrick terrace property, identical to every other house in the street, which led at one end to the High Road with its small shops and bustle, and the other into a maze of similar roads to our own but with less-imaginative numerical names, such as First, Second and Third Avenue.

There were three bedrooms, and downstairs a front room – rather less sacrosanct than those I would later discover in South Wales, where they were reserved for use only on special occasions – a living room, a kitchen containing a boarded-over bath against the back wall, and an outside lavatory. For me, the most exciting feature of the house was the coal cellar, accessed from outside through a circular iron manhole, and inside via a staircase off the kitchen.

When the coalman arrived with his horse-drawn flatbed cart I danced with excitement as he carried the sacks on his back into our miniscule, uncultivated, front 'garden'. He wore a strange leather hat that extended into a flap covering his back and shoulders, and as he funnelled the coal down through the manhole into the low-ceilinged cellar, clouds of dust erupted as if from an underground fire, blackening my face almost to match his as I kicked or threw any spilled lumps of coal into the hole.

Horses were a source of wonderment to me: why were they so malleable and obedient, I wondered, given their great size and strength? My Nan fobbed me off with the explanation that there was something in the eye of a horse that made it see human beings as three times the size they actually were. With this reassurance, I would feed the coalman's horse with sugar cubes on my flattened hand (though being sent out with a shovel by Nan to pick up horse droppings for our sparse back garden was less agreeable). The same went for the milkman's and the baker's horses when they arrived on their respective deliveries. They were clad in ancient sets of harness that must once have been like those worn by the police horses that occasionally trooped along our street, all shining brass and glowing leather. But the harness on these tradesmen's beasts was now as dull and unpolished as their coats as they stood patiently alongside the gutter with a feeding bag around their necks or slurping from a bucket of water while their handlers came indoors for a cup of tea.

The most puzzling to the comprehension of small children were the meter readers. They counted out pennies, sixpences and shillings emptied from the metal boxes under the stairs with tiny dials on the front, sorting the higher value coins into gleaming towers on the kitchen table before pouring them into his satchel, leaving Nan only a few of the coppers.

Sometimes, an unkempt old man would appear at our door, Ernest's brother, Uncle Bill. He had been wounded in the war and was said to have a silver plate inserted into his head. If he arrived at mid-morning, the coast would be clear, but sometimes he called nearer the time Ernest returned from work, making Nan extremely agitated, for her husband threatened to throw him out of the house if he ever encountered him there. Uncle Bill, wearing a strip of medal ribbons on his coat, played an accordion and begged on the streets, like many ex-soldiers from World War One were still doing in the 1930s. Nan would give him whatever change she had in the house and something to eat before anxiously entreating him to leave.

Ruth, a dynamic, attractive young woman – she was, I now know, a younger sister of my mother – was another caller, sometimes accompanied by friends: I wonder whether my mother was among them. Ruth would laugh and giggle, raise her skirts to reveal stocking-tops and suspenders as she danced around the kitchen, until my Nan, primly Scottish, would call her a 'hussy' and order her out. Soon after the end of the Second World War she disappeared, and her body was found years later in Epping Forest beyond the Wanstead Flats: it was concluded that, grieving over her husband, a shady businessman who had killed himself, she simply walked into the forest to die. As a teenager, I remember visiting them both at an impressively large but remarkably under-furnished house in Hampstead where she gave me one of his tailor-made suits. It was only slightly too big for me.

But when Ruth was cavorting around our table it was the time of the Great Depression with its toll of unemployment and poverty. Uncle Vic next door, with his teeming young family, would have shouting matches over money – or the lack of it – with his second wife, Ada. The rows made me unhappy, for I loved his two daughters from his first marriage, Glad and Cath, and their brother, Peter.

In the house on the other side lived the Benton family, headed by Joe, who had a secure job with the Royal Mail and kept racing pigeons in a wood-and-wire loft at the bottom of his garden. They had a baby daughter, Josie. Money circulated, I'm sure, between the three houses to meet particular crises, but I never went without my weekly pre-decimal halfpenny to spend at the sweet shop around the corner, with its wide window-ledge on which we children would sit, gazing at the jars of multi-coloured sweets on display. However distracting the more expensive temptations, we knew that a halfpenny would pay for a bag of fizzy, tongue-numbing sherbet, with a stick of liquorice to dip into the bag, and possibly a packet of cigarette 'sweets' as well.

One job given to Peter Hopkins and me was to be sent periodically to a nearby shop carrying an 'accumulator' – nothing to do with betting, but a chemical battery for our large wooden-cased wireless set. It was heavy enough to need the two of us to carry, and carefully, as it was filled with liquid we were untruthfully warned was acid, rather than distilled water. We also had a wind-up gramophone, which stood next to the aspidistra plant in the front room, but I cannot remember any of Nan's records, which were rarely played anyway.

In the accumulator shop we'd buy a 'blue dolly', a whitening agent used in the clothes boiler for the Monday morning chore of washing day. Nan would scrub the laundry on a ridged zinc board before passing it through the mangle, with we boys competing for the privilege of straining at the handle that turned the rubber rollers through which the clothes were squeezed part-dry. Then the washing would be festooned on the garden line, lifted just clear of the droppings from our Airedale terrier, Judy, who would sadly meet her end from a septic cat-bite after I had left for my new life at Spurgeon's.

Sundays were different in the 1930s, with people dressing in their best clothes (even the Hopkins family, who were not churchgoers), and sitting down together for a meat-and-two-veg dinner (nowadays known as lunch), and for tea, when visitors might be welcomed. Tea often included the cockney delicacy, winkles – pins were inserted into the tablecloth beside each plate and used to manoeuvre the tiny marine gastropods, winkling them out of their shells to eat with brown bread. And there were shrimps, not the gigantic, bright red creatures sold nowadays as prawns, but tiny, fussy, highly salted, greyish pink miniatures bought by the pint from street vendors and consumed with Heinz salad cream, still on the market today as a cheaper alternative to mayonnaise. The big teatime treat, however, was tinned peaches with Nestle's (always pronounced 'Nessles') condensed milk, also out of a tin: I still retain a nostalgic preference for canned peaches over fresh ones – at least, those not kissed by a Mediterranean sun.

On Sundays, too, nearly all the shops remained closed by law, but if anything urgent had been forgotten in our household, we boys were sent to the so-called Jews' shop in the high street – because they closed on the Jewish Sabbath, they were permitted to open on the Lord's Day.

But quite unknown to me, a storm cloud was gathering over my carefree head, even before I was old enough to enrol for the local school. I still don't know the details – I imagine there has seldom been a more secretive family than the one I was inducted into – but my guess is that Nan's devotion to me may have started to be seen as detracting from the attention she might otherwise have been devoting to her own grandchildren, Rene's Jean and Mina's Ian.

Her daughters' husbands were kind but unassertive men, so any such pressure – if it existed – would doubtless have come from their wives. Uncle Alf (Johnson), married to Rene, almost made the British wrestling team for the Amsterdam Olympics in 1928, if only, he claimed, he hadn't had to carry heavy furniture upstairs to a new flat the night before the team selection trials. Mina's husband, Uncle Fred (Rowse), worked at a metal foundry and was part-time chauffeur to his employer, Mr Spinks, who successively owned an American Packard saloon and a Jaguar SS ('the Jews' Rolls Royce' according to Uncle Fred): Fred would sometimes give us children a ride in these unimaginably glamorous vehicles, but usually any outings were in the firm's van.

Much later, I learned that Nan consulted a Rev. Hipperson, minister at the Baptist church at the end of our road over what was to be done with me. It was he who recommended that I should be placed with Spurgeon's, an orphanage founded in 1867 by Charles Haddon Spurgeon, a famous Victorian evangelical preacher closely identified with the Baptist Church. From that moment on, my fate was decided.

Following my uncomfortable baptism in the Belfast sink by Miss Barker, the nurse, on the day of my arrival at Spurgeon's, I met another boy admitted on the same day. We were bathed, our clothes were taken away and replaced by the institution's uniform of grey tweed jacket and short flannel trousers, and a fine-toothed 'bug comb' was scraped painfully across our scalps in search of fleas, before we slept top-to-tail, in a single bed.

A day later, we were taken to Birchington on the Kent coast, where what seemed to me a huge mansion housed the orphanage's infants' department: over the iron gates was the 'SO' cipher, along with the Biblical injunction, 'Feed My Lambs'. There we learned how to march in crocodile columns, attend church with amazing frequency, live together in greater harmony than existed among the older boys at Clapham, and made sure never to walk on the lines between the paving stones for fear of being eaten by a lion. This game also served as a diversion from the stares of people in the street gazing at children all marching in step in a fashion more customarily expected of soldiers.

I remain puzzled all these years later why incarceration for most of my childhood should have been the preferred choice of the family for my future. After all, two older brothers of my mother were living in or near Manor Park, both closer in blood to me than my second cousins, Nan's daughters, yet I saw hardly anything of them unless we happened to encounter them in the street, when they or their wives would stop for a brief chat with Nan. Rene and Mina, and their mother, one would think, had a good deal less moral responsibility for looking after me than my real uncles, to say nothing of my own mother, who had quite vanished from the scene.

Nan and Ernest's health may have been failing, judging by the fact that they both died only a few years later – first, Ernest, and then my Nan, who on losing him had returned to her homeland of Scotland, where, incidentally, my mother still had a multitude of siblings. Katherine's father, James Paterson, the often-absent patriarch of this family of (by my count) eight offspring, I knew as Uncle Jim, completely unaware that he was my grandfather. He was still alive in 1946 or 1947, living it was said, with a much younger woman at a hotel in Bloomsbury. According to rumour, he had an adventurous life, once fleeing the Gold Coast (now Ghana) with the remaining funds of an about-to-be bankrupt gold mine where he was manager. As a teenager I met him several times, valiantly trying to keep up with his consumption of beer through the cloud of tobacco smoke from his reeking pipe, but he had as little to say about my mother's whereabouts or the identity of my father as all the rest of them: children in those days were not permitted to ask questions, and in any case, I was too reticent to delve into their secrets.

No-one ever enlightened me over why I had to be disowned, but during the war I discovered my birth certificate. With the space for my father's name left blank and the truth of my status suddenly overwhelming me, it struck me that the stigma of illegitimacy borne by the child was heavier in those days than any disgrace visited on the parents.

Many in my position have cheered Edmund's 'God stand up for bastards' speech in King Lear:
Why bastard...when my dimensions are as well   compact, my mind as generous, and my shape as true as honest madam's issue?

But Shakespeare made Edmund a villain, thus undermining an otherwise encouraging message to bastards yet unborn. The laudable aim and purpose of Spurgeon's, I would like to think, was to ensure that in character, at least, I would not grow up to resemble Shakespeare's notorious bastard.

Chapter 3

FOR a child, life in an orphanage before and during the war meant living under two different systems, each as detached from the outside world as an enclosed religious order, which in some senses, Spurgeon's resembled. Almost everyone – teachers, matrons, cooks, nurses, and children – lived within or nearby the institution's walls, obliged either to enforce the official system or react to it.

In the name of charity, and Jesus, Spurgeon's Orphanage was religious, controlling and punitive. The hundred and eighty to two hundred boys (the numbers fluctuated) had their own set of rules and conventions, as rigid as those of the authorities.

There was an element of the convent as well as the monastery about Spurgeon's, for there were girls there, too, but they lived entirely separate lives, largely unseen by us. They were enclosed in their own duplicate facilities for living, school, and play. Even brothers who had sisters on the 'girls' side' were allowed to see them only on allotted visiting days in the company of whatever relatives they possessed.

The institution had originally been founded in makeshift premises in Stockwell in 1867 by Charles Haddon Spurgeon 'for the care of fatherless or motherless boys'. Twelve years later, when he had raised the money for a purpose-built orphanage (pre-dating the larger and more numerous homes for unwanted children created by the more famous Dr Barnardo) were girls admitted, though in fewer numbers than boys. Most of my schoolmates were Londoners, but I remember the arrival of five Basque refugees from the Spanish Civil War who spoke little English and, despite the place's Baptist affiliation, were taken on Sundays to a Roman Catholic church: they were soon moved elsewhere. There was also a black child, about seven years old, who joined us in the middle of the war and was the object of great curiosity, but he stayed little more than a fortnight before he was taken away:

I scarcely care to remember how he was forced to drink black ink, and rubbed vigorously with a white towel to see whether his colour came off.

The pre-war orphanage was constructed on the lines of a small city square, its entrance on the Clapham Road, Stockwell, with two sides containing living accommodation in terraces of three-storey terraced houses, each divided into dormitories, staff accommodation and classrooms, and linked at one end by a communal play hall for use in wet weather, an infirmary, and a dining hall, workshops and offices at the other: I'm partly imagining this because I never saw anything other than the half provided for the boys. We had a tarmac playground, with at one end a high, steeped embankment topped by an insurmountable wooden fence: presumably, the girls' playground was on the other side, though I cannot recall ever hearing them at play.

On the boys' side, a broad wire-fenced shrubbery ran along one side of the playground, and beyond it, an expanse of lawn, also embanked at one end, thus entirely shielding the girls' side from our vulgar gaze – theoretically, at any rate, since I never remember anyone saying, 'Come on, let's go and have a peep at the girls'.

The lawn was used mainly for an annual pageant (and its endless rehearsals) put on for the entertainment of the orphanage's board of governors, donors, and friends or relations of the inmates, with the children performing for them. There was no state aid – though a year or so before my time, the pageant was given royal patronage with a visit by the Duke and Duchess of York (later, King George VI and Queen Elizabeth) – Spurgeon's relying entirely on charitable giving, much of the money coming from the congregations of Baptist churches up and down the country, sometimes even from abroad.

Also for fund-raising, the orphanage trained some boys in the art of ringing hymn tunes on sets of miniature bells mounted on racks. One boy returned from such an outing, having performed at the Reverend Hipperson's Manor Park Baptist church, where a sixpence had been pressed into his hand by my Nan to pass on to me (illicitly, for we were not permitted to possess cash not held on our behalf by the staff).

I only took part once in the annual pageant, probably in 1937 or 1938, having lost out a year earlier because I had broken my right leg in the playground while riding on the shoulders of another boy. For my one pageant performance I was dressed up in a kind of black cat suit to play a 'lost minute' in a tableau on the theme of time: along with a score of other boys I marched stiffly around the embankment stage as we swung our arms and legs alternately once a second, chanting, 'All is not lost – we'll yet save time' to the tune of – if I remember rightly - Westminster Chimes. Above us an older boy on a throne, attired in a long robe and a white beard as Father Time, held a scythe against the background of a huge silver disk representing the sun. We were instructed that we were representing the multitudinous minutes lost by wasting time.

Cricket and football were never played on the lawn, only in the playground, with coats for goalposts or a block of wood with three sticks inserted into drilled holes for a wicket. When it rained, we spent our free time in the play hall where there were sets of small lockers, one for each boy. Many boys happily pursued their own hobbies, building model aeroplanes from scraps of wood, constructing cranes from pieces of Meccano arriving as cast-off gifts, or making little theatres in cardboard shoe boxes, with toffee papers creating a son et lumière effect when viewed with a torch through a hole cut in the end of the box. More boisterously, we played a game called Jimmy,

Jimmy Knacker, with one team of seven or eight boys crouching, as in a rugby scrum, against a corner wall of the play hall, while a second team vaulted as far forward on to their opponents' backs as they could get, before jumping up and down, pretending to be galloping on horseback, shouting, 'Jimmy, Jimmy Knacker, one…two…three!' for as long as it took for the pack beneath them to collapse.

There were always indoors games, sometimes cigarette cards coming from goodness knows where, or marbles, five-stones, or postage stamps, each craze dependent on raw materials from outside. These would suddenly arrive among us, presumably donated by well-wishers, like our sporting equipment – cricket pads and gloves with no protective stuffing left, bats held together by copper wire and insulating tape. We also received piles out-of-date comics – in our monastic life, we never went near a newsagents. One tends to remember the classics – Hotspur and the Wizard, in my case, but one cartoon strip in a less elevated comic has remained with me all my life. It showed Minnie Mouse picnicking with the twins and proudly handing them a slice of her home-made cake. 'No!' said the twins in unison as she proffered the plate, to which, as the adult in charge of teaching them manners, Minnie demanded, 'No what?' 'No fear!' they replied.

I also remember at Reigate, the orphanage's home during the war, an enormous number of Victorian Penny Black stamps coming into our possession, some in multiple sheets and others affixed to envelopes bearing addresses in immaculate copper-plate handwriting. Suddenly dozens of boys had their own collection of Penny Blacks, until by the process of swapping and bargaining, a few determined collectors cornered the market: goodness knows what they might be worth today.

From covetousness, I stole the stamp album owned by a bigger and more aggressive boy. When I was caught and forced to hand back the album, the beating I received put me off stamp collecting for life. I think this must have been related to the incident where I was stabbed with a knife – I still have the scar in the middle of my back where the blade fortunately skidded against my spine – but I preserved the Mafiosi spirit of omerta, an article of faith among the boys, by not reporting it. Unfortunately, when I cut the wrist, right to the bone, of another boy in some quarrel, he denounced me, and I received six of the best.

Apart from such occasional woundings, the usual childhood ailments tended to sweep simultaneously through the entire school, and measles and chickenpox must have been over and done with very early in my stay at Spurgeon's for I have no recollection (nor record) of them. What boys did tend to suffer was impetigo with its sores around the mouth treated with a staining purple ointment, ring-worm, which obliged the victims' heads to be shaved, and boils. The latter were dealt with at the infirmary, where the nurse administered kaolin paste boiled up in its tin on a gas ring, spread on a piece of lint, covered with a heat-retaining green material called pigskin, which was slapped on the pullulating, inflamed swelling, before the neck was bandaged. We had a schoolmaster called Mr Tadbury, who, confronted by the sight of a pupil with a bandage around his neck would attract his attention in class by shouting, 'You there! The boy with the towel round your neck!'

Every week, in an attempt to reduce these afflictions, we lined up to get our dose of 'white mixture', a chalky medicine with the most revolting taste: so horrible that each boy was instantly handed a Garibaldi or 'dead fly' biscuit to take the taste away. We were also given a not unpleasant substance called 'malt' which was sticky and sweet, presumably a dietary supplement.

Mealtimes at Stockwell were hazardous occasions because the two systems, the official one and the one operated by the boys, would merge. Before each meal we lined up on the playground in house order: each house had up to thirty boys aged between six and fourteen. It always struck me as exceedingly odd, particularly after I began reading books like The Fifth Form at St Dominic's and comics featuring public schools, such as Red Circle school in the Hotspur and Billy Bunter's Greyfriars, that none of the orphanage's houses bore a name. I used to wonder why they weren't called after Raleigh, Drake, Frobisher, Howe, Nelson, Wellington, Napier, Gordon, or other national heroes whose heroic deeds featured heavily in our history lessons. Instead, they were bleakly numbered, from No.6 to No.12, the missing No.1 to No.5, presumably accommodating the girls – I do not know for certain, and it's too late to find out, for the place was first flattened by German bombs and later replaced by council flats.

I was boy No.14 in House No.8 – 8(14) was stencilled on to my clothing by way of identification: at least twice a day there was a roll-call, and I would answer '14' when my name was called. Otherwise surnames only were employed by the staff, and we boys seldom used first-names except to distinguish between brothers: nicknames were the preferred form of address between ourselves. These were as cruel as you'd expect among schoolboys anywhere: boys with hair-lips were automatically called 'Monkey', the red-haired were 'Ginger', the overweight were known as 'Fatty', 'Bunter' or 'Moonshine'. While I was wearing the plaster cast on my leg and needed help in getting around, I was nicknamed 'Gaffer', presumably because, like a foreman, I issued orders rather than requests: fortunately, the name never stuck.

Once 'on parade', as the pre-mealtime outdoor assembly was known, we were under the control of a Mr Beazer, a short, peppery ex-soldier who also performed the duties of maintenance man, bustling around the place with a large handcart piled with broken chairs needing repair, or painting some corner of the premises. On parade, however, he was a sergeant-major, inspecting each boy's hands, including fingernails, and boots for cleanliness. If you failed Beazer's inspection you were sent off parade, which meant forfeiting the meal.

Once he was satisfied with our turn-out, and the grubby malefactors had been dismissed to mooch around the playground or play hall until the meal was over, the rest of us marched along the drive in front of the houses to the dining hall. We moved four abreast, stamping our right foot every fourth step. This foot-stamping routine – I believe it was a ceremonial Light Infantry parade-ground drill practised by the army in Victorian times and known as 'marking the fourth' - was so close to Beazer's heart that if the sound that echoed off the tarmac was too ragged or half-hearted he would order the whole school back before bedtime to march around the playground for an hour while he shouted army-style imprecations at us without, of course, blaspheming.

So to please him as we marched to the dining hall, those of us beyond his immediate gaze leaped into the air on the fourth pace to come down with a satisfying crash using both feet. However, this exposed us to a further hazard, for our classroom teachers and the matron in charge of each house lined the pavement at intervals. Anyone caught faking the drill, or committing the crime of talking to another boy, would be pulled from the line, often painfully by the ear. Removal at this stage also meant missing the meal.

Under the boys' own unofficial system of governance, it was incumbent on one's friends to make up for the food lost to those sent off parade. So we would pocket the thick slices of bread and thinly-spread butter or margarine (known as 'licks' or 'bread and look-for-it') for distribution to the hungry.

Nor were these the only dangers when we ate. Bullying was rife, and Sunday teatimes were the climax for arrangements made under duress by the weak to assuage the strong. This was the only meal unsupervised by the matrons, with just one teacher in charge of the dining hall, unable to be everywhere at once. The meal generally consisted of bread and fish paste or bread and jam, accompanied by a piece of fruit cake. This cake acted as currency in the game of extortion played by the bullies: to avoid being tortured or beaten the target had to promise to hand over his piece of cake to his tormentor on the following Sunday.

Failure to pay up meant plunging into a circle of more harassment which could be escaped only by hiding from cake creditors behind groups of other boys, or by staying close to members of staff when bullies were around. The best thing that could happen to those on the run for failing to surrender their cake was for squabbles to break out between the bigger boys – like the humans in the movie Jurassic Park they would be saved from destruction by the dinosaurs attacking each other.

There was a fenced-off corner of the play hall reserved for boot cleaning, with a foot-rail around the walls forming a ready-made boxing ring. When a fight erupted small boys ran around shouting, 'Slog in the boot shed!' and everyone crowded into the space behind the rail, fervently encouraging one's friend or one's enemy's enemy on to victory. If Beazer or a teacher was in the vicinity the fight was soon stopped and the participants marched off to face a higher justice, which meant four to six strokes of the cane. Otherwise, victory or defeat was acknowledged when one contestant was bleeding from the nose at a volume generally regarded as satisfactory.

The blacking supplied in the boot shed was of a brand called Day & Martin's and came not in a tin but as square blocks in grease-proof paper, a cross between liquorice and ebonite: to apply it efficiently it was necessary to spit on it and, with a piece of rag, work it up into a sufficiently gooey state to transfer to boots for polishing with a rag, and then shined with a brush.

The orphanage lifestyle was accepted, perhaps because most of us had never known, or had forgotten, any other. Our public loyalty was to the boys belonging to our own house: all others were regarded as outsiders. Affections and hatreds were equally fierce, creating an atmosphere of constant conflict.

Once the orphanage had been forced to move out from Stockwell to a safer and more permanent wartime home at Reigate in Surrey, institutional life began to change. Attempts to continue the harsh disciplinary regime that hid behind the iron gates on the Clapham Road were gradually weakened by the porous boundaries of the new location and, once properly settled in to our new home we started to make illicit forays into the town and the surrounding countryside.

In our spacious new surroundings we boys enjoyed more sporting activities, as well as fresh pursuits designed to help the war effort, such as growing vegetables and raising pigs and rabbits, all entirely novel to the majority of us who had known little but London. With a proper pitch to play on, cricket assumed more importance, with a pavilion on one boundary and the Edwardian splendour of St David's, the former fee-paying prep school the orphanage had taken over, on the other.

Now we started our cleaning duties before breakfast, continued during lunchtime, and resumed in the evening – the old Beazer parades and the ritual of stamping our right foot every fourth pace thankfully abandoned at Reigate. But what with the housekeeping chores, caring for the pigs and rabbits, and working our large vegetable allotments, we sometimes managed only by being let out of classroom lessons to work, not unlike the boys of Dotheboys Hall under the caring regime of Mr Wackford Squeers in Dickens's Nicholas Nickleby (though in the greater cause of national self-sufficiency, for the pigs were taken away and slaughtered elsewhere). We were also in unpaid demand during the summer by teachers with houses around the grounds to mow their lawns.

Curious 'outsiders' – local Reigate boys - also made incursions into the orphanage grounds, perhaps seeking to make friends with us (a possibility I only now appreciate) and were violently seen off by us, acting from a basic tribal instinct.

Bird nesting was actively encouraged – no-one thought it wrong in those days and tree-climbing was a routine part of childhood – so many of us built up impressive collections of eggs, developing the skills, according to choice, of blowing or sucking out the contents without damaging the shells, and presenting the eggs cushioned in cotton-wool in display boxes, neatly labelled, for sale or barter.

As discipline became more difficult to enforce money began to take the place of the piece of cake doled out on pre-war Sundays. If you had any coins (paper money was beyond our imagination) they might still be hidden in the knot of our ties, or even buried at a secret spot. As a way of discouraging this developing monetary economy, we were lined up by headmaster Dr Green and made to chant over and over again in unison, 'No boy owes any other boy any money!' This was a customary form of instruction by the gentle Green, who seemed to think that, like primitive tribesmen, if everyone joined in the condemnation of wicked practises, all would be bound to obey: I remember another of these occasions when he was warning against the dangers of piles, and we had to chant, 'Every boy will avoid sitting on wet wood'.

Older boys began to make forbidden unlawful expeditions beyond the orphanage, the possession of money allowing them to gain admittance to the cinema in nearby Redhill, when they would recount the plots of the films they'd seen to goggle-eyed juniors. When I became courageous enough, with other boys, to sneak out to visit the cinema one Saturday afternoon, the first film I saw was Captain Blood, starring Errol Flynn. One of my companions suffered for the rest of his schooldays, never able to live down his moment of over-excitement when a soldier was aiming his rifle at the unsuspecting hero and Mitchell leapt from his seat to shout, 'Look out, Captain Blood!'

Among my close friends, an old copy of Baden-Powell's Scouting for Boys fell into our hands, but we were hypnotised less by the injunctions to godliness, cleanliness and general good behaviour - stuff with which we were already over-familiar - than by the sections on field-craft and tracking which we first studied and then put into practice in the Dell, a small copse on one side of the orphanage grounds. Later, we would go AWOL into the outside world to hone these skills in the miles of Surrey heathland around Reigate. An attempt by the authorities to found for our improvement a troop of the Boys' Brigade, a church organisation, proved a flop when we saw that membership required us to wear pillbox caps of the kind seen on hotel bellboys in American films.

While our diet was boring, we never went hungry: nor did the staff suffer. We were well aware that the kitchen staff themselves made off with food they stowed on their bicycles when leaving work at the end of the day: history relates that food rationing encouraged widespread pilfering in wartime Britain and Spurgeon's was no exception.

It was probably the atmosphere of simmering violence that always seemed to pervade the orphanage that led to the precipitate departure of most of the matrons in the spring of 1943. Whether this was a revolt by the staff defending their right to punish, or, possibly, some alarm on the part of the institution's governors, the trustees, that stories of boys being brutalised had begun to spread beyond the boundaries of Spurgeon's, a general relaxation of the old discipline gradually followed.

Paradoxically, we had all been happier in 1940 and 1941, despite the bitterly cold winter, when the leaves of evergreen shrubs were encased in ice, icicles formed inside our dormitory windows, the entire plumbing system was constantly frozen solid, and most of the boys developed chilblains. When the Battle of Britain erupted, Reigate offered an exciting front row seat to the dogfights overhead for boys fascinated to the point of mania by the sight and sound of the sinews of war. The German night bombings that followed later on had us fleeing our beds for the shelters as the sirens sounded night after night. Sometimes we had to run with the swish of shrapnel falling around us – and in the morning, still clutching our blankets, we would pick up small pieces, most likely not from bombs but exploded anti-aircraft shells.

A lull in the air war in 1943 in our part of the country followed, and a certain tedium enveloped our lives as the location of the fighting shifted to Africa and the Far East, leaving us, now schooled in sensation, jaded and dissatisfied. As D-Day arrived in June 1944 our neighbouring Canadian army camps emptied out as their occupants joined the struggle on the beaches of Normandy. Then the Germans launched the first V.1 rockets over southern England and the war became closer and more personal again.

We were standing in the playground one morning, lined up during the break for the daily ration of half-a-pint of milk introduced by the government for every schoolchild, when, familiar as we were with the sound of all types of German bombers and fighters, we heard a strange new noise from an aircraft quite different from any we had encountered before. Suddenly, the engine cut out and a black object with stubby wings bearing German markings on its slim, tubular fuselage flew low and silently over our heads, disappeared over a hill perhaps a half a mile away, and exploded, sending up a plume of black smoke. We all cheered lustily, assuming that a new type of enemy fighter had been shot down by the RAF, though there was no sign of a Hurricane or Spitfire pursuing it. We realised soon enough that the object was our first V.1 rocket.

Over the next few months we became accustomed to hearing their rumbling moan overhead, always in daylight hours, forcing us to duck under our desks as the rocket motor cut out, presaging the missile's final glide towards its random target, before we resumed our lessons.

But the Germans, of course, had a more terrifying new weapon up their sleeves, one that did not attract the V.1's contemptuous nickname of Doodlebug. The V.2, the world's first weapon-grade ballistic missile, unlike the V.1 offered no warning of its approach.

Amid the general anxiety created in government circles, and among the population, as the number of casualties from V.2s mounted, it was decided that the orphanage must be moved away from the danger (though they were mostly falling further north, in London). For me, it was to lead to a profound change in my life.

Chapter 4

It was just another school day in Stockwell when I was called out of my class by the headmaster who, to my astonishment, told me that I had a visitor: no-one had visitors except on appointed visiting days. I walked, under his escort, along the drive to the orphanage gates, where my mother, Katherine, was held at bay as though in quarantine a yard or two outside on the Clapham Road. She greeted me with a kiss – embarrassing for a tough eight year-old unused to such displays of affection – and a brief introduction, before walking me to a waiting, bright red sports car with a leather strap across the bonnet. My mother slipped into the front passenger seat alongside the man who was driving, while I squeezed into the tiny space behind them.

We drove off at a roar, but we hadn't gone very far when we stopped outside a department store called Bon Marché in Clapham Junction. While the man waited outside in the car, my mother and I entered the store's impressive portals, where she told me that we were going shopping and that she would buy me anything my heart desired.

But I was too confused at being taken out of school and meeting a mysterious woman who said she was my mother – I was none too sure what a mother was for – to think of asking for a train set, a toy car, a bicycle, a horse, or a puppy: any thoughts of acquisition I might have had in my more dreamy moments simply withered away. My main preoccupation as we traipsed around the various department stores with her holding my hand was to wriggle free without appearing rude, excusing myself frequently to blow my nose or fidget in some other way to break her unwanted grasp.

Asked several times what I would like her to buy me, I displayed a stubborn unconcern, eventually plumping, for want of any desire to choose anything at all, for a snake belt – an elasticated two-tone belt with an S-shaped metal buckle in the form of a snake. I picked it solely to avoid having to make any selection that would show me up as greedy. The reality, however was that a belt was something I would not be allowed to keep anyway, because our trousers were held up by braces.

Apparently, my choice did not please my mother for she continued to search for another gift for me. Finally, she lighted on a black beret, removing my school cap, which I stuffed into my jacket pocket, to fit her purchase at the proper angle on my head, and inviting me to admire my new look in a mirror. I, of course, hated it, but by now she was in a hurry to get out of the shop and back to the waiting car.

I resumed my seat in the back as we drove through the streets of London. I was certain that all the people on the pavements were staring at me wearing this ludicrous beret, even if it was the little red sports car that they were actually gazing at: clearly, marching along the pavement on public roads with other Spurgeon's boys and being stared at by passers-by had not made me any less self-conscious. Unable to bear the humiliation any longer, I removed the beret and threw it under the wheels of the London bus close behind us, unnoticed by my mother or her companion. Eventually, we pulled up at a large house in a quiet tree-lined street. Once inside, I was taken into a large ground-floor room containing a polished dining table surrounded by a set of large chairs. My mother gave me some magazines to read, saying that she would return in a few minutes and disappeared elsewhere into the house with the car driver. Everything was silent except the ticking of a large clock on the marble mantelpiece, the magazines were uninteresting and she seemed to be gone for hours.

When my mother and her companion returned, there was a rush to the car outside in the street, and we drove straight back to Stockwell:

perhaps she had been given a time by which she must have me back at the orphanage. Leaving her friend in the car, she took me to Spurgeon's gates, fumbled in her handbag, and produced a tiny snapshot, kissed me, promised that she would be back soon to take me out again and drove away.

I rubbed her kiss off my face and returned to the classroom, the object of universal curiosity. Later, alone, I studied the snapshot, showing it to no-one else. It was of a woman, undoubtedly the dark-haired lady who had just taken me out, wearing a cloche hat and a light coat over a floral dress, walking along a seaside promenade. Alongside her was a man – not, I noted, the one who had taken us out in the car. I carefully tore the photograph down the middle and threw away the unknown man, hiding the image of my mother in a little green Bible my Nan had sent me.

The weeks then the months, passed with no more appearance at the gates by my mother and no letter to say when she might be coming back to see me. I tore up the remaining part of the snap, threw the pieces down the lavatory and pulled the chain: it took several pulls before the remains, stubbornly floating on the surface of the water, disappeared. I never heard from my mother again.

My upbringing at Spurgeon's did not lack the presence of a dominating woman. I had been allocated to House No.8, which was presided over by a woman we called Tilly (though never to her face). Extraordinarily, for a substitute 'mother', I never did learn her actual first name, and I have used a version of her surname here in case she has relations still living I would not wish to upset.

Tilly was the most competitive matron at Spurgeon's - or so I thought: other boys in other houses might have believed the same thing about their own overseers. To be sent off mealtime parades for failing to reach the required standards of hygiene was regarded by her as a cardinal sin, bringing utter and abject disgrace on the entire juvenile population of No.8 and, worse, on herself. It was punishable not just by the deprivation of food, which applied to any boy breaking the rules, but additional particularised, humiliating, and disagreeable penalties.

These might involve spending the hours between the end of the school day and bedtime brushing one's hair with a stiff bristle brush, or cleaning boots without any polish. As our heads were virtually shaved by a visiting barber every few weeks, leaving little more than a tuft at the front and back of our pates, I dare say all this brushing could have saved us from baldness in later life.

Domestic penalties meted out by Tilly were in some ways worse than the cane. They not only included the hair and boot brushing routines mentioned above, but face slapping, punching and scratching, having our mouths washed out with soap for some verbal infelicity, or being made to stand in a cold corridor at night, bare-footed on a stone or lino floor wearing nothing but a nightshirt, while everyone else slept: all this reinforced by regular daily ridicule, mockery and sarcasm.

The greatest sufferers under her regime were bed-wetters. These unfortunates were required to rise before the rest of us responded to the 7 a.m. morning bell and proceed, still in their nightshirts, to the communal bathroom to dunk their soiled sheets. Anyone who had wet the bed but failed to wake up in time was forced to run the gauntlet of the other boys, who flicked wet towels stingingly at their bare legs and pummelled them as they ran between the beds clutching their sheets, while we chanted, 'Wet-bed! Wet-bed!' on their sorry way to the bathroom: Tilly would add her blows to ours. It seemed to work as a cure, of sorts, for bed-wetting.

One humiliating moment I recall was my Nan coming to visit me a couple of years before the war, when I was unable to go to the door of the house to greet her because I had lost one of my boots – obviously needed if I was to accompany her outside. Inviting her in, Tilly gave a running commentary as I hobbled, half shod, from one place to another in a desperate search for the missing boot while she enlarged on my awkwardness, carelessness, my inability to concentrate, and my general inadequacy. Choked with angry tears I eventually found the boot in a place where I had already once looked, certain that she had deliberately hidden it so she could mock and belittle me in front of Nan.

By contrast, the moment in Tilly's tender care I have treasured for the rest of my life, came one morning in the summer of 1939 at Stockwell. Unlike the boys in the other houses, we Number Eighters were given an extra parade, conducted by our obsessive matron, requiring us to line up on Saturday mornings (this was the day of the week dirty clothes were exchanged for clean), a shiny pair of boots on our feet, and another – our spare pair – placed on the ground in front of us. And we had to carry our underpants in our hands for inspection.

This event took place in the alleyway behind the terrace of houses, in front of open-fronted sheds where sheets, pillowcases, counterpanes and curtains were hung to dry. In an echo of the entire school's daily parades, anyone failing Tilly's more exclusive scrutiny was barred from attending the tuck shop, which was open only on Saturday mornings and where we were allowed to spend one penny of our own money, doled out by the matron and accounted for in a small accounts book she kept. This was money occasionally sent to us, handed over on visiting days by relatives, or from the one shilling each boy was presented with during our Christmas Day dinner under the will of an ex-internee of the orphanage, designated an 'old scholar'. This shilling was collected up from the table by the matrons before the coin bore a boy's fingerprint: we were not allowed to possess any money except on Saturday morning, and then, of course, only if they were in credit, for it was orphanage policy not to give pocket money.

On that particular morning in the alley, at the furthest end of the line, Eric Wright and I were awaiting our turn to be inspected. Eric came from Devon and was short, with a ruddy, round, freckled complexion, and hair as black as Day & Martin boot polish. At the far end of the parade line, our matron's eagle eye turned to examining boys' underpants, worn for a week, for signs of accidental soiling. Eric tugged at the sleeve of my jacket. 'Hey, Pete,' he said excitedly, 'Guess what? I saw Tilly's knickers on the line this morning and they had fart marks inside!' The pair of us collapsed to the ground laughing hysterically, unable to stop, the reason hidden from everyone else. We were, of course, banned from the tuck shop, but still burst into uncontrollable laughter for weeks afterwards whenever either of us reminded the other of that wonderful, unforgettable moment.

Tilly was a well set-up woman in her late thirties or early forties, I imagine (it is not easy for children to gauge accurately the age of adults), and she wore glasses (which I once triumphantly knocked off her nose in a struggle). Her hair was always set in a bun, and she was the possessor of quite shapely breasts and legs: she also wore dresses that would have been quite daring, I realised later on in life, if the space within the deep V-neckline hadn't been filled with a concealing piece of lace known, I believe, as a modesty-vest – not an item for which there is much call today.

At Stockwell before the war, where we were always running up and down the stairs of the houses, Tilly insisted that no-one must ascend behind her, and anyone descending must, on reaching the floor below, avert their gaze, presumably to avoid us staring at her legs or under her skirt. What was so curious about all this was that most of us were not yet even aware of sex, except as an unknown something that was, for unexplained reasons, dirty and reprehensible. So while we would recite jokes we'd heard about Scotsmen's kilts or old ladies with parrots stuffed down their knickers, we had no real notion of sex, except that it all had something to do with bodily functions and was disapproved of by our carers.

Discipline took many forms at Spurgeon's and was by no means confined to Tilly. It was imposed at different levels according to who was imposing it and the severity of the crime. She and the other matrons never administered the cane, so serious offences – damaging or losing property, talking in class, and fighting - were dealt with by the male teachers (in my time I recall only one female teacher, a Miss Douglas, who was so quiet I hardly noticed her existence), and for very serious matters, the headmaster or the superintendent. Boy-on-boy violence was frequent, but only in the afternoon of Christmas Day was it officially encouraged, when wrestling matches were organised among us by a junior teacher while the rest of the staff went off for their festive dinner.

Christmas was an altogether strange event. It was prepared for weeks in advance, with many school lessons taken up with rehearsing carols, making paper chains to be festooned around our dormitories and classrooms, and drawing Christmas cards in a copied design of holly, bells and robins, with seasonal greetings handwritten in gothic lettering. Things moved towards their crescendo with the staff – especially Tilly - becoming more and more bad-tempered as December 25th approached. So bad was Christmas Eve, when more screaming was directed at us and more punishments inflicted, that we called it Devil's Eve.

It is my impression that caning was administered slightly less frequently for 'social' crimes like fighting and defiance of the authorities at Stockwell before the war than it was after the orphanage went to Reigate (one old scholar has boasted that, pre-war, he was caned three times in a single day by the same teacher). Once a day was more than enough for me, although in the early days at Reigate the ratio declined, broadly, to about twice a week.

Corporal punishment was to be seen at its worst when practised by one particular teacher. He was something of a Jekyll and Hyde character, for in addition to his whackings he taught us calligraphy. Faced with the wartime shortage of paper he devised an ingenious writing contraption from framed pieces of glass painted black on one side, which we would cover in whitewash with a small sponge. On this device we engraved alphabets – he was keen that we should master gothic script - by cutting into the dried whitewash with the rubber block from a bicycle brake. Then a little water on the sponge would clean off the surface ready for re-use.

This teacher also entertained us at night in the cellars during air raids with highly dramatic readings of the novels of Charles Dickens: we would weep over the trials of Oliver Twist or exult in the good fortune of Pip in Great Expectations, inculcating in many of us a lifelong love for Dickens.

But when he turned into Hyde, he would order an offending boy to bend down, his head held in a stranglehold by a classmate, while he himself marched to the other side of the classroom from where he launched into a little run, followed by a theatrical leap as he brought the cane down from a great height on to the victim's backside.

His method, which he boasted was modelled on a punishment once meted out in the Royal Navy, no doubt succeeded in terms of shock and awe, but I can say from long and frequent experience was nowhere near as painful as routine strokes of the cane delivered by a teacher from a firmly-anchored standing position.

Whichever way it was administered, caning was not only physically uncomfortable but intended as a humiliation, the latter dealt with among the boys by adopting a stoicism which made it a matter of pride not to cry during or after receiving one's strokes: weeping not only lost the sympathy of the other boys but exposed cry-babies to jeering and bullying as well.

Running away from the orphanage was the equivalent of a capital crime. Those who absconded had to take certain precautions, somehow accumulating some money, sneaking through the front gates at Stockwell, folding their sock-tops to conceal the orange-and-blue stripes and hiding their caps bearing the school's SO cipher. Most runaways were promptly sent back, sometimes with a policeman escort: only once in a while did they find themselves welcomed home by their families, in which case we never saw them again. Before the war, those whose escape effort failed, were punished in front of the entire assembled school, receiving sixteen strokes of the cane distributed equally between their hands and bottoms: for greater effect, they had to wear gym shorts.

These were important occasions, accompanied by lurid lectures on how running away inevitably led to a life of crime, drunkenness, degradation and failure, but as counterpoint, such homilies were also tempered by an opposite and uplifting picture – tales of old scholars who never ran away, stuck to the straight and narrow and thereby did well for themselves in the outside world: surprisingly often, for Spurgeon's had no apparent nautical connections, these exemplars often turned out to have become sea captains.

Whether the multiple canings, from the one or two on the hands to the four to six strokes regularly administered for 'serious' crimes, such as theft, impudence and fighting, were recorded in a punishment book I have no idea: but I very much doubt it, given the casual frequency with which the cane was inflicted. Had such a book existed, it would be an interesting record of crimes in the war between teachers and pupils at Spurgeon's.

Caning, of course, was practised in schools of almost every kind in those days, and I do not think they had any lasting affect on me or my companions at Spurgeon's: certainly not the consequences engendered, so we're led to believe, in some public schoolboys, who thus acquire a taste for chastisement in later life, given, received, or both, in a sexual context.

Tilly's punishment regime, however, never appeared to be administered with love in a this-hurts-me-more-than-it-hurts-you kind of way, nor was it tempered by any subsequent sign of affection. She was allowed the occasional day off, but I do not recall a single occasion when she spoke of attending a play, seeing a film, going to a concert, or even hearing a sermon in the world outside, and certainly not of having a man in her life.

Whatever drove her, I believe her power must have been corrupting both to her and to us, so that when she and I finally parted, in peculiar circumstances, there were no fond farewells or happy memories (apart from what I still fondly think of as the Eric Wright Knicker Bombshell) or regrets in my heart at her going.

At Reigate, overall responsibility for discipline lay not in the hands of Mr Holt or his colleagues but with a non-teacher, Mr McLaren, whose title was Superintendent. It was McLaren who inflicted a more than usually severe caning on me and three other boys after an odd incident in Reigate in 1943. We had been taken to see a dentist in the town and, following the inspection of our teeth, were awaiting a member of the staff to escort us back to the orphanage. There was, I admit, a little horseplay going on, and someone knocked into a spindly, tall and thin item of Victorian furniture I now know to be a 'what-not', on the top of which was perched a cardboard collecting box for a charity unconnected with the one under whose aegis we were being raised. The box fell to the floor and its contents – only a few pennies, for who feels charitable at the dentist's? – spilled out. We were scrambling around to pick up the money and get it back into the box when the receptionist entered the waiting room, uttered a shriek, locked the door as she retreated, and telephoned the superintendent.

In a few minutes he arrived, completely misinterpreting the situation at a glance and marched us back to the 'Homes' as they liked to call our place of education and residence, where he straight away gave each of us eight strokes of the cane for theft. In fact, there had been no theft, but he was not interested in anything we might have to say in our defence.

Things had became particularly tense at the time, as though some unseen domestic crisis was developing – not among the boys but the staff. Then, quite suddenly, McLaren and most of the matrons, including Tilly, and all but two or three of the teachers disappeared without any announcement to us boys, and no goodbyes, sentimental or otherwise: I did not even see them go.

Within Our Gates, a quarterly publication circulated to the institution's friends and donors (though the boy who found a copy on McLaren's desk and excised the word 'Gates' in the title, replacing it with 'Prison', achieved the unusual feat, after a thrashing, of being expelled from an orphanage) printed nothing of substance on the departures of staff.

Like us, the readers for whom Within Our Gates was intended were told nothing of substance about the event or events that led to the staff exodus, but were merely assured that 'all goes well, the children are healthy and happy...the future is bright and promising', along with the statutory 'thanks to the heavenly Father for his goodness, mercy and guidance through a period of difficulty and stress'.

All that remained of Tilly after she'd gone was an opened parcel found in her room and addressed to me. It was from my Nan, who was by now dead, and it had been posted a year or so earlier in Scotland: it contained no letter, but a woollen scarf, blue on one side and grey on the other. All I could conclude was that Tilly had not given it to me because (a) the scarf was not in the correct school colours, and (b) we did not wear scarves, however cold the weather. Or, with the old adage in mind, that what the eye doesn't see the heart doesn't grieve over, she simply confiscated Nan's gift from spite and then, oddly, hoarded it.

Even as I write this, on some inexplicable level I might even have loved Tilly, just as children can love abusive parents. I'm certain, however, that the consequences for me would have been worse had it not been for two events, one preceding and one following her departure from my life. The first, which probably toughened me psychologically, was the unannounced appearance at the orphanage of my mother, and her disappearance. And the second (covered in Chapter 6) just over a year later was when I was thirtteen and the Nazis started to bombard southern England with what proved to be Hitler's last-ditch terror weapon, the V-2 rockets, I was precipitated into the warm and loving home of a Welsh coal miner, his wife, son and daughter.

Chapter 5

Apart from bullying, excessive punishments, and a necessarily tedious, if plentiful, wartime diet, there were other aspects of institutional life that had to be endured: one was the pressure exerted to make up our young minds about religion.

I experienced a start of recognition years later when, no longer a churchgoer, I read the great hell-fire sermon in James Joyce's autobiographical novel, A Portrait of the Artist as a Young Man. The shivers it sent down my spine recalled the numerous sermons I had sat through in my time at Spurgeon's, homilies that invoked the near-certainty that I would go to hell, the message ameliorated only by the assurance that repentance could save me from that awful fate.

Unaware that this was standard religious blackmail, my reaction, once I had reached the age of thinking seriously about such things, was always the same - a moment or two of genuine wobble depending on the oratorical power of the preacher urging me to save my soul, followed by an equal determination that I would prefer not to be saved at that particular moment, thank you very much.

This internal struggle was never aroused in me when I read the sermons of the founder of the orphanage, Charles Haddon Spurgeon, in a collection called Swords Into Ploughshares, which was available as approved reading in the orphanage. Spurgeon may have stirred huge congregations to fever pitch, and there is abundant evidence that he did so: he was preaching to 12,000 people at the Surrey Music Hall in London on 19 October, 1856, when some miscreants shouted 'Fire!' and his congregation stampeded, killing seven people. Spurgeon attributed the disaster to the malevolence of Satan. But on the page, the sermonic fire was missing. Another count against him was the number of photographs of him I was confronted with all over the orphanage, off-puttingly like the images of those other hairy paternalists, Karl Marx, Leon Trotsky and Sigmund Freud, whose images I would encounter in the outside world.

Nor did the general run of the many preachers I heard in childhood possess the galvanic Joycean impact. Most, like our headmaster, Dr Green, offered simple messages, uninspired and uninspiring. However, I can remember one visiting preacher who did thrill me. He was a Rev. Channon, nicknamed Herman Goering by us boys for his supposed resemblance to the commander of the German air force whose bombers were then droning over our heads every night on their way towards London. Channon had charisma and an exciting preaching style, his foot always hard down on the wages of sin pedal.

Despite his efforts, I had made my mind up that I would not be a believer when I was about ten years old and fast approaching the moment when, among the Baptists, one had to decide to accept the Lord Jesus into one's heart by undertaking the sacrament of 'adult' baptism – they did not believe, like other Christians, in baptising babies. I was always conscious from my Bible studies, too, that the Old Testament, with its violence, wrath, vengefulness and sex, had much more appeal to my schoolboy imagination than the gentle Jesus meek and mild message of the New.

So when the time came, at the age of eleven, to make my public avowal to Jesus I took a deep breath and declined, while the rest of my classmates, for whatever reasons, accepted. The day they were to be baptised arrived, and I too went along to the church in Redhill, Surrey, near the orphanage's wartime home in Reigate, but as a spectator. I wore my Sunday suit, while they were dressed in cricket whites: I sat in the gallery of the church, while they queued below me at the front by the 'table', as the altar was called, preparing to be immersed in the tiny pool that was hidden, boarded over, during regular services. As each of them in turn joined the minister, standing up to his waist in water, to be completely immersed in the name of the Lord Jesus Christ, I sat nervously in the gallery.

Mine was not a crisis of faith – a phrase I had never encountered - but a simple refusal to conform. It probably had less to do with belief or disbelief (at eleven there's usually time to change one's mind) than with discovering an issue on which I might defy authority: I suppose it was in a sense a political gesture.

I knew that I would be disappointing my teachers and matrons, particularly Mr Tadbury, for he occasionally tried to inculcate a respect for religion in us in a less hectoring way than his colleagues. A tall man with a great domed bald head, a long neck with an oversized Adam's apple emerging from a stiff collar large enough for a horse, he often recalled his army service in Mesopotamia (now Iraq) in the First World War when he refused to be deterred by his fellow soldiers throwing boots at him as he knelt by his bed in the barracks saying his prayers. Perhaps a heart-to-heart talk with Taddy might have changed my mind, but I can recall no such conversation – as opposed to lectures - ever occurring with any member of the staff. But I had always been a star pupil at our regular Bible classes, committing to heart large tracts of scripture which I was able to recite at the drop of a hat. And I could entertain my fellows by knowing where to find the words 'piss' and 'shit' in the holy scriptures. Studying the Bible also proved useful in later life for arguing with doorstep evangelists.

In a way, the lack of a response from the authorities to my defiance was quite galling, but to their credit nothing really changed as a result of my stand and I experienced no persecution on this score, not even from Tilly. I still attended Bible classes and services in the school chapel, for all these activities remained more or less compulsory, even though I had become a baptism denier (strange how that word has come into general use, as in Holocaust deniers and climate change deniers, when during and after the war it referred only to the fineness of women's nylon stockings).

The fact is that the whole ambience of my life at the orphanage had been as geared to worship as that of a monk. We prayed publicly together every morning and every night. Grace was said before and after every meal, even if, out of immediate earshot of authority, we mumbled our own version – 'We thank the Lord for what we've had/A little bit more and we would be glad...' On Sundays we attended church services morning and evening, with Sunday school in the afternoon. Sunday lunches were cold: Mr Fox, the cook, and his underlings were not permitted to work on the Sabbath. And no games or pastimes were permitted.

The blanket of pressure towards an acknowledgement of the Christian faith with which I was smothered for ten years did have some effect. I adore the beauty of the King James Bible, recognise with gratitude the debt that our literature and culture owes to Christianity, sometimes even find myself singing hymns while driving along a motorway, and found myself flirting briefly with Catholicism in my early twenties. All this, I think, makes me a cultural Christian, but a doubter all the same.

In addition to the emphasis on religion, there were features of life at Spurgeon's that echoed the existence of boys at the smartest and most expensive public schools (or the version of them I read about in comics), but without the tuck boxes and postal orders. Our school motto, Sequimini Optima (Follow the Best) was Latin, but Latin was not part of the curriculum. That is probably why our slang for flight or fight was not the public school 'cave!' but the cockney 'Skid!' Another ritual we shared with our betters was chapel on Sunday mornings when we sang the same immemorial hymns, led by Dr Green in his academic gown and mortarboard, and on certain high days warbled our school song – his own composition - the words of which I still remember:

Sequimini Optima, Sequimini Optima,
This is our motto and this is our aim,
We'll always try to play the game
And seek to win an honoured name,
Not resting on our founder's fame
But trusting Him who long since came
To be exemplar, guide and friend
Through youth and manhood to the end.
Sequimini Optima, Sequimini Optima.

Only in school did we escape the prayers and religious exhortations, perhaps because we were classified for educational purposes (and presumably inspected from time to time, though I saw no sign of it) by the London County Council as a state elementary school, the lowest pre-1945 order of education from which only a very few escaped from Spurgeon's to the next rung up, the central school, or higher still, the grammar. I never in my day heard of a Spurgeon's boy going to university, and a scrutiny of Within Our Gates between 1939 and 1953 compiled by Bill Mager, a contemporary of mine at school, contained not one report of such an event. Nor was 'uni' ever held up as an ambition we should aim for: indeed, I don't think I ever heard the word university from any teacher.

The orphanage continued to teach us within its own walls until we reached the age of fourteen. If we were not considered bright enough to pass a public exam we left. I remember only a few boys at Reigate who were allowed out daily to attend other schools as scholarship holders. This situation lasted until the Butler Education Act went through Parliament just after the war, when Spurgeon's lost its educational status, its children thereafter attending ordinary community schools, with the orphanage becoming simply a home or hostel. This change marked the end of the old enclosed Victorian orphanage, but it happened after I had already left.

Schoolwork was crude but effective, unashamedly concentrating on the three Rs, rammed into our heads by a copious use of the cane. This was not as traumatising as it might seem: it was the system, unquestioned, a normal part of life. And very few boys, it's worth noting, left Spurgeon's unable to read, write and comprehend basic arithmetic.

I am also beholden to Spurgeon's for bestowing on me another great gift. One of its educational precepts was learning by rote: not just the times-tables or simple childhood rhymes and mnemonics, but quantities of poetry. We would walk up and down the football field muttering the words while reading the prescribed pieces over and over again. Then we would be rigorously tested. Excerpts from the Bible were memorised at weekends, with the difference that prizes, usually uplifting books, were awarded for the ability to recite from the Good Book.

Thankfully, at least snatches of what I learned remain with me to this day, and I've never understood why rote learning is scorned by modern educationalists as damaging to young minds: childhood is the time when one is most capable of learning, and remembering poetry word for word is exercise for the brain.

One serious weakness in the schooling was the scant attention paid to music. There was the school choir, of course, but it was almost entirely confined to church and Christmas music, and once your voice had broken the choir had no further use for you. The bells some boys were taught to play hymns on, used for fund-raising purposes by the orphanage, had disappeared after the Stockwell premises were bombed: otherwise, no instrument was taught. For a while, during the war, we had a visiting singing teacher, and when he disappeared there was a patriotic period when we learned the national anthems of most, if not all, of the nations in the wartime alliance (I could still, if needed, offer a cracked rendition of the Czech national anthem, Oh, Homeland Mine, which I always thought was by Dvorak but now know, thanks to Google, was composed by one Frantisek Jan Skroup).

Jazz was frowned upon, not regarded as 'proper' music. Years later, in New York, I attended a concert by the avant garde jazzman, Thelonius Monk, which rather confirmed for me a sniffy attitude towards jazz, but I did eventually come to enjoy the traditional form, perhaps confirming that it is a taste most appreciated by the elderly, for most of whom it has formed an ever-present musical background to our lives.

The consequence of all this is that I have turned out to be a musical ignoramus, though I was once accused by my composer friend, Donald Fraser, of having more CDs of Elgar's music on my shelves than the great English composer ever actually wrote.

It was Don Fraser who gave me the most enthralling musical experience of my life. At the time – the late 1980s – he was a near neighbour in West Sussex, living in a house constructed around Edward Elgar's old garden studio. Having invited me one day to join him at the keyboard of his Steinway, Don invited me to play in any way I liked at my end of the piano, using the black keys only, while he played a piece of what I took to be classical music at the other. I obeyed, striking the keys at random, but the effect was quite magical, as though it was I who was producing the music: the experience left me close to tears.

Despite my ten years at the orphanage, probably because of this acquired reserve or detachment – even hatred - I developed towards authority, I never attained the rank of prefect with its attractive blue and gold enamelled badge, which was in the gift of the headmaster. And I was most certainly never in the running for most popular boy in the school, a title awarded each Christmas along with a watch for the winner. The only holder of the title I can remember was called, somewhat spectacularly for an orphanage boy, Basil van Sertima.

Friendship was the core value among the boys, involving utter loyalty to those in one's own house and the creation of defence pacts against all other boys and all members of staff. We endlessly discussed wild revolutionary plots among.

One plan we No.8 boys rehearsed in conversation was to smash poor devout Mr Tadbury over the head with an iron bar one particularly boring, rainy wartime Saturday afternoon when he was due, as the teacher on duty, to make his two-hourly inspection to check what the occupants of our hut were up to during the weekend. What we might do then, with a teacher lying unconscious or dead, I don't recall but, of course, exhilarating though it was to fantasise, our revolution never came to pass.

Occasionally, Nan or her daughters might come to see me on the monthly visiting days prior to the outbreak of war, but often I was left with the coterie of boys who were without visitors, concealing our envy under a cover of sarcasm towards those more fortunate than ourselves. Once, we saw the chairman of the orphanage governors at a visiting day. He was a Mr Higgs, chairman of a large London building company, and presented a quaint sight as he strode along in a frock coat with striped trousers, a shiny top hat, a gold watch chain stretched across his waistcoat, and a large diamond glittering from the centre of his cravat: a perfect Grosz cartoon image of a bloated 1930s capitalist plutocrat.

But once the war came everything changed, with visiting days suspended, and the orphanage itself removed from London. At the age of eight, I heard the declaration of war made over the wireless by prime minister Neville Chamberlain at 11 a.m. on 3rd September, 1939. The moment war broke out I was nursing blisters on my hands at a house in Godalming, Surrey, where we had been evacuated and billeted on local families. I had spent the morning at a patch of empty ground opposite the house, having become intrigued watching an old man cutting the long grass with a scythe. I asked him if I might try it myself, to which he readily assented, so much so that I did the rest of his work for him: hence the blisters.

It was all too clear to me that the family in Godalming resented having me foisted on them. The father was a commercial traveller, and had a new black Ford Prefect car with an aeroplane symbol on the bonnet. They had a couple of children and a large, scary Chow dog. I was not permitted to eat with the rest of the family but left in the kitchen to consume an unvarying diet of lemon curd sandwiches, and to be growled at menacingly by the dog. The one person in Godalming I remember as friendly was a motor mechanic whose workshop I would pass on my way to school classes, and who greeted me on our very first encounter with the words, 'Hullo, Peter Paterson'. It took me a while to realise that he knew my name from reading it on the top of the cardboard box containing my gas mask.

We assembled in the open air for classes on most days – it was the glorious 1940 summer – equipped with the only schoolbook that had survived the evacuation - Robert Louis Stevenson's Treasure Island: we could scarcely have been more fortunate. After a few months, we left Godalming for St David's in Reigate, which was to be our home for the rest of the war, interrupted by another transportation to South Wales for a few months in 1944 when the Germans started their V.2 rocket bombardment.

Among my pals – along with the rest of the country's juveniles - I constantly fantasised about joining the RAF, hoping against hope that the war would last long enough for me to climb into the cockpit of a Hurricane or Spitfire to shoot down German Heinkel and Dornier bombers. I prepared by studying wartime booklets explaining the theory of flight and how to fly, learning the outlines and performance figures of all German and British – and, later, American – aircraft.

One speculation, when I was about twelve, was induced by the idle study of ants' nests, wondering whether existence, which I understood from religious studies lasted but a brief moment of time, was much the same for me as for them. Were the scale and dimension of our life spans different from that of the purposeful ant with its burden of eggs and leaves? Was I an insect in some larger world, where a boot could be brought down on my head in the same way as we boys stamped on the ants, and our lives and everything that happened to us mere products of imagination that really did begin and end in a mere flash of time? Philosophy, I've often thought since, should be taught in schools, to help children make some sense of the abstract thoughts and concepts that constantly pass through all our minds from infancy to old age.

It was slipping into such habits of thought, questions of who we are and why we are here, that helped persuade me that I was somehow in the wrong place, the victim of some terrible mistake and that the error or errors which resulted in my being sent to the orphanage could somehow be rectified. But something was about to happen that confirmed that I now did emphatically belong where I was. It occurred when I went to one of my Nan's daughters, Auntie Mina, for a summer holiday in 1942. (The orphanage encouraged the idea that such families as its charges possessed should have 'their' boys take holidays with them at summer and after Christmas: maybe they were not keen to develop Dickens-style Smikes spending every minute of their entire school lives 'Within Our Gates'.)

It was while playing in the Anderson air raid shelter in Mina's garden in Carlton Avenue, Manor Park, that I found my birth certificate. It bore a dash in the space reserved for the father's name and I knew enough at the time to realise that this made me a bastard.

This discovery must have been the reason why I behaved so badly during the fortnight I was with the Rowse family. To itemise but some of my crimes: I stole their sugar ration to cram into sandwiches I consumed in the secrecy of the lavatory, and in a rage fired an air rifle at Auntie Mina – fortunately a sheet of glass deflected the shot – and I bullied my coeval, their son, Ian. Nevertheless, she and her husband, Uncle Fred, were courageous enough to ask me if I would like to stay and make my home with them, and to be a brother to Ian. With scarcely a second's hesitation, I declined their offer. The holiday was coming to an end, and I was more than eager to get back to my companions in the orphanage. And, following my discovery of my birth certificate, inside Spurgeon's walls was perhaps the one place where illegitimacy mattered not in the slightest: I've no idea how many of us were the offspring of unmarried women, but the condition must have been common enough to be seldom, if ever, mentioned, let alone employed as an insult to hurl at one another.

The underlying truth was that I was now homesick for the place where all the other boys were more my brothers than any outsider could possibly be: it seems that I had become thoroughly institutionalised, and content to be so.

l to r: Peter Paterson, Ian Waller, Nicholas Bagnall, Nicholas Garland

Chapter 6

AS they arrived in the South Wales town of Neath in early July 1944, a scene of confusion awaited our train full of evacuees from the south of England fleeing the threat of German V.2 rockets, Hitler's last throw in his aerial bombardment of Britain.

For the outnumbered staff of Spurgeon's Orphanage, whose children occupied a part of the train, it must have been a nightmare, for in preliminary consultations with the London County Council they had apparently been assured that their boys and girls would be housed as a single unit – subject, of course, to the sexes being kept separate.

Instead, individuals swooped down on the train like brigands in the stories we consumed in schoolboy comics of the days of the Indian Raj, carrying away as many children as they could fit into their cars. These were the so-called 'billeting officers', whose job was to place the children in private homes across a wide swathe of South Wales, who knew, or cared, little of any bureaucratic promise made to Spurgeon's.

Five of us boys were snatched from the throng of children carrying a small rucksack containing a few clothes, and round our necks a spare pair of boots. After a thirty-minute drive we arrived at a hall, where there were already a few evacuee children – strangers to us, as they would remain - sitting at tables. Remarkably swiftly, they disappeared, probably to other villages, leaving only the five of us behind, with no matrons or teachers from Reigate to be seen.

We were brought a meal of fried eggs, bacon, and chips, the first food we'd had since the sandwiches supplied by the orphanage had been wolfed down during the first few minutes of our train journey many hours earlier. Now, as we ate, we realised that the people bustling around us were not speaking English, and the blue-ringed plates before us bore a word we could not get our tongues around - 'Cwmllynfell'. We huddled together, trying to work out where we were, and why. For a little while the thought took hold that we must surely have been captured by the Germans, and we determined to take our first opportunity to escape.

There was clearly some difficulty with our little group – perhaps someone realised that an error had been made, that we had not been expected, that our names were not on any list. The adults conferred in what seemed an excitable fashion in their strange tongue before, one by one, we were taken away. I was the last to go, and not a little scared as I was placed in a car, the driver remaining silent until we pulled up outside a detached stone house, the first in a row struggling up a steep hillside. He walked me along a path made of compressed chippings of coal. Behind us, with darkness beginning to fall, was a bleak stretch of tufty grassland with a scattering of sheep, and above, the massive outline of a mountain full of thick shadows, and of a shape that instantly reminded me of pictures I had seen of Table Mountain in South Africa.

I had arrived at the home of the Evans family, though I was met at the door only by their daughter, Megan, a girl of about seventeen, and their son, Donald, a couple of years older, and the girl appeared to be arguing with some vehemence with the billeting officer, who eventually, with a shrug, turned on his heel and left. They both surveyed my forlorn and tired form with what I read as disappointment, Megan, contemplating my spare pair of boots, their laces tied together, asking rather sharply, in English, 'What have you got boots round your neck for, boy?'

Inside, I was immediately offered a meal, politely refusing it on the grounds that I had just eaten. But I was overruled by Mrs Annie Evans, who promptly cooked me more eggs, more bacon, and more chips, accompanied by several large slices of bread and butter, the latter providing me with my first word in their language, 'bara menyn'. Still unaware that a part of Britain might speak a different language from English, I did examine the idea that my hosts did not sound guttural enough to be Germans, but might conceivably be another of our enemies, Italian. As I ate heartily, I had the chance to study them, taking in the blue scars across the nose and cheekbones of the grizzled patron of the household, Dai Tom Evans, the comfortable roundness of the bespectacled Mrs Evans, the angular, beaky-nosed bossiness of the self-confident Megan as she apparently lectured her parents, and Donald, handsome, blue eyed, with regular features and curly fair hair, like his father, saying very little.

It was Megan who explained to me what was happening. I gathered that the family had only recently been freed of an evacuee, a boy from London, and felt that they had done their bit for the war effort in this direction. Also, if they had to have another evacuee, which they considered unfair, they would prefer a girl. So they intended to put their case to the billeting officer next day. Until then I could stay.

I looked around the room where I was eating. It was dominated by a large black range set into the chimney alcove, with two ovens separated by an open fire in a raised grate. This was clearly the Evans's living room, with a large window covered by maroon curtains now concealing the common I had seen on my way in, a sofa under the window on which Dai Tom sprawled, a wooden armchair for Mrs Evans, and dining room chairs around the large table for the rest of us.

After a night under what felt like a hundredweight of blankets and sheets on top of a ballooning mattress, in a bedroom shared with Donald, I explored the house – which was called Bryn Mair, on a road equally bafflingly signposted, Ochr-y-Waun (meaning Road to Gwauncaegurwen, the next village to the east), details I would need if an escape plan was to be formulated, though the Evans's ability to speak English, albeit in a weird accent, was reassuring.

I was shown the scullery/kitchen where I was to wash and clean my teeth, for the house had no bathroom, and I surprised Megan and Mrs Evans by stripping off to the waist, orphanage-style, for my ablutions. There was also a large walk-in larder, with a large ham, already cut into, sitting on a slate shelf, and others hanging from hooks. From our agricultural activities at Reigate, I knew I was among a community of pig-keepers.

Outside, there was a vegetable garden with a few flowers around the edges, and a path leading to the outdoor privy with its wonderful view of the Black Mountains. On a sunny morning you could sit on its comfortable boarded wooden seat, neat piles of sliced-up newspaper – the *Daily Herald* and *Llais Llavur* (*Labour Voice*) - at the ready beside you, and simply by kicking open the door, commune with nature above the roofs of a couple of intervening houses, their roofs well below the sightline of the mountain scene: this was a loo with a view.

When I awoke, Dai Tom and Donald had already disappeared off to work at the coal mine at dawn, and Megan soon left for her job at the local co-operative store. I was alone with Mrs Evans, an intensely shy woman who, I was to discover, seldom ventured out of the house.

I scarcely needed Mrs Evans's encouragement, with both of us standing shyly tongue-tied, to go off and explore the village, meandering down the main street which consisted for a while solely of houses, except for a fish-and-chip shop containing two full-size billiard tables: eventually I was to find there were nine such tables in the village, most of them combined with chippies, and I eventually got to play on all of them, once I was trusted not to rip the green baize table covering with the end of my cue. Then I came to a section with shops on both sides, on the left the ironmongers under the blue-and-white sign of Llewellyn Jenkins, and on the right, the Co-op, a two-storey building with a large grocery department, and on the upper floor a clothing store. Megan, in her shop assistant's apron, came skipping out to see her latest evacuee making good use of his time, and called to her friend, Jenny, to leave her post in the grocery to come and meet me.

I fell utterly in love for the first time in my life as I beheld Jenny's tight-curled red-hair, her laughing brown eyes, and her lustrous figure. It was a passion that was to end in pre-teen frustration and jealousy when I later met her fiancé, a bus driver – a calling seen as glamorous in a coalmining community where families did not wish their sons to follow their fathers down the pit and few other careers were available: Donald's misfortune was his father 's disappointment that he should be working at the pit.

I wandered further down the street past the working men's club on my left. I now came to what was the heart of Cwmllynfell, with the thoroughfare widening into an approximation of a square, flanked on one side by the Miners' Welfare Hall, where we had been brought for distribution the evening before, and opposite, a large church, known as 'the chapel', its extensive cemetery confining not only those who died of old age but men killed in their prime in mining accidents, as well as the graves of the victims of a late 19th century cholera outbreak buried at the outer edge of the graveyard by the road: included among this group was an elaborately carved In Loving Memory stone for an Enoch Powell, the significance of the name I only realised many years later when a politician of that name divided the whole of Britain on the question of immigration and race, a man I came to know quite well.

The Miners' Welfare was also the village cinema, concert hall, library, and the most spacious of its many billiards emporia. Alongside was a bowling green, surrounded by a stout hedge, its manicured grass an entirely different genus to the coarse growth on the common opposite Bryn Mair. The Evans's first injunction to me was never, on any account, to leave their side gate open, for the sheep would walk in and destroy their garden: it was an iron rule for every other dwelling in the place, but one sacrosanct haven against the advance of pesky ruminants and coarse unkempt grass, was the bowling green. I seldom saw anyone play on it, but its growth and texture was studied minutely by old men, sufferers from the mining disease of pneumoconiosis – coal dust on the lung – who peered lovingly at the lawn for hours on end before making their halting and wheezing way home at the end of their painful daily promenade.

Soon, my friends had found their own way to the hall, where we compared notes on our new quarters. Bert Stredwick was the luckiest, finding himself billeted at the village sweet shop, run by a Mrs Watkins, a sophisticated lady who spoke authoritative middle-class English and proved a good and generous friend to all of us. Time has wiped the identity of our fifth companion from my memory, though John Smith and his brother Barry were with the Bevan family. Soon afterwards Mr Bevan, also a miner, became victim to a ghastly underground accident, stepping over one of the hawsers laid between the rail tracks on which ran the open trucks, or 'tubs', carrying coal through the tunnels, just at the moment the donkey engine powering the traction system was started, whipping the cable up between his legs and hurling him into the roof of the tunnel. Miraculously, he survived, but his recovery extended long after we returned to Reigate.

We were to learn a great deal about coal mining in the months of our stay at Cwmllynfell, something that was to stand me in good stead later in my life when I became a writer on labour and industrial affairs, and again, when I was involved in the Moorgate disaster, a London tube crash possessing many of the characteristics of a mining accident since it took place below ground in a tunnel in pitch darkness, killing more than forty people.

We often found ourselves playing around the village square – we spent much time trying to spear fish in the stream behind the Miners' Welfare (now, sadly, inaccessible to children) – and no longer contemplating escape: on the contrary, we were immensely happy to be away from the orphanage. On the square, miners would be awaiting the arrival of buses to take them home to surrounding villages, black-faced from their work, squatting on their haunches against the kerbstones like so many rooks perched on telegraph wires. And, shades of Alabama, they were not allowed to sit in certain seats on the buses which were reserved for women going shopping and not keen on getting their clothes covered in coal dust.

We learned about the un-merry King Coal from incidents like Mr Bevan's misfortune, and more by playing among the old mine workings that surrounded the village. These were known as 'drifts' or 'levels', with the workings simply dug into an incline into the earth, and then abandoned when the more easily accessible coal had been exhausted. Often, the old equipment was left behind, and we spent many hours manoeuvring tubs back on to the rails and rolling them into a drift, to hear them hit the wall with a resounding and satisfying crash. With the advent of 'open cast' mining years later, many of these drifts were disinterred by great machines tearing up the earth to win cheap coal: this fate would eventually overtake the common opposite Bryn Mair, ruining the foreground to the mountain scene from the house.

At home, too, there was no escaping this harsh, elemental industry's presence. Every night Dai Tom and Donald came home from work, black from head to foot, and Mrs Evans would prepare a large galvanised iron bath, moved from its peg outside the back door to a place in front of the range in the living room. Dai Tom and Donald would, one by one, wash and scrub themselves into a great soapy lather, with Mrs Evans pouring extra buckets of warm water over their heads from a tap on the range. But neither of them would allow her to wash their backs, except on the last day of their working week: they held to an old belief of miners that washing weakened the back. Sitting in his bath, Dai Tom himself demonstrated the dangers of his calling: in the black rectangle that remained on his back there were three deep round white holes where bullets of rock had penetrated from explosives going off prematurely underground. On his face, too, the blue scars were from wounds caused by sharp chips of coal driven into his skin as he wielded his pickaxe against the coalface.

One way in which I could show my gratitude to the Evans's for taking me in was to help them with their domestic supply of coal. Each mining family was entitled to a ration from the pit, dumped beside the road. I volunteered for the task of transporting the coal in a wheelbarrow to our cellar – actually the shell of an old stone-built ruin attached to one side of the house. The coal came in huge chunks, some several times larger than the wheelbarrow, and had to be broken up with a sledgehammer. This was heavy work, but nowhere near what it must have been like below ground, where coal was painstakingly hacked from narrow, often wandering and elusive seams, the miners working on hands and knees in pitch darkness but for the lamps on their helmets.

We also learned of the poor state of labour relations in the mines. Dai Tom told me how, before the war, he had spent months out of work with no unemployment pay because there were so many men bearing precisely the same name on welfare rolls – in his case, David Thomas Evans – with officials refusing to pay out, ostensibly for fear of fraud. There was a deep anger and bitterness against the mine owners, which was to change very little when the pits were nationalised by the Attlee government three years after the war, although the miners themselves, according to government propaganda, were now, with the rest of us, part-owners of the industry.

One day, our little gang was playing on a hillside overlooking the Cwmllynfell mine, named by the miners, in a classic example of Welsh humour, after the old London prison, the 'Clink'. Below us, on a sunny day, the entire workforce – perhaps three hundred men - were attending a meeting in the pit yard. One after another impassioned speeches echoed up to our high perch, often accompanied by shouts and jeers from the listening miners. One of the first speakers was Dai Tom, who was chairman of the miners' 'lodge', or union branch. Another, in opposition to him, came from a lad of Donald's age: it was clear, although the proceedings were entirely in Welsh, that this was a dispute not only about politics, wages and working conditions (there were no pithead baths or showers in those days) but between generations as well. At home, Dai Tom explained that there was agitation for more pay, but it was his duty to maximise coal production for the war effort, which meant preventing strikes: on this occasion, he won the argument. A thoughtful, intelligent man, he had also – possibly on the strength of having been in the trenches in France in the Great War – been commissioned as a captain in the local Home Guard. I would secretly play with his Sten gun while he was at work: fortunately, the bullets were stored elsewhere (I was told on a 2008 visit to Cwmllynfell that during a restoration of the Evans's old house, a quantity of ammunition was found in the eaves and handed in to the police: clearly, this was Captain Evans's ammo dump).

Some years later, Mr and Mrs Evans visited me in London. It was the only time she had ever left Wales, and only his second, the first a stopover en route to northern France and the Great War. So frightened were they by the traffic and crowded streets that they took a piece of chalk with them whenever they left my house, marking walls and pavements to ensure they would be able to find their way back.

Cwmllynfell stands at the northern end of the Swansea Valley on the border of what in those days were Glamorganshire in the south and Camarthenshire the north. The Clink produced anthracite, a particularly high-grade type of relatively smoke-free coal, which was curiously clean once the dust was washed off: as Donald demonstrated for me, you could put a piece between the clean sheets on your bed overnight and it would leave no mark. One man in the village made handsome carvings from anthracite, including a bust of Paul Robeson, a revered figure among the socialist miners.

Before Thatcher, Scargill, and the global warmists ruined it, mining was a largely rural industry, the pits standing amid often beautiful countryside, around them rushing rivers full of great stones and waterfalls with plenty of natural swimming holes. We evacuees took ourselves off on whole-day hikes into the mountains, discovering the source of rivers emerging from the rocks, marvelling at Neolithic standing stone circles, stampeding great herds of wild Welsh ponies and delighting as they wheeled like migrating birds in their gallop across the bare hillsides. For a boy, the mountains were pure heaven.

Even better for me, I realised just how much in such a short time I had come to love the Evans family, even if I never brought myself to call them Uncle and Aunt, always sticking to the Mr and Mrs formulation of our initially awkward relationship, even after it developed into mutual affection. One incident brought home to me how much, in a short time, I had come to depend on their love and approval.

The crisis arose when one day Mrs Evans announced that she had lost a ten shilling note – not far short of £20 in today's money. And it was all too plain that she regarded me as the suspect. I remember walking out onto the common with our Welsh corgi, Sandy – my only friend, I thought - feeling that my entire world had come to an end, and deeply depressed at the thought that Mrs Evans or anyone else could regard me as a thief. Hours later, I returned, slinking into the house, trying to remain unseen and expecting to be banished from my new, wonderful home. But to my unutterable joy and relief, the ten shillings had been found during my absence, tucked away at the bottom of Mrs Evans's handbag. Did she ever really think I had taken it – that I was, in Welsh, a 'bachgen drwg', or wicked boy? Later, while basking in our restored affection, I was sitting on the floor in front of the fire while she ironed clothes at the table behind me. Stepping back, the steel tip on the heel of her shoe tore out a verruca from the sole of my bare foot. She was shocked at having caused me hurt but to my childish mind, her remorse seemed a kind of atonement.

Apart from billiards and snooker, with an occasional outing on the train to the seaside at Mumbles, close to Swansea, leisure activities in Cwmllynfell were few. As was crime, with little to disturb the resident policeman who, I discovered many years later, was the father of the great actress, Sian Phillips, with whom I may well unknowingly have shared the school playground more than sixty years ago. An occasional film would be shown for one night only at the Welfare Hall, and sometimes there was a concert by a visiting choir, but otherwise, apart from the mountains on our doorstep, there was little to do – which, I would say, applied more to the adults than to us youngsters.

Dai Tom would adjourn for a few pints to the working men's club a couple of evenings a week – occasionally, he took me there, but would never allow me, at thirteen, anything stronger than a soft drink, or 'pop' as it was called. Inside the house there was no alcohol at all, not even in the sacrosanct front room, used only for events of high importance, like funerals or weddings.

Some of my happiest moments were when Megan, her friend Jenny, the object of my lovelorn passion, and I would walk several miles along the railway track to the larger village of Brynamman, over the Carmarthenshire border, to attend the cinema there on Saturday nights, lighting our way on dark winter evenings with a torch. One of the sights of Brynamman was the village pervert, who week after week danced in front of the cinema queue apparently masturbating under his grubby raincoat: men giggled and women averted their gaze. In winter, we had to abandon the picture show several minutes before the final credits came up, to catch the last bus back to Cwmllynfell.

Although we had experimented at Reigate with dried laurel leaves wrapped up in rice-paper pages torn from a Bible, it was in Wales that we all started smoking tobacco. Able only to afford a paper packet of five Woodbines a week, once they'd gone up in smoke we spent hours turning the empty packet inside-out, the art being not to tear or crease it.

But our Welsh idyll was about to change. We evacuees attended the village school, usually in a small classroom of our own, with part-time Welsh teachers. But suddenly, we had word that the orphanage had tracked us down and was sending a master to take charge of us: it turned out to be the teacher who practised on us the Navy style punishment technique, running up to the boy he was caning and leaping ferociously into the air to bring the stick down on his victim.

He duly arrived, and was offered the hospitality of the home of the minister of the chapel, Reverend Roberts-Thomas, who had already taught us how to sing a popular rugby ground anthem, Calon Lan, in the original Welsh.

On the first morning at school attended by our nemesis, there had been a playground fracas between the Welsh and English boys, in which I was caught red-handed throwing the cap of a Welsh lad over the wall of the school. The English teacher decided that this was an opportunity to re-establish orphanage-style discipline publicly and quickly. With the entire Welsh school, teachers and pupils alike, pressing their noses to the glass panels separating our classroom from theirs, they watched him give me four strokes of the cane (he must have remembered to pack the stick with his luggage), two on the backside and two on the hands.

When I arrived home, news of my caning – a practice unknown in the local school - had already spread through the village. That evening, our house was crowded with neighbours invited by Dai Tom and Mrs Evans to view the weals on my backside – conveniently, it happened to be my bath-night – and to tut-tut over my swollen fingers. It was proposed, possibly by my foster-father's Communist brother, Jack, that everyone should go down to the minister's house to give our teacher a taste of his own medicine. I pleaded with them not to do so, for the moment would come when we would have to return to the orphanage and he would be even less well-disposed towards me. My appeal was accepted and he escaped an awkward, probably painful confrontation.

The V.2 threat that had led to our move to Wales disappeared as the Allies advanced in Europe. We were to return to Reigate just before Christmas 1944. Our Welsh foster-families saw us off on the bus from the Miners' Welfare Hall to Neath station, weeping copiously to see us go and waving furiously until we were out of sight: we waved, and were sad, too, but our thoughts were full of apprehension over the loss of freedom that lay ahead.

Worrying over what was to come proved a waste of energy. In a matter of weeks after I arrived back at Reigate I received news that while in Wales I had passed an examination allowing me to go to a secondary school at the unusual age of fourteen (the normal age was eleven), and I would be fourteen early in the new year. Nor had I the faintest recollection of even sitting such a test, let alone passing one: was this, I wondered, yet another kindly act by my Welsh hosts?

So when, in 1945, I left the orphanage, armed with my benefaction of ten shillings, the suit of clothes, and the Bible, I had a destination. I headed for Guildford, not very far from Reigate, where I was found digs and enrolled with the Wandsworth Technical Institute, a London state school evacuated to the Surrey town some years before. And this new school, significantly, was co-educational.

Cwmllynfell had been an ecstatically happy place for me and my orphanage companions. It had been my first real taste of home life, apart from wartime holidays with my aunts, since I entered Spurgeon's at the age of four, and I responded by loving the Evans family with all my heart. Their obscure pit village with its kind-hearted people matched the 'warm-cold village' described in one of Dylan Thomas's poems, for an icy north wind swept down from the great mountain above us (we borrowed Thomas's words for the title of the Harlech TV documentary about the village I made with John Morgan in 1974).

For several years I spent my summer holidays in the village, cycling the two hundred miles from London to be reunited with Dai Tom, Mrs Evans, Megan and Donald, and re-tracing my evacuee wanderings in the mountains.

Then, in the late 1960s, Dai Tom died, but not before I had dropped everything and driven to be at his bedside in hospital, where he lay, bright yellow from jaundice, a side-effect of the cancer which in turn was the product of his pneumoconiosis. As I held his hand, he said, 'Peter Paterson always turns up.' 'Like a bad penny,' I responded. 'No,' he said, 'like a good penny,' and tears streamed down my face. Then Mrs Evans died when I was abroad and unable be at her funeral, followed by Megan, not long married, and with a young son.

Her funeral was held at a tiny Georgian chapel high in the Black Mountains, not far from Craig-y-nos Castle, the home of the Victorian soprano, Adelina Patti. As I stood among the mourners, the chapel surrounded by trees bent and stunted by the incessant winds, with rooks wheeling noisily overhead protesting at the invasion of their privacy, it all presented a picture of desolation, sadness and loss. I have not been back since Megan died, except briefly during the writing of this book. The Clink has closed down and Cwmllynfell looks neglected and moribund. But in a happy life, I have seldom been happier than in those five-and-a-half ecstatic months I spent there.

Chapter 7

WHEN puberty coincides not simply with the first time you've noticed that girls exist, and your first encounter with them arrives in the close confinement of a co-educational classroom, a young man has a problem.

This was the situation facing me when I arrived to enrol at the commerce department of the Wandsworth Technical Institute, a school evacuated early in the war from south-west London to the sylvan delights of Guildford, a place not yet encumbered with supermarkets and traffic jams. There, I was to learn shorthand, typing, double-entry bookkeeping, elementary economics, and a general curriculum of English, maths, history, French, and geography.

Before very long, however, news arrived that the Wandsworth Tech was returning to London, and that the commercial, or secretarial, side was to be hived off into a new and separate foundation, to be called the Balham and Tooting College of Commerce.

My digs in Guildford were presided over by a gentleman who worked in an old-fashioned tobacconists shop in the high street, and at home remained, so far as I could see, in a state of permanent incommunicado with his wife. He spent every evening reading in his armchair, steadily smoking his way through a packet of Black Cat cigarettes, and drinking numerous bottles of Guinness before, at 10 o'clock sharp every night, he stomped wordlessly off to bed.

At school, I quickly became friends with two fellow pupils, brothers Ron and Len Fowler – the former always known as Chick. Measured against the divine Jenny back in Wales, the girls in my class at Guildford seemed callow but, nevertheless, there was still a certain something about them that fascinated me. My state of confusion towards them was expressed in a spiteful fashion, shoulder-barging into them when we passed in the corridor, pushing their books off their desks, cutting them dead if we met outside school: a general pattern of boorish behaviour.

This changed a little when the school returned, under its new name and in new premises, to London, and Jenny's charms faded when I heard she'd married her bus driver. My new place of learning was housed in an Edwardian school building on Tooting Broadway, and was headed by Mr Banham, a rotund and jolly man who insisted on treating his pupils as if we were older then we were, like honorary university students: the contrast with the orphanage was dizzying. Soon my attitude to the girls around me began to change, too, though I cannot say I saw much difference in theirs towards me, at least for a while.

I started by observing small changes in them - when they'd washed their hair (a once-a-week event so far as I could gather, the day changing as girls provided themselves with an excuse not to go out to play). I saw, too, how badly their thick stockings were holed, how many buttons on their blouses were left undone, and the come-hither looks they seemed to give to more favoured boys – a tiny, enviable minority: the rest of us hated these fortunate fellows and boycotted them. I was also measuring my cleverness against the girls in lessons and classroom discussions, and trying hard, not with much success, to better them.

While I was still in Guildford, I had got to know the Fowler boys' parents, Len, who had a one-man building and decorating business, and Cath, who worked in the bomb damage compensation department of the Inland Revenue at Somerset House. Immediately on hearing that the Wandsworth Tech was returning to London, the Fowlers offered me lodgings with them.

They lived in West Kensington, in those days a less salubrious address than it is now. In fact, their small terrace house in May Street long ago disappeared in a slum clearance scheme, though in my eyes its only fault was the lack of a bathroom. But cleanliness had an altogether lower priority in our post-war subsistence existence. I can remember with a shudder that a thick layer of grime covered my ankles as I removed my socks at night.

This state of filth was rectified once a week by a visit to the municipal baths, three-quarters of a mile away in the centre of Fulham. On Saturday mornings, I would go there for a bath, costing six old pence.

There appeared to be a distressing lack of trust between the municipality and the customers at its bath-house (not to be confused with its more modern usage), for the taps were situated out of the user's reach, on the outside of each cubicle. There was always a queue and when you were called, a filled bath was ready and waiting. If, however, a tentative dip of the toe warned that the water was too hot for comfort, it was necessary, without running naked into the corridor outside, to warn the baths attendant of the fact by shouting out the number of your cubicle, as in 'More cold, Number Seven!' It was hard to get the balance right, for often enough the attendant would disappear for a while with his badge of office, a giant spanner, leaving the cold tap running, at which point you would hop out of the bath and start yelling in a panic, 'More hot, Number Seven!'

Life with the Fowler family was a delight. They were by no means rich, and under Mr Fowler's tutelage, I learned to darn socks, mend my own shoes, buying the leather in square sheets at Woolworth's, cutting it to size, and then, using a last and a sharp curved knife to trim the new sole to shape, before banging in the little nails all the way round, to the detriment of one's fingers. Rubber heels could be bought ready made, but it was something of an achievement when one learned how to fix 'blakies', or quarter-moon shaped spiked metal corners to save vulnerable leather heels from wearing down too quickly.

We were kept extremely well fed by Mrs Fowler despite the continuation of rationing long after the war was over. She never threw away the paper in which butter was wrapped, keeping it to rub around the frying pan or cake tins to prevent them burning. She also hoarded bowls of beef and lamb dripping when the rations allowed a Sunday joint, which we spread on our bread enthusiastically, a custom I continue to this day (toasted, with Marmite): years later, when food had again become plentiful, she would still include a bowl of dripping when she arrived with Christmas presents for my children.

Intellectually, we were constantly challenged by Mr Fowler, who, anticipating the disputes I engaged in years later at the *New Statesman* and the *Spectator*, insisted on having an argument about absolutely everything. His fount of truth was the *Daily Express*, and in an echo of his wife's hoarding habits, he never threw a newspaper away, until our living room was piled high with copies in every corner. Anything his sons or I might say, he instantly contradicted, forcing us to defend our thesis whether it was simply an observation on the weather, a remark about politics, or the merits of the library book we happened to be reading. Like the Marx Brothers' song, Mr Fowler's glorious attitude was, 'Whatever it is, I'm against it'.

He was the man who taught me to argue, not in the way of factual schoolboy disagreements over the relative firepower of the guns on a Spitfire and a Messerschmidt 109, but forcing one to present and marshal facts, produce convincing rebuttals to his arguments, however heated, or on occasion threatening, our debates might become. Sometimes we argued each other to a standstill, glowering across the kitchen table, and stalking off to bed without a 'Good Night'. Then, next day, we would resume verbal hostilities. I owe this kindly and delightful man more than I can say.

Meanwhile, I found myself getting on a little better – or bolder - with the girls at the Balham & Tooting College of Commerce. I was first bitten by the pangs of love towards a girl called Clare Mudd, a name, with its echo of the old saying about the clarity of mud, struck me as cruel. She had lovely brown eyes and long straight hair delightfully curled up at the ends, glowed with the health of a playground hockey star, and was frightfully well-spoken (years later, when we met again, she asked me, 'Peter – whatever happened to your cockney accent?' and I explained that it had disappeared of its own accord, which was quite true). Like John Betjeman's Joan Hunter Dunn, she athletically filled my dreams.

After a while I was invited to visit Clare's home in Streatham, but mortified to discover that the occasion was not à deux, but a party for a group of her friends that included some of my schoolfellows, the gathering presided over by her mother. Their flat was the antithesis of our house in May Street, with carpets, curtains, lamps, pictures, no piled-up newspapers, and a general atmosphere of middle-class comfort. Then I noticed that the object of my desire seemed to be behaving in an excessively friendly fashion towards another boy: his name was Darley, but I thought of him as Darnley, second husband of Mary Queen of Scots, who was blown to pieces by dynamite – a fate I devoutly wished on my perceived rival.

Thanks to Darley, my affections switched to Jean Airth, dark haired, with a pale heart-shaped face, and an expert in strategic button unfastening who seemed to turn the white blouse of her school uniform into an alluring invitation to seduction. Seduction never occurred, of course, but I did go to the cinema with her a couple of times, not daring to do more than shyly grasp her hand in my sweaty paw as she concentrated on the picture. I scarcely noticing the shadows dancing across the screen at the Tooting Gaumont.

Eventually deciding that I was not cut out for the softer, sweeter aspects of life, I threw myself into sports, playing cricket and football in the local parks and taking up boxing at a boys' club in Shepherd's Bush. It was there that the boxing trainer brutally urged me to concentrate less on girls and more on the ring: 'You can't box and wrestle, too,' he warned with a knowing leer.

I chose boxing as a pastime because towards the end of my time at Spurgeon's I became aware that I had developed an inclination to fly into rages, and I'd read that pugilism was a way of dealing with problems of aggression. Perhaps, unknown to me, I had already been cured by Mr Fowler's argument academy and had no need of the noble art, but I was also inspired in my choice by reading an autobiography of Gene Tunney, world heavyweight champion in the 1920s who twice conquered Jack Dempsey, the Manassas Mauler: Tunney was something of an intellectual and out of the ring corresponded with George Bernard Shaw.

To supplement the training I was getting at the boxing club, out of curiosity I started to pop into a tiny professional training gym in Fulham. The gym's owner, a small, elderly and out-of-breath man called Darkie Hughes, had been trainer to Joe Beckett, British heavyweight champion in the 1920s. A boxing ring filled two-thirds of the premises, a shower and a lavatory occupied little more space than a telephone box, and Darkie's office, decorated with old posters advertising boxing matches, took up nearly all the rest, leaving just enough room for a heavy punchbag and a punch-ball.

Weighing ten stones at the time – five pounds too heavy for the lightweight division, and seven pounds too light for welterweight, I began sparring with some of the professionals. I made friends there with Tommy Barnham, an extremely classy lightweight and scion of a well-known Fulham family of street traders and taxi drivers. His boxing had been interrupted by four years in a German prison camp after his Royal Navy ship, HMS Barham, was sunk, and he was now in the process of re-starting his career. He would mistily recall his ship visiting New York in the early days of the war, when British sailors were besieged by girls who regarded it as a patriotic duty to entertain them. Taken by one New York female to the cinema, he was surprised when, under cover of darkness, she started to undo his fly buttons. 'What did you do?' I naively enquired. 'I gave her half an hour to let go,' he said.

Tommy, who was also a bookie at the dog track that in those days shared Chelsea football club's Stamford Bridge stadium, ran a drinking club in the North End Road. His manager was an ex-fighter called Arthur Boggis who owned a chain of 'continental butchers', which meant he sold horse meat, traditionally repugnant to the British palate even at a time of meat rationing. Boggis provided the several fighters he managed with horse meat steaks, each unappetisingly surrounded by bright yellow fat, but not all accepted this dietary reinforcement: Tommy fed his manager's offerings to his pet greyhound.

Another habitué of Darkie's place was Frankie Ronan, a promising heavyweight, blond and handsome enough to have been the model for Michelangelo's David in Florence, but sadly endowed with the brain power of the Carrara marble. Frankie once assured me , as though he had studied the matter deeply for many years, that the one absolute, incontrovertible difference between the sexes was that men grow hair on their big toes, while women never do. Sadly, after a few winning fights, he was found drowned in the Thames – accidental death was the coroner's verdict.

Ben Perry, Barnham's bag-carrier and corner-man, might have lived at the gym, were there the space. His great claim to fame was that he had been the last man to fight a woman opponent in the British professional boxing ring – something that had briefly been permitted by the Boxing Board of Control just before the war but then abandoned (intersex boxing is now, I believe, making a comeback). The bout took place at the Olympia stadium in West London as a foot-of-the-bill novelty, and by all accounts - except his own – poor Ben received a pretty good hiding.

All went well for me until I was sparring one afternoon with a former army light heavyweight champion of South-East Asia Command, who landed a terrible blow to my solar plexus. I was floored, and unable to get my breath for what seemed five minutes. This was deemed a 'liberty' by Barnham, who remonstrated with my opponent, though it was hardly his fault that I succumbed to the punch after happily volunteering to be the punchbag.

My boxing career, such as it was, continued alongside my other sports, and I had a few amateur fights at various Territorial Army drill halls and public baths until after I was called up into the army in 1949. But any thoughts I might have had of becoming a professional boxer came to an end when Darkie introduced me to a boxing manager, a swarthy man in a camel-hair coat, a porkpie hat, sporting an Errol Flynn moustache, and – very unusual in those days – sunglasses. He was called Doi Lorenzo, and he offered – this was in 1948 and I was 17 - to sign me up for a four-round professional fight at Hammersmith Baths against an opponent 'yet to be chosen', to take place in precisely a fortnight. My share of the purse – subject to deductions for training expenses and the manager's cut - was to be £12, which was rather more than quadruple my monthly income. On the wise advice of my friend Barnham – 'Look at my ears and the shape of my nose – you don't want to do that,' he said - I declined Mr Lorenzo's offer. I had to concede that Tommy's features were heavily deformed – flattened doesn't take account of their lumps - despite his reputation as an exceptionally skilful proponent of the noble art.

Having watched Tommy in hard and bloody fights over fifteen rounds with the French champion, André Faméchon, and against the great stylist, George Daley of Blackfriars, it was obvious that the professional ring demanded skills and tenacity of a considerably higher order than my three-round amateur contests. After boxing once in the army, I gave up the fight game for good.

Then there was cycling. The entire Fowler family was keen on it, the parents riding a tandem on weekend trips to the country, and Ron and Len taking part in time trials: massed bicycle racing of the kind they go in for in France was banned on the public roads in Britain, so in a time-trial, racing cyclists would be released from a starting point at half-minute intervals officially to race not against each other but against the clock over a course of 25, 50 or 100 miles. You might overtake, but it was forbidden to ride immediately behind another competitor to shield oneself from the wind, or to spread across the width of the road and cause danger to other traffic as well as yourself. Obviously, these rules were often ignored in practice.

I was soon enlisted as a cyclist, rising at dawn on Sunday mornings to rendezvous with our fellow club members, usually at Hammersmith

Broadway – we were called the Belle Vue Cycling Club after the pub in Parsons Green where the committee meetings were held and members gathered to discover times and meeting places of events. We would usually ride out to Slough for the weekly time trial, strip our bikes of saddlebags and mudguards to minimise weight and maximise speed, and set off on our usual 25-mile race, the route finally returning to the starting point. There we would enjoy a fry-up breakfast at a café, compare our racing times, and ogle any girls who'd come along to watch their boyfriends, before heading off to the south coast, to Brighton, Eastbourne or Worthing, for a brief look at the beach, and then, via a sit-down meal at a pre-booked village teashop on the way back, getting home after dark. Once, we were all immensely elated at being stopped by the police for speeding as we rode down the hill through Preston Park and into Brighton at more than 40 mph. Within ten years, our place at the cafés and teashops – and the seaside - would be taken by Mods riding scooters, followed in another decade by weirdo Hell's Angels on big, showy motorbikes.

But cycling in the first decade after the war, when few people – certainly in my circle - had cars, was a national preoccupation. One of the great sporting heroes of the day, alongside heavyweight boxers Bruce Woodcock and Freddie Mills, middle-distance runners Sidney Wooderson and Roger Bannister, and cricketers Bill Edrich and Dennis Compton, was Reg Harris, the (professional) sprint cycling champion of the world. He put on exhibitions at cinemas to great enthusiasm, riding his bike on rollers on the stage.

When one day I found a set of second-hand rollers in a junk shop I carried them triumphantly back to May Street and installed them in the narrow corridor immediately inside the front door. This had the advantage that the walls on each side prevented the bike toppling over – it took a little time to get the knack of cycling while standing still

- and the disadvantage that the rollers made a roar like the yet-to-be-invented Comet jet airliner when anyone got up to speed. Eventually, at Mrs Fowler's insistence, they had to go.

An indication of what journeys could be achieved on a bike in those pre-motorway days, was an Easter tour half a dozen of us made in, I think, 1949 or 1950. We met at dawn in Hammersmith Broadway and lunched in Worcester, before riding on to Ludlow in Shropshire, where we stayed the night. The following morning we rode over the ancient trackway, the Long Mynd, as a detour, before continuing south to Ross-on-Wye, and putting up for the night in a hostel over a gents' outfitters, where we were fed delicious country eggs and bacon. The following day we rode back to London in the pouring rain.

I left the Balham & Tooting College of Commerce at the age of sixteen with a clutch of Royal Society of Arts certificates. Any progress I made was thanks to a wonderful English teacher called Miss Smythe who, the antithesis of my teachers at Spurgeon's, seemed to believe in me, encouraging me to read widely and to write. It was plain to me, too, that Miss Smythe favoured her male pupils over the often cleverer girls, to which I raised no objection. On leaving school I secured a job as an office boy with W.T. Henley's Telegraph Company (curiously, the first of four firms I would work for with the word Telegraph in their title), and my new employers insisted that I continue my education by granting me a day off to attend the Kingsway Institute, just behind the Aldwych in central London, on condition that I also went to night school twice a week, so as to gain even more RSA certificates.

Henley's was a manufacturer of electric cables with a subsidiary making car tyres, its head office in Hatton Garden, a street in Holborn mostly occupied by diamond merchants. At the northern Clerkenwell end, a tobacco factory wafted the pungent aroma of its Skipper and Bondman pipe tobaccos over the entire neighbourhood. One of my tasks in Henley's advertising department, just before Christmas, was to wrap and despatch tobacco pipes to be sent out to the company's business contacts as genteel bribes.

I spent much of my time filing the department's correspondence, often consisting of letters between Henley's and a trade body, the Cablemakers' Association, a cartel that, when I had long gone, faced exposure by a government enquiry into price-fixing, leading to its members being fined a surprisingly small sum for distorting competition.

Gradually, however, the pointlessness of my working life dawned on me: hardly anyone seemed to consult the files I so carefully, if spasmodically, placed in those grey marbled boxes. Assuming that I would not be staying too long at Henley's, I greatly reduced my workload by screwing the accumulating pile of unfiled letters into paper balls and stuffing them down the backs of the fluted radiators around the office.

Years later, Henley's office block was demolished. When I heard the news, I idly wondered whether the wrecking ball had uncovered my crime. And those tedious hours as an office boy came flooding back to me when I wrote a piece for the *New Statesman* about an experiment in a car factory in Sweden where, to relieve the tedium of the assembly line, work was rearranged to allow the workers, instead of each attaching one component as the production line moved past them, to co-operate in small groups to build entire cars. The scheme had to be abandoned because it caused greatly increased psychological stress: it was found that on the assembly line, the workers led a rich inner life in their heads, but building a whole car interrupted this process, imposing unbearable strains. My article from Sweden bore the witty headline, 'Wild Raspberries', a rudery I probably indulged in when the time arrived for me to abandon clerking for a reporter's life.

Chapter 8

WHAT was at least a theoretical solution to my difficulties with girls, and the choice of a career, both occurred almost simultaneously in the spring of 1948, when one evening, listening to the radio at the Fowlers, I heard Victor Sylvester giving a dancing lesson over the air.

'Slow, slow, quickstep, slow...' intoned the bandleader and dancing instructor to the nation. I knew that an ability to dance was the essential prerequisite to dating girls, allowing one to clutch them in one's arms without even being introduced, and beyond that, who knows what bliss awaited?

I heard of a place in Balham where dancing lessons were to be had without having to wait the interminable period it would take to absorb Victor Sylvester's weekly sessions on the wireless, even when supplemented in the more popular newspapers by diagrams of feet moving in various directions. So I hastened to Balham to enrol.

When I arrived, the prospects looked less promising. This was the heyday of public dancing, from village hall hops to the thé dansants of smart hotels, and around our way, the Hammersmith Palais where, gossip reported, it was possible to pick up an easy girl at any time. But first you had to learn the wretched steps, and here in Balham, the number of would-be learners must have reached more than a hundred, with a queue around the block. I waited my turn for a while before impatiently walking to the front (to an inevitable chorus of jeers from the crowd fearing I was queue-jumping, a serious social solecism) to find out what was happening, and how long it might be before it would be happening to me.

One woman was conducting the classes, with another attending to the gramophone providing the music, each in turn taking a man on to the dance floor. It was clearly going to be a very long wait, but we were accustomed to waiting in those days from the butchers and greengrocers, to the buses, the public baths on a Saturday, the cinema, the doctor's surgery, and the Telfer's pork pie factory in Fulham where they sold a bag of broken pies for a few pennies at the end of the week, mopping up the beer and providing a cheap protein supplement to our diet at a time of continued food rationing.

The queue consisted largely of men in their twenties returned from the war, and youngsters (but no girls). Settling down to wait, I started a conversation with the next person in the line. I learned he was Alan Trengove, that he, too, lived in Fulham, though at the smarter end, Hurlingham. More importantly, he told me that he was a reporter on a local newspaper.

'Wow!' I told him, hugely impressed, 'That's what I would like to do,' suddenly realising – or imagining - that this was what I had wanted all my life. 'Well,' he replied, 'there were two of us, but the other fellow got the sack today.' He told me where the office was situated, and I decided to take an unauthorised day off from Henley's to try for the vacancy.

Next morning, I presented myself at a suite of rooms above a bank in what is now Fulham Broadway, but in those days was called Walham Green, as was the underground station opposite, to apply to become a reporter on the *Fulham Gazette*. I enquired at a desk where a girl awaited people who wished to place an advertisement in the paper, and was directed to an office occupied by a Captain Tucker, the company secretary.

Tucker continued using his military rank long after returning to civilian life, a practice widely disapproved of by the time the war had been over for three years. He was a very fat man built on the same lines as the husky-voiced film actor, Sydney Greenstreet, inseparable partner of the diminutive Peter Lorre in my favourite films of the 1940s, Mask of Demetrios, The Maltese Falcon, and Casablanca. He seemed to pour over the edges of his chair like a suet pudding overflowing the bowl, his jowls shaking in the same way as a bulldog's. Slightly intimidated, less by his unusual size than my own nervousness, I informed him that I was applying for the vacancy of reporter.

Witheringly, Mr Tucker told me there was no such vacancy, though perhaps they might need an office boy. I said I was already an office boy and didn't wish to continue as one. At that moment, an even stranger figure entered Tucker's office.

A tiny man, his head an assortment of grey hair tinged with ginger forming a halo around an expanding bald patch, he was holding what I later learned to call a galley proof – a column of type printed on a long, narrow sheet of paper – in front of, and very close to, his face. He wore thick glasses, behind which his eyes constantly watered because of the smoke from the cigarette clamped between his lips, the ash left to grow until it tumbled down the front of his suit, waistcoat and tie.

Without a word to me, Mr Sam Soester, editor and proprietor of the *Fulham Gazette*, jerked his thumb in my direction, asking Tucker, 'What does he want?' With a dismissive shake of his head, the company secretary replied that I was seeking a job as a reporter but had been told they didn't need one. The editor swung round, still holding the galley proof but peeping at me from behind one edge. 'Can you write shorthand?' he asked. 'Yes,' I said, 'at about 200 words a minute.' To my relief and joy, he said, 'Right, when can you start?' and abruptly walked out of the office, leaving a discomfited Tucker to work out the details.

The fat man was clearly enraged, gazing at me as though I'd removed his dinner from under his nose. 'I have to tell you,' he hissed, 'we would pay an office boy 35 shillings (£1.75) a week. A reporter only gets 25 shillings.'

I wouldn't have cared at that moment if the remuneration had been twopence a week – I was about to embark on a calling which, apart from a couple of years off for my national service, would absorb, delight, and satisfy me for the next 59 years, bring me fun and friendship, and immense amounts of freedom, allowing me to observe people from all walks of life, and to travel the world. And somehow I already knew all this would be so. I was to be a reporter, the most glamorous job I could imagine. And I've never had the time or the inclination for another dancing lesson since.

Despite my elation, the meagre pay represented a sharp drop from my Henley's salary. I still had to meet the cost of lodging with the Fowler family, but it was ameliorated by their generosity in instantly reducing my rent on hearing I would now be earning less. My activities suffered because there was little money for lifestyle or wardrobe, though members of the local press were able to enjoy perks, like free admission to the two local cinemas and a press ticket to Fulham FC – but not its neighbour, Chelsea.

My first assignment, on a Monday morning, was to produce an account of a wedding that had taken place two days earlier. Its news value lay in the fact that twin brothers had married twin sisters – but both couples were unavailable for interview because they had already, as our *Gazette* reports invariably indicated, 'departed for their honeymoon'. (Later that year, a slip-up when the metal type was being laid out prior to printing the 'wedding page', fused a report on a young couple's nuptials with an account of a golden wedding, resulting in the no-doubt surprised readers being informed that the happy couple in their seventies 'left for their honeymoon in Brighton ... with a *Gazette* reporter who called to congratulate them'.)

The address I was sent to was a flat in a council block – is it probably only my imagination that it was called Clement Attlee House – occupied by the mother of the two bridegrooms. Full of confidence, I interviewed this lady over several cups of tea, cramming my notebook with the information she gave me, before returning to the office.

There, I sat down and typed a report of the wedding, before submitting it, an hour or two later, to editor Soester. He glanced at it, pointing out that I had omitted to mention the name of the church where the ceremony had taken place, ordering me to return to my source for the information.

It was a hot day, the 'contact', like the majority of people, in those days, did not have a telephone, and the flats were some distance from the *Gazette* office, but not far enough to justify the expense of a bus ticket. Once more I toiled up the stairs, this time remaining at the front door while the lady identified the church for me, before returning to the office to insert this crucial fact into my copy. Again I submitted it.

This time, the editor rebuked me for not naming the officiating clergyman, and sent me back again. This wearisome process continued over the course of much of the day. I must have returned three or four times to the flat as I wearily sought information on the presents given to the bridesmaids, their names and a description of theirs and the bride's dresses (plus that of the bride's going-away outfit), my self-assurance draining away with each succeeding visit. I ended the day hot, miserable, and desperate to forget all about this wretched, humiliating double-wedding with all its complications: it was some time before I appreciated that Sammy Soester had taught me a sharp and necessary lesson.

There was more trouble to come. One of my tasks at the start of each week was to visit the police station to see the Incident Book, a record of the constabulary's activities over the preceding week. One day I was intrigued to find an entry recording that the caretaker of the local spiritualist church had been knocked down by a car while crossing the road.

I was surprised that this did not rate more than an end-of-column paragraph, but part of my job was to write a short headline for it, and almost without thinking, I devised 'Was He in a Trance?' which I intended as a humorous comment. This duly went into the paper, and immediately drew an angry letter from the spiritualists, rightly pointing out that as well as mocking their beliefs the headline displayed a certain callousness towards the injured caretaker.

Sammy Soester called me in and delivered a fierce lecture on my folly which, he said, but for the generous spirit of the offended party, might have cost the paper thousands of pounds in damages. Chillingly, he went on to say that with something like this on my record, I would automatically be blacklisted by every newspaper in Fleet Street, as though such a list existed and he had access to it. My career was blighted from its very start.

I never did warm to Mr Tucker, whom I subsequently learned represented the paper's creditors because, left to Sammy, the *Gazette* was technically bankrupt. But I really liked and admired the editor and understood his irritation at receiving letters like the one I had provoked. Local newspaper editors need to navigate their way among a range of business, political and religious interests, and voluntary organisations, particularly so since the *Gazette* faced competition from two rivals in Fulham – the larger *Chronicle* and the smaller *Fulham Advertiser.*

One exception to Sammy's supervisory role was the sports pages, a subject of which he knew little. These were sub-edited by Alan Trengove, so he and I would write accounts of the football or cricket matches we'd played over the weekend and give ourselves starring roles with flattering headlines. Once, Alan came to one of my fights and wrote a glowing report: fortunately, on that occasion I managed to emerge the winner on points. To this day, however, he sternly denies glorifying his own role on the sports field, attributing any perceived exaggeration to over-enthusiastic reporting by the non-journalist sports club secretary charged with submitting reports to the paper by Monday morning. I, however, always voracious to be noticed, am happy to plead guilty to indulging in sports page self-promotion.

Early on most weekdays I would cycle over to Alan's house in Hurlingham Road and, long before jogging became popular, we would go running in Bishop's Park, alongside the Thames close to Putney Bridge, before returning to his house where his mother made us breakfast before we went off to the *Gazette*. When I went into the army, he emigrated to Australia to become a reporter on the Melbourne Herald and, later as a sports writer, eventually specialising in tennis. When he was posted to London by the Herald two decades later, we spent family holidays together, and we still meet once a year when he reports Wimbledon.

One substantial perk we possessed on the *Gazette* was a press pass for Fulham Football Club, which was enjoying one of its brief periods of glory in 1948, achieving promotion from Second to the First

Division under its then manager, Fred Peart. We were seldom able to use the pass, however, because either we were ourselves engaged in our own sporting activities or Sammy allotted us other tasks on Saturday afternoons. For me this meant covering the constituency activities of our local MPs, Dr Edith Summerskill and Michael Stewart, both Labour. I felt sorry for Dr Summerskill's daughter, who would be ordered by her mother to dictate from memory the contents of her mother's speech, word for word, to any reporter derelict enough to arrive too late to hear it delivered in person by the MP.

Dr Summerskill was a famously aggressive and courageous feminist who, in her time, protested against a wartime security poster bearing the witty slogan, 'Be Like Dad, Keep Mum', on the grounds that it disparaged women's powers of discretion as well as the wartime role of working women. She also pressed for a law to compel husbands to reveal their earnings to their wives, something Harriet Harman was still trying to do in 2008. She campaigned vehemently against boxing, demanding the sport's abolition (a subject I failed to raise with her), and magnificently faced down the derision she endured on introducing whale-meat and a South African fish called snoek into the British diet while she was a food minister in the post-war government.

The far less colourful Stewart occupied a number of more senior ministerial posts than his constituency neighbour but was quite the most uncomfortable figure I ever saw on a soap box, a humiliation this quietly-spoken and pedantic individual regularly submitted to by holding regular street meetings on Saturday afternoons, despite the fact that sometimes, apart from his agent, I constituted his only audience. He would eventually rise to become Foreign Secretary, and was one of three occupants of that post in Labour governments between 1964 and 1970 who, once they had left office, were convicted of drunken driving (George Brown and Patrick Gordon Walker were the others).

A girl reporter on one of our competitor papers, the *Fulham Advertiser*, was Gwyneth Morgan Phillips, the daughter of Morgan Phillips, a powerful politician and general secretary of the national Labour Party whom I would get to know quite well later in my career. After a short time in the job Gwyneth contracted TB, and her mother, Norah, would invite young people, myself among them, to entertain her daughter in the evenings after we had finished work, at their house off the Fulham Palace Road, where she was confined to a sofa in the Phillips's living room. We were a little in awe of her: before becoming a reporter, she had reputedly been a singer in a night club in Amsterdam.

Our little soirées would be interrupted by the arrival home, by taxi, of Gwyneth's drunken father. Morgan would rantingly order us all out of his house, leaving his wife and daughter humiliated, embarrassed and dejected.

Once, I regret to say, it was I, rather than her husband, who upset the pleasant and hospitable Norah Phillips. Theatre criticism comes with the territory for a local reporter, however unqualified they might be (so far, my only experience of the theatre had been a performance of She Stoops to Conquer, starring Donald Wolfitt, while at school) and it took her a long time to forgive me for a slightly unflattering review of her role in an amateur production at Fulham Town Hall of the tedious socialist classic, The Ragged Trousered Philanthropists. After her husband's death, she was given a life peerage, campaigning in the House of Lords against shoplifting. Gwyneth happily recovered from her illness, became an MP, and married another (they were later divorced), eventually becoming, as Gwyneth Dunwoody, a famous

House of Commons battle-axe, chairman of the Transport Committee and one of the few women backbench MPs of the Blair era to make a substantial reputation without ingratiating herself as a 'Blair Babe'.

Life for most people was pretty grim in 1948, with food still rationed – even bread and potatoes, which had never required a ration book to be flourished in food shops during the war. People in Canada, Australia and the United States, sent food parcels to help the British poor, to be distributed by local councils.

In Fulham it was decided that the parcels should be presented to old age pensioners in a ceremony at the town hall presided over by the mayor, Mr Horton, who made a little speech of thanks to the (necessarily absent) donors. While the young had benefited from food rationing, because it gave them a balanced if meagre diet, the elderly had suffered grievously. Many instinctively sacrificed their rations to their children or grandchildren, and watching them at the town hall that morning in their threadbare clothes, hollow cheeked, grey-skinned, and shuffling, it was easy to see the terrible strain the war had placed on people who had never known prosperity even before the outbreak of hostilities.

Yet at the time, I was deeply shocked to see an unruly throng of old people abandoning the rules of queuing as they pushed, shoved and snatched to seize the largest parcels for themselves, producing a near-riot in the town hall vestibule. Now in old age myself and looking back to that occasion sixty years ago, I'm sure I can feel great sympathy for a much more ill-used generation than my own, even if I could never bring myself, even today, to jump a queue in the way they did.

Only a year after starting on the *Gazette* I received my call-up papers for the army, but not before I accomplished a tangible change to my little world – perhaps the only real one I can claim to have secured as a reporter. After a short 'campaign' – it took only one or two stories in the paper - London Transport was persuaded to move a bus stop on the busy New King's Road from a narrow section of pavement with no room for the gigantic prams – a kind of sidewalk equivalent of today's Chelsea tractors – in which babies were wheeled about in those days. I suggested – no, demanded, that the bus stop must be re-located to a wider, safer place a few yards away. To see a huge organisation respond to one's written words was a heady experience for a 18-year old tyro reporter, particularly as his future experience would demonstrate how rarely such instances occur. Of course, with more experience in the ways of state bureaucracies I now realise that they never respond with such speed. The decision to move the bus stop had probably already been mulled over for months by multiple committees, the flattering timing of the arrival of a bus-stop-moving work team so soon after my article appeared no more than pure coincidence.

Chapter 9

IT was as a National Serviceman, during which, like Hitler, I reached the lofty rank of corporal, that I made the acquaintance of two people at the other end of the chain of command - Field Marshal Lord Montgomery of Alamein and General Dwight D. Eisenhower. Not, I should make clear, that I knew them in a social sense, but slightly closer, at any rate, than the Good Soldier Schweik's relationship to the Archduke of Austria.

But before becoming connected to such exalted figures I had first to undergo the basic training endured by all recruits, whether destined to be a clerk or a commando, finding myself living in a hut near Aldershot with fifty other apprentice soldiers, constantly being shouted at and – once again - punished for clumsiness, slowness, idleness or breaches of the rules, making the experience spookily like going back to the orphanage. The place was Deepcut Barracks, a place that was to become notorious more than half a century later following a spate of apparent suicides among young soldiers who had volunteered rather than, like us, being pressed into the army.

I've no idea how many conscripts committed suicide while serving their compulsory term of national service, but although the regime at Deepcut was fairly tough, nothing like that occurred in my time there. However, I was familiar enough by now with the dynamics of group-living in an all-male environment, feeling no sense of homesickness or alienation and therefore suffering less than those of my comrades dragged from a comfortable home existence (friends have often suggested I would adjust with equal ease to a term of imprisonment).

I was able to take a detached view, observing 18-year olds far from home quietly weeping into their pillows for their mothers while others, natural bullies, exploited the timid. All of us hastily incorporated four-letter words – the quadrilateral reprehensibles used so freely by the shouting and bellowing NCO instructors - into our own vocabularies. The language thing was new, with its rhythm accommodating the F-word several times in each sentence: 'Oh, botheration!' was about the only curse we ever heard from the staff at Spurgeon's.

We conscripts came from all parts of the kingdom, but in my hut it was soon obvious that a handful of boys from London were determined to rule the roost. As well as the route marching, saluting, and rifle drills, we all had to endure more irksome and messy chores, like applying a greenish-coloured paste known as blanco to our belts, gaiters and ammunition pouches, as well as bringing our boots to a brilliant shine aided by the vigorous application of a toothbrush handle to eliminate tiny wrinkles in the leather of the toe caps.

One night, a couple of the London youths approached me to demonstrate a new, faster method for blancoing they had discovered. They showed that a shaving brush remarkably speeded up the job, as well as achieving a better finish. I graciously accepted their invitation to borrow the brush they were using to 'bull' my own kit.

Next morning, I awoke and made my way blearily to the washhouse clutching my sponge bag, only to find that my shaving brush was missing. I realised that when the Londoners had been so friendly to me the previous evening, what I had been using was my own brush to apply the blanco. Failing to see the funny side, I flew into a rage and attacked one of them. It finished with my opponent lying bleeding and half-conscious on the floor while I nursed a broken hand.

The consequence of all this was that, although I recovered my sense of humour and made peace with my antagonists (who refused to lay a complaint of assault against me) I was unable to hold a rifle or finish my training, which still had ten days of the six-week course left, with nothing for me to do but hang around the barrack room with a plaster cast on my hand while everyone else carried on without me. I was also a mere spectator to the climax to any recruit's induction into the army – the final passing-out parade on the barrack square with the newly-created soldiers marching up and down, stamping their feet in a fashion that would have delighted old Beazer back at Spurgeon's. Nevertheless, I was presumed to have completed my training, the necessary stamps were inserted into my records, and I awaited my first posting.

At Deepcut, after the first phase of training was completed, one collected weekend passes, rattling down to the railway station nearest the barracks in an army lorry packed full of youths boasting in lurid terms of what they would be doing to their girlfriends when they got home. The distance to London by rail was too short to qualify for free tickets except for prolonged home leave, so a technique was adopted – probably inherited from earlier generations of soldiers – to avoid paying the fare. When we reached Waterloo station we would charge off the train in a great mass, ignoring the ticket collectors at the platform gates, each of us waving a ten shilling note. The desperate collectors would grab one or two soldiers, who would immediately proffer the fare money (amounting only to a couple of shillings, and therefore requiring change to be given), leaving everyone else to sprint safely into the station concourse and away. Some weekends this ploy failed to work: military policemen were lined up to enforce the authority of the ticket collectors.

My first posting turned out to be a temporary clerical job at the Citadel in Plymouth, an old stone-built fortress with enormously thick walls, where what the army called a TEWT – a Tactical Exercise Without Troops – was taking place. This involved a lot of paper work being shuffled between different offices as a theoretical battle was fought out through an exchange of memos between generals and staff officers. (There must have been a problem finding a distinguishing acronym for a Tactical Exercise With Troops.)

While at Aldershot I had become friends with George Metcalfe, son of the northern sports editor of the *Daily Mail*, and before his call-up, a reporter on the Hampstead & Highgate News. His first posting was to attend a course lasting several weeks at the Army Records Office.

George's job, amazingly, allowed him as much access to the army's levers of power as any general, which he swiftly seized, for he wrote to me at Plymouth to offer three possible postings, any one of which, he airily announced, he could grant me. The first was to the British military mission in Saigon, where the French were engaged in their bitter war with the Viet Minh to retain a hold over their then colony of Vietnam. The second, I have now forgotten. And the third was to report to the headquarters of the Brussels Treaty, a forerunner of NATO, housed at Dover House in Whitehall, just opposite the Cenotaph.

Unaware that Vietnam would a few years later become quite the story it made when the Americans took over the struggle from the French, and that some familiarity with Saigon might have made me a hot piece of journalistic property, I plumped for the home-town option of the Brussels Treaty, and within a few weeks I'd duly become a Whitehall warrior: when I reported for duty George was the first person I met.

The military wing of the Treaty, an alliance between Britain, France, Belgium, the Netherlands and that military giant, Luxembourg, was headed by Field Marshal Montgomery. Unlike the tales we had heard during the war of his disciplinarian ways, life at his headquarters at Dover House was extremely relaxed or 'cushy' as the army term would describe it. We lived at our own homes, had no need to wear uniform except on Fridays when we reported at an army office in Great Scotland Yard, just off Whitehall, to collect our pay, and spent a great deal of our working time playing table tennis. One of our offices was where Charles I spent his final night before his execution precisely 300 years earlier at the Banqueting Hall on the opposite side of Whitehall.

I mostly found myself working for General David Belchem, Monty's chief of staff, who had been the army's youngest brigadier during the war, and was beside him when he accepted the surrender of the German army at Luneberg Heath, marking the end of the war in Europe.

The Field Marshal usually preferred writing personal letters and memos by hand – often, ominously, in green ink – rather than dictating to me, to George, or to the several other nascent journalists spending their eighteen months' national service in such comfort and ease while other unfortunates fought in the jungles of Malaya, faced mad hordes of Chinese troops in Korea, went crazy with boredom on guard duty at remote bases in Germany, or – worst of all - worked down the mines as Bevin Boys.

Belchem was amused by his boss's writing style, complaining one day when we were deciphering the great man's latest script, which I then had to type up, 'The Field Marshal keeps his punctuation in a pepper pot, and sprinkles random commas, colons and semi-colons all over the page once he's finished writing.' But if his punctuation was poor, Monty certainly believed in the power of his own signature; one evening the young officer who acted as his aide-de-camp rushed into our office to borrow a pair of braces, as the Field Marshal's elasticated hold-ups had snapped just as he was preparing to leave the office to present the prizes at the amateur boxing championships. A corpulent staff sergeant, named Pawley, removed his own army issue white, non-stretch cotton braces, having no fear that his trousers would fall down, and they were rushed to Monty. Next morning they were returned by the messenger, inscribed, 'Thank you for the use of these braces' and signed, 'Montgomery of Alamein.' Maybe they'll turn up one day on the Antiques Roadshow.

I had many opportunities to study Montgomery, sitting in on group discussions or conferences in his office overlooking Whitehall, occasionally taking dictation from him, and reading his correspondence. Years later, when stories began to circulate after his death in 1976 that he had a homosexual taste for young men and boys, I did not believe it: nor do I, to this day. The one deep attachment obvious from his correspondence, to which I was privy, was towards his daughter-in-law, then living with his son, now the second Viscount Montgomery, in Hong Kong.

The two character traits I most remember about the Field Marshal were his acquisitiveness and his hypochondria. I have never encountered anyone so terrified of the common cold. At the onset of the infection he would sit at the head of a long conference table with a towel over his head and a steaming bowl of Epsom salts beneath his beaky nose. If this failed to cure it, he would retire to his house in Hampshire, a converted mill, until he recovered.

An example of his acquisitive nature was his remark on the radio during a trip to America that he had just discovered peanut butter – a delicacy virtually unknown in those days in Britain. Immediately he said it, manufacturers of the substance began sending him samples of their product by the crate-load: they were shipped to his house, Isington Mill, where they remained, presumably, unless he became addicted to the stuff, until his death. On a visit to the Mill on some errand or other, I saw a cornucopia of goods acquired by or gifted to Britain's greatest soldier, including one of the caravans, presumably the property of the army, he had used as a headquarters during his wartime campaigns, and a brand new, unused, dispatch rider's motorbike, still in the grease it was packed in when it rolled off the manufacturer's production line. He also hoarded the German army's document of capitulation, provoking some MPs to demand its return as the rightful property of the state: I don't know whether they succeeded in forcing him to surrender his prize.

The army also supplied Monty with his own aeroplane, an Avro Anson twin-engined workhorse, formerly the property, I believe, of the French racehorse owner, Marcel Boussac. Dover House had a branch office in France, at the Château Henri IV near Fontainebleau, and we shorthand writers were sometimes airlifted over there in the Anson. These trips involved hard work, for a change, with long hours and no time to enjoy the delights of this pleasant part of France, the attractions of which, so we were informed, included an extremely popular one-legged prostitute. The Anson was also used by all ranks to ship cigarettes, whisky and gin back to austerity-ridden Britain. Soon enough, however, we would turn our backs on London for the dream experience of any national serviceman of our generation as we moved to Paris.

Even at that time, barely five years after the end of the war, the city was a delight. There was no sign of the destruction we saw all around us in London, and Paris had not yet been marred by the skyscrapers erected in the Pompidou years that disfigure some of the finest views from the centre of the city. One indication that the French were getting back to normal was a strike by bus and underground workers in progress as we arrived, and for some days afterwards. Army lorries were drafted in to provide public transport, filled with pretty girls laughing and waving on their way to work: it was just like the newsreels of the crowds welcoming Allied troops into the city after the Germans were ejected.

Our move followed the Brussels Treaty Organisation being subsumed into SHAPE – Supreme Headquarters Allied Powers Europe – and our new office was the Hotel Astoria on the Champs Elysée, the building from which Hitler reviewed his troops after the collapse of France in 1940. Our work remained the same as it was in London: planning for the eventuality of a Russian invasion of Western Europe. Despite my earlier flirtation with the Communist Party, no-one ever asked me about any dodgy affiliations I might have had in civilian life, and I was permitted to read documents relating to matters sufficiently sensitive to be designated not just Secret or Top Secret, but Metric Top Secret (and, of course, I had signed the Official Secrets Act).

The notes I took at meetings and conferences, together with other secret papers, were locked up every night in the office safe by a captain fulfilling one of the few responsibilities demanded of him – even so, he would often leave the task to me when he wished to leave early.

In Paris the French were understandably adamant after their recent disagreeable experiences that they did not wish to see people in the uniforms of foreign armies on their streets. So I continued as a soldier in civvies, living no longer with the Fowler family in West Kensington but in a tiny pension overlooking the old cycle track, the Vélodrome, in the St Didier quarter of the haute monde 16th arrondisement of

Paris, just off the Place Trocadéro. My workplace was a converted bathroom at the Astoria with an oblique view from the window on to the Place de L'Etoile, now, of course, renamed Place General de Gaulle, and its centrepiece, the Arc-de-Triomphe. Nor did it take me long to discover that life in Paris left little time for table tennis.

The Field Marshal had now become (oxymoronically) the Deputy Supreme Allied Commander, Europe, or in one of the alphabet soups beloved by the military, DSACEUR. The Supreme Allied Commander, SACEUR, was General Eisenhower, Monty's D-Day boss, a man I was to meet from time to time and who, in common with most of the American military, was impressively courteous: unlike any British army officer I ever met, his first gesture on meeting 'other ranks' like myself, was to shake their hand.

When I started going out with dark and pretty Marie, from Normandy, an assistant at a grocery shop on the Avenue Kléber which announced itself on its sign simply as 'Buerre Oeufs Fromages', I passed a carton of Lucky Strike, bought at the American version of the Naafi, the PX, each week to the concièrge so that she would not notice when I brought my girlfriend to my room for the night. By now, after a shaky start, I had quite shed my fear of girls, thanks to the general British notion of Paris as a sinful and lustful place.

SHAPE eventually outgrew the Hotel Astoria – since pulled down – and we were moved out of the centre of Paris to a new purpose-built headquarters, a sprawling complex thirty miles outside the city, identified by the British as Marly-le-Roi, and the Americans as Rocquencourt. Before leaving Paris, however, we were privileged to occupy one of the finest viewing points for the Liberation Day parade on July 14th, 1950. The Field Marshal, in mufti, along with his multi-national staff, was to watch the march-past along the Champs Elysées informally from a balcony of the Astoria.

I squeezed on to the balcony with everyone else, hearing French army tank engines starting to roar somewhere to our right in the direction of the Place de la République. Opposite us, a regiment of French paratroopers was lining the route. As the sound of the tanks grew closer they were drowned out by a formation of jets flying low overhead. The French paras were called to attention, but the man precisely opposite our balcony put his rifle between his knees, removed his beret and tucked it under his shoulder-strap, produced a comb, and started to arrange his hair.

I could see a look of indescribable astonishment and disbelief cross the Field Marshal's features. Then, just as the parade was about to draw level, the soldier, with perfect timing, swiftly reversed his movements to be standing rigidly to attention, just in time. How bothered was Monty, I wondered years later, when SHAPE had been wound up and the French resigned from the military wing of its successor, NATO? Not too much, I suspect, if he remembered this incident.

Philip Hope-Wallace and Guiness Bird

Chapter 10

George Metcalfe, the private soldier who somehow secured for himself the powers of a member of the general staff, and used those powers to arrange my luxurious National Service existence in central London and Paris, was in touch with me again when I was about to return to civilian life and hoping to resume my career as a reporter.

There was a snag, however, for while enjoying myself in Paris I had happily signed on in the army for an additional six months. Somebody had found a little-known clause in the regulations that permitted this brief extension so as to avoid disruption in Field Marshal Montgomery's office during the time we were due to move from the Hotel Astoria into SHAPE's new headquarters at Marly-le-Roi.

Most National Servicemen kept calendars on which they marked off the remaining time they had left to serve. A few enjoyed life enough to become regulars, signing on for periods of years, but very few, I imagine, agreed as I did to continue serving six months more, when all about me couldn't wait for their 'demob'.

When I was called up in 1949, national service lasted for eighteen months, but was then, because of the Korean war, extended to two years. By voluntarily staying on beyond the statutory time, I automatically lost my legal right to return to my old job on the *Fulham Gazette*. Just as well, for that impoverished paper would have had to sack one of its two reporters to re-employ me.

But George was now on the *Fulham Chronicle*, the oldest-established paper in the borough and part of a larger chain of local newspapers. He wrote to tell me that the *Chronicle* had need of a reporter. I arranged to see Arthur Sly, the editor, and was hired.

Arthur Sly was both sleek, with his silver hair and bank manager's demeanour, and stout, a man of tremendous gravitas, hugely respected as a member of the Fulham establishment. He never spoke without first emitting a little cough, like a butler politely seeking your attention, and except for extremely important council meetings where the level of council tax, known in those days as the rates, was being fixed, he seldom did any reporting himself, confining his efforts to writing the leader column and the gossip column, politely known as his notebook.

Outdoor reporting was the responsibility of the chief reporter, John Pryke, neatly dressed and moustached, like an English version of the Hollywood comedy star, Adolphe Menjou. He assigned reporters to their tasks, including a New Zealander, Graham Birkett, who had flown Catalina flying boats in the Pacific during the war, and Pryke's son, Peter, who would later join the *Daily Telegraph's* parliamentary staff. On Thursday, publishing day, once our one and only edition had safely gone to press and Arthur Sly headed for home, John presided over our weekly editorial game of pontoon, or vingt-et-un, in the office.

Pryke senior was also the Fulham correspondent, or stringer, for most of the national newspapers, and if any of us came across a story that was deemed worthy of a wider audience than our local rag, it would be sent off to the *Mail* or *Express* in Pryke's name. When the payments arrived, he would disburse the money to the underlings, making a modest deduction to meet his own tax bill.

In 1953, when excitement over the forthcoming Coronation was rising to fever pitch, some jokey acquaintances, seeing a naïve and inexperienced reporter approaching, persuaded me that a costermonger in Fulham had received a message from Buckingham

Palace asking if they might borrow his horse, apparently similar enough in appearance to one in the royal stables, to make a matching pair to draw one of the less important coaches in the Coronation procession.

The tale of the horse obviously struck me as a good story. I was introduced to the sincerest costermonger who ever existed, and his horse, which made up in character what it lacked in appearance, and assurances were sworn on a stack of Bibles that the letter containing the request from the Palace was genuine – it was just not possible to see it with my own eyes because the recipient had been sworn to secrecy. I hastened to tell John Pryke that we had a great story. He, in turn, sent my scoop to the *Daily Express*. I was disappointed when the tale failed to appear in the columns of that week's edition of our own paper, but I found it rather close to press day so I imagined it would appear the following week. And, of course, I eagerly scanned Lord Beaverbrook's great organ each morning, hoping to see my story, with a picture of the soon-to-be famous horse, on the front page.

There was no sign of it, and after a few days John showed me a cheque and an account he'd received from the *Daily Express*. The cheque was a handsome one - for 10/6d, or half a guinea (52 ½ p) – but the accompanying handwritten details baldly stated, 'Horse NOT for Coronation'. The reputational damage at Fleet Street level was done not to me but my senior colleague, 'Pryke of Fulham', as he was their agent, but he never complained.

Before long I began to think it was time for me to move on to get closer to Fleet Street. I was growing tired of the trivial lot of the local reporter, shut out from the big stories and events. The one court we regularly attended was the coroner's court at Hammersmith, which covered a number of West London boroughs and was presided over by a sardonic coroner (a lesser character than the great Mr Bentley-Purchase, the St Pancras coroner, whom I was later to encounter, a genuine eccentric who foreswore the evil of wearing socks). The Hammersmith incumbent became greatly irritated by the sight of half a dozen reporters sprawled on the benches on one side of his court reading the morning newspapers while waiting for an inquest into a death in their own borough to begin. 'I would remind the gentlemen of the Press,' he would say sarcastically, halting the proceedings and gesturing towards us teenage scribblers, 'that this is not a public library reading room.'

Inquest juries were drawn randomly from among passers-by in the street. Not all enquiries into sudden or unusual deaths earned the attention of a jury. For example, every couple of months group inquests were held into the routine discovery of aborted or discarded foetuses scraped from the filters of a riverside power station, all unnamed and unwanted, cast into the Thames by their unknown mothers. These were such a routine event that they went unreported in the papers. Yet when the police found a back-street abortionist or a qualified doctor alleged to be conducting abortions, it was regarded as Page One news. It was as if fishing had been declared a crime but only a few skilful anglers were ever prosecuted.

Policemen assigned as coroner's officers – their job was to trace relatives of the dead, or witnesses whose evidence might be needed - also manned a small mortuary and laboratory at the rear of the premises for the use of visiting pathologists. Coroners' officers delighted in showing us prized specimens in jars of the largest penises removed from the bodies of the dead, and other curiosities, before we all adjourned to a pub across the road to recover from the grisly sights we had just seen.

An additional sense of excitement always pervaded any coroner's court where the glamorous figure of Dr (later Professor Sir) Francis Camps, arrived to give evidence at an inquest. Employed by the Home Office, he was usually accompanied by his beautiful, red-haired assistant, and was unusually friendly and approachable by comparison with most professional witnesses one encountered. I was to meet him again a few years after I had left the *Chronicle* while covering the investigation into the suspected Eastbourne murderer, Dr John Bodkin Adams.

I was staying at the New Inn at the Sussex resort when Camps arrived, and I exchanged cheery greetings with him at the bar. That evening, we reporters got wind of a police operation, and the reason for Camps's presence became clear: the bodies of two elderly and wealthy women, former patients of Bodkin Adams, were to be disinterred from their graves in the town cemetery. The weather, just before Christmas 1956, was bitterly cold so I wore a pair of pyjamas under my clothes and equipped myself with a half-bottle of whisky (of a brand I'd never encountered before) to help me survive the rigours of the night. There was not much to see – the police erected tents over the section of the graveyard being excavated - but it was noticeable that they were working at one end of the graveyard, at the bottom of a slope.

A local policeman told me that water had turned this end of the cemetery into a quagmire, causing the bodies to swell and burst out of their coffins. Camps worked the rest of the night in the mortuary examining and dissecting the bodies. Yet there he was next morning at breakfast in the hotel as perky as ever, buttering his toast, spreading it with marmalade before delicately slicing it into quarters and popping the segments into his mouth and chatting with his delectable assistant. At the neighbouring table, my own mouth was ringed by third degree burns from the suspect whisky with which I had fortified myself the night before.

To get on in journalism before the age of media studies there was a generally prescribed route to be taken, and one essential qualification: shorthand. Reporters, few of whom in my early days had been to university, would generally start on a local weekly before moving to a provincial evening or morning paper, from whence the jump could be made to Fleet Street. Some people took other routes, perhaps working for trade papers or starting out as office boys on national papers or news agencies and, once they'd started shaving, moving into a staff job, but in most cases the common denominator for aspiring journalists was shorthand. Quite a few leading female journalists began as editorial secretaries, though a notable exception was Rita Marshall, a top-grade Fleet Street reporter who became the first woman news editor of *The Times*. She had the advantage of a father who was a lift operator at the *Daily Express*. He successfully interceded with Lord Beaverbrook one morning, while taking him up to his office, to give Rita a job as a reporter.

As Sammy Soester and Arthur Sly were the only press lords I had met, I knew that my best bet would be to try the provinces. I travelled up to Coventry to be interviewed for a job on the *Evening Telegraph*, but failed to get it. Then I saw a job advertised on the *Western Daily Press* in Bristol, and this time I was successful.

Chapter 11

Joining the *Western Daily Press* from a Fulham weekly was tantamount to a footballer being transferred from the third to the second division. Bristol was a bustling city with a range of industries, and boasted a brand of bareback-riding capitalism whose leading lights proudly called themselves Merchant Venturers. Bristol's assets included tobacco factories, aircraft manufacturing, and financial services, a spread that ensured that during recessions it was seldom hit as hard as other places dependent on only one or two industries. It also possessed a busy port that had flourished during and after the boost bestowed by the slave trade.

When I arrived the city supported no fewer than three daily newspapers, the morning *Western Daily Press*, the *Bristol Evening World*, owned by Northcliffe (now Associated) Newspapers, and the *Bristol Evening Post*: the *Daily Press* and the *Post* were locally owned. The city was also a cultural centre, with several theatres, including the 18th century Old Vic, the florid, curlicued Hippodrome, and a permanent repertory company at the Little Theatre. Religion was still a powerful force, the city attracting ambitious clerics like the politically influential Mervyn Stockwood, of Bristol's St Mary Redcliffe church, subsequently a Canon of St Paul's Cathedral, and one of the founders of the Campaign for Nuclear Disarmament.

Artistically, Bristol could show itself to be somewhat less progressive. It had a fine museum, but when its curator, the distinguished scholar Hans Schubart, daringly acquired a Henry Moore piece for the city, the acquisition was greeted by a roar of philistine disapproval the moment it went on display. To my untutored eye the piece looked like a Roman curaisse, or body armour, giving it a romantic and historical air. Some critics ludicrously complained that the piece had no head, a blemish more appropriately applying to the city council majority who rejected the sculpture, given the rising value of Moore over succeeding years. Schubart was humiliatingly forced to return the sculpture to the artist.

The *Daily Press* occupied a remarkable building of a wedge shape not unlike the New York skyscraper, the 1902 Flatiron Building on Fifth Avenue. Its roofline was decorated with Grecian urns, one of which was jokingly said to hold the ashes of the great Gloucestershire cricketer and local hero, Dr. W.G. Grace. The interior, however, was clad in wood panelling, behind which, in a patented process, the cavity to the exterior brick walls was filled with sawdust.

This made the building an exceptionally high fire risk and it was a sackable offence to smoke anywhere in the office except in one entirely stone-built room on the ground floor. This produced an unusually democratic atmosphere for a newspaper, since almost everybody smoked in those days (and tobacco was one of Bristol's great industries), so that everyone from the editor, Mr Shapcott, to the machine-room hands, gathered in the smoking room at various times during the day.

Times were tough for the paper, and competition in a crowded local media market was fierce. One trusted machine hand, it was said, was paid a little extra to guard the gauge registering the number of copies printed each day by covering it from prying eyes with his raincoat. He was required to memorise the total before turning the counter back to zero and then reporting the true figure to the managing director.

I arrived at the paper a little after school-leaver Tom Stoppard joined the staff, and it was the future playwright, demonstrating huge enthusiasm, who showed me around the regular newsgathering places, such as police stations, the port authority, and the council offices.

Socially, Bristol was an entirely new experience for me. We wandered out of the office to assemble in mid-morning at Carwardine's coffee house, where we would meet the theatricals – among them Dorothy Reynolds and Julian Slade, creators of the joyous musical hit, Salad Days; Peter O'Toole, who was appearing at the Bristol Old Vic and, it was whispered, conducting an affair with a girl reporter on the *Daily Press*; and actors with visiting shows at the Hippodrome.

When Noel Coward visited Bristol, John Tidmarsh, one of my new colleagues who subsequently became a stalwart of the *World Service* of the BBC, was sent round to the great man's hotel to seek an interview. Reportorial cunning enabled him to discover the number of Coward's room and his knock on the door was answered by the great actor and playwright wearing, as one would expect, a resplendent dressing gown. 'Ah, Mr Coward,' said John, 'I'm from the *Western Daily Press* and I've been sent to interview you.' One hand on his chest thrust Tidmarsh out into the corridor while the other swung the door shut, as Coward dismissed him with the immortal line, 'Silly go-ahead boy! '

I found digs with a pleasant young couple in a small terraced house in Clifton, but felt a sense of relief in bidding farewell to this temporary home on leaving Bristol, for the wife, her husband out early to work, would insist at breakfast time on placing my hands on her breasts , where numerous lumps turned them into bags of marsh mellows, while she discussed the treatment she was receiving at the Bristol Royal Infirmary. It may sound extremely naïve, but there was not the slightest sexual element or embarrassment on her part in sharing with me her anxieties concerning an intimate part of her body. I, however, I did have to overcome my embarrassment.

I stayed only about a year with the *Daily Press*, for I had become engaged and was anxious to return to London. My happy stay in Bristol unfortunately ended with a slight unpleasantness. In the 1950s the names of reporters rarely appeared above their stories and authorship was the anonymous 'Our Own Reporter', or 'Our Own Correspondent'. Personal by-lines were starting to creep in, but were confined to specialist columnists and critics, or occasionally granted as a reward for a particularly good story. So when I was asked to stroll around the city persuading people to give me their thoughts on the forthcoming Christmas holiday, and the article appeared with my name at the foot, albeit in tiny letters, I was quite pleased.

Then I saw that the rest of the page was covered with Christmas advertisements, obviously solicited specially by the paper's advertising department to go with the article. Known in the trade as 'advertorial' this is something that happens with depressing frequency today, but back then journalists jealously guarded a separation between advertising and editorial content.

So, far from being pleased to have my first and only by-line in the *Western Daily Press*, I felt ashamed at seeing my name in what I rather pompously regarded as a sordid commercial context, and felt I had been treated deceitfully.

My next step towards an admittedly rather broad and unfocused ambition – all I really wanted was to get a reporter's job in Fleet Street – was frustrated when I was talked out of the first job I applied for.

I'd seen an advertisement by the *Exchange Telegraph* news agency for a reporter to help cover the Law Courts, and interviewed by Mr Byrne, the editor of *Extel*. I was anxious to boast that I already had some knowledge of the court system as a result of occasional moonlighting as a note-taker when the divorce division of the High Court – a moveable feast in those days – was sitting in Bristol. What I didn't tell him was that I had never been required to transcribe a single line from my shorthand notebooks, nor to write a story based on anything I'd heard in court except to provide the paper with a list of names for publication: in fact, I was forbidden to do so.

This was because my role was confined to hearings of undefended cases. However, to overcome any tendency on the part of reporters earning a few pounds in this fashion to take their duties lightly, we were sternly warned of the existence of a powerful official called the Queen's Proctor, who had the right to overturn a divorce petition if he suspected collusion by the parties in presenting their evidence of adultery, cruelty or desertion.

Because of an intervention by the Proctor or an appeal, even years after the case had been heard, the shorthand writer was under a strict obligation to produce, word for word, everything that had passed in court. And if he failed to come up with the goods, he would have to pay for the case to be re-heard, which would cost some frightening sum.

However, the job Mr Byrne had on offer was not for an official shorthand writer, but a reporter to write news stories based on civil cases, including libel actions, commercial disputes, and such lip-smacking legal dramas as alienation of affection and breach of promise cases – both sadly missed by Fleet Street since their abolition – where the rich would sue over a broken engagement, claim damages or compensation for a mistress allegedly enticed away by a rival with gifts or other blandishments, or even to force the return of gifts bestowed upon a discarded paramour.

A kindly man, what worried Mr Byrne on learning that I was about to be married, was that reporters were not paid during the long vacations enjoyed by the Law Courts, and that I would need to find other work to make up the shortfall. 'Go back to Bristol,' he advised, 'and I will contact you when something more suitable comes up.'

As good as his word, he called me a few weeks later to offer me a full-time staff job as a general reporter. The upshot was that in 1953 I was plunged into the most hard-working period of my life, before or since – once I had recovered from appendicitis, which struck me within a day of starting the job.

On a typical working day, the *Extel* news desk would call me at breakfast time, sending me off to attend a court hearing anywhere around London, perhaps to report the brief arraignment of a newly-arrested murderer or bank robber, to cover a press conference, or dash out to the airport to witness the arrival or departure of some dignitary.

I remember an outing to Heathrow to see the Foreign Secretary, Anthony Eden, returning from negotiations in Switzerland on the conflict between France, the colonial power in Vietnam, and the rebel Vietminh, forerunners of the Vietcong. In those days the press facilities at Heathrow consisted of a Nissen hut tucked away at the edge of the airport, and we were allowed to greet incoming statesmen, film stars and other notables as they came down the steps of the aircraft, questioning them on their way to the hut where press conferences were held. (I recall this particular occasion because someone noticed that Eden was wearing a black tie and asked whether this was due to a bereavement: 'No,' replied Eden, slightly taken aback, 'I always wear a black tie with a blue suit'. A swift ad lib, but probably not quite a truthful one for an acknowledged dandy).

Television news was then in its infancy, and the first news producers fancied themselves as film directors, trying to manipulate press conferences into film sets rather than occasions for the more numerous writing press to do their work. They would address a crowd of newspaper reporters in the hut while their cumbersome equipment was being set up, telling us to imagine a white line drawn across the floor which on no account should we cross. On one occasion we were even urged by a director, preposterously wearing a Hollywood-style fur coat, 'Please look as though you are taking notes', thinking, I suppose, to add a little colour to the proceedings and apparently unaware that taking notes and asking questions was what reporters were for.

So irritated did we become with these would-be Cecil B. De Milles that we would indulge in a little sabotage, chattering loudly while they were trying to do their interviews and absolutely refusing to take orders from such upstarts. We won the odd battle, but as most people now derive their news from TV bulletins or the web, we newspapermen lost the war.

The rest of my job was parliamentary reporting as part of the agency's four-strong parliamentary reporting team. At around 5.30 or 6 p.m., after *Question Time* and the main opening speeches of the day's chosen debate, with everyone else adjourned to the bar, apart from some unfortunate backbench MP addressing an almost empty chamber, I would cross the road to Norman Shaw's crenellated fortress on the Embankment which then housed New Scotland Yard, headquarters of the Metropolitan Police. There I would hang about until 11 p.m. awaiting any news that might be dispensed by the crabby and unforthcoming public relations staff. The information was usually terse and came in typewritten form conveyed to us, like chickens being fed, through a tiny hatch by an unseen poultryman:

we were fearful only that we might be caught on the hop should the most famous and frequent post-war prison escaper, Alfie Hinds, then at large for the third time, suddenly be re-captured.

Thankfully, my tedious nightly Scotland Yard vigil didn't last too long before I started to be given my evenings back (but always 'on call'). And when Parliament was not sitting I was out on the road covering every kind of story, including the political party conferences each autumn, general elections, by-elections, strikes, disasters, and sensational cases in the provincial criminal courts. Life was good.

Early in my time with *Extel* I made the acquaintance of Tom Driberg, newspaper columnist, Left wing MP, eventually a member of the House of Lords, and – something that immediately became obvious to me – homosexual. The unsuitable setting for this encounter was Lambeth Palace, where we were covering an important occasion in the calendar of the Church of England, the Convocation of Canterbury, and the press table was positioned between the clergy and the bench of bishops, presided over by the Archbishop of Canterbury. When the morning session broke up Driberg, heavily built and jowly, approached me, grasped my hand in his, and introduced himself, 'I don't think I've seen you about before – if you want any help or advice please don't hesitate to telephone me at *Picture Post*,' (in those days a famous publication, the British equivalent of America's *Life* magazine). He seemed unwilling to let go of my hand, and I was in a hurry to get to a phone to send my story to the office.

In the following months I was frequently approached by him in the environs of the House of Commons and sometimes on Westminster underground station: I regarded him as a pest and took to ducking behind a pillar when I saw him. To be fancied by Driberg was an experience I apparently shared with Mick Jagger, Aneurin Bevan, even James Callaghan, and doubtless many, many others, as he pursued his promiscuous ways.

Over the years, however, I came to know him reasonably well, enjoying his sharp conversation and his acute slant on his fellow politicians. It was also impossible not to notice his extraordinary rudeness towards the underclass, particularly waiters, which may, of course, have been another variation on his sexual proclivities: I know that this aspect of his character embarrassed Conor Cruise O'Brien, Michael Foot, and other Left wing luminaries, in whose company I would sometimes meet him. As a former gossip writer – he had written the William Hickey column on the *Daily Express* – he was himself the object of gossip, and an alleged remark of Churchill's when Driberg, surprisingly, announced that he was to be married, was much circulated. An aide is said to have reassured the astonished Churchill that the bride was an extremely ugly woman. 'Well,' the old prime minister is supposed to have observed, 'Buggers can't be choosers.'

Towards the end of his life Driberg bought a flat in the then new Barbican development in the City of London, where one evening he showed my wife and me around: everyone was eager to see what these surprisingly cheap flats, sometimes derided as council dwellings for the better-off, were like. Opening the door to the second bedroom, which contained no furniture but was stacked almost wall to wall with large Victorian paintings in their ornate frames, he announced, 'There's my pension.' And sure enough, Victorian art, then deeply unfashionable, was soon to come back into favour, though a little too late for Driberg, who died in a taxi in 1976, aged 71.

I was a little surprised to discover on making an occasional pre-lunch visit to the office of my employers that the morning routine was quite a contrast to my own frenzied rush. My patron, Mr Byrne, would be sitting among the teleprinters and typewriters in his newsroom playing chess and drinking coffee for hours on end with his more senior staff, among them the soon-to-be-famous Alan Whicker.

I can't say that the future presenter of Whicker's World, Around Whicker's World, Whicker on Top of the World, Whicker Down Mexico Way, Whicker's New World, The World of Whicker, and the rest, was just another foot-in-the-door reporter in a dirty raincoat. On the contrary, he was as elegant, smoothly-spoken and agreeable in those days as the much-loved TV star Whicker would become, and the neatly-trimmed moustache and horn-rimmed glasses were already part of his image long before he stepped into a TV studio.

But when Parliament was sitting, the central part of my work remained my daily reporting from the Commons. The very first exchange I covered at *Question Time* on my first day as a parliamentary reporter came from a Labour MP, Philip Noel-Baker – a pacifist and minister in the previous government who was to be awarded the Nobel Peace Prize a few years later. His question was directed at Winston Churchill, less than a year from his retirement as prime minister: it was the peacenik versus the war leader.

The great man heaved himself slowly to his feet, grasping the edge of the table in front of him, to offer Noel-Baker a standard monosyllabic ministerial answer, 'No, sir,' to the question printed in the order paper. It was now Noel-Baker's right to ask a supplementary question, the subject at issue being what in those days was still known as the 'atom bomb'. Noel-Baker appeared to be seeking information that even I appreciated could hardly be answered truthfully without offering state secrets to our then-enemy, the Soviet Union.

Churchill rose again to respond. 'The answer to the Right Honourable Gentleman's question,' he said, 'depends upon the accurate assessment of a variety of imponderables.' As this sentence emerged, I was not wondering how on earth something imponderable could be assessed accurately. My problem was how to get the sentence into my notebook (imponderable, is an awkward word to write in Pitman's shorthand). I set off at the top left-hand of the page in speedy style, but palms sweating, my pencil nervously spiralled down to the bottom right corner with me fearing I would never be able to read the squiggles back: I didn't need to worry because it was already burned into my memory.

Churchill's performance at the despatch box that day certainly shamed those Tory politicians of the time who regarded the great war leader at eighty as a feeble geriatric barring the way to a glorious new chapter to be written by his long-time successor-in-waiting, the handsome and dapper Anthony Eden.

When Churchill at last stepped down from the premiership, Eden sensibly called a swift election, securing a workable majority of 58, the future seemingly set fair for him after his years of waiting. My role during this 1957 election was to follow Herbert Morrison, deputy leader of the Labour Party, on the campaign trail. He was by then a declining political force: he would make an ill-advised bid for the leadership of the party when Clement Attlee stood down and was easily defeated by the younger Hugh Gaitskell. A fascinating but now largely forgotten character, Morrison's name is sometimes invoked in profiles of a contemporary politician, Peter Mandelson, whose grandfather he was. Born in Lambeth in 1888, he lost an eye when he was run over by a horse and cart, and left school at fourteen. In a sense, he created modern London as leader of the London County Council, unifying the transport system, creating the Green Belt, and building the present Waterloo Bridge, which was opened in 1942 while he was Home Secretary in Churchill's wartime Cabinet.

Things were simpler in the Fifties, so to accompany Morrison on the campaign I merely had to telephone and ask him for his schedule of meetings, rather than going through the impenetrable public relations and security bureaucracy surrounding politicians today. His first foray from London was to East Anglia, and he suggested I accompany him in his car.

We were driven by Morrison's second wife, Edith, a Lancastrian with an irrepressible instinct for speaking her mind, but a hopeless navigator. During one of our enforced detours, the veteran politician recalled the wartime coalition, clearly aggrieved that Churchill had never said a word to his Cabinet colleagues about the development of the atom bomb, or the decision to deploy it. 'The first I ever heard about it was when the news of the bombing of Hiroshima and Nagasaki appeared in the newspapers,' he told me.

It is hard to imagine now, but in those days in the villages of Suffolk and Norfolk – our starting point - farm workers were reluctant to emerge from their cottages or place election posters in their windows when Labour Party canvassers arrived with their loudspeakers and leaflets, for fear of offending their farmer or aristocrat (or both) landlords. So when the Morrisons arrived with the local Labour candidate it was like visiting a series of ghost towns. One consolation came with my first sight of a young, articulate, alarmingly excitable and red-faced Labour politician, George Brown, at a public meeting we attended in the country town of Stowmarket in Suffolk: I would have been astonished had I been told that forty years later I would write a biography of the brilliant but wayward Brown.

A week or so later I was with the Morrisons in the North, where the inhibitions so apparent in the East were absent. Among Herbert's many engagements was a meeting of miners in a village outside Rochdale – his wife's home town. We were running late and the audience had been packed into a school classroom for an hour on a warm night. Nevertheless, he was determined not to short-change his audience, settling down into a lengthy lecture on the subject of foreign affairs.

This was not the ideal subject for him to choose, for he had served a brief and disastrous term as Foreign Secretary in the course of Labour's precarious 1951 government, facing much ridicule from the press on his performance. Morrison put the miners of Rochdale on the rack, serving up his disappointments as great successes, until they must almost have expired from boredom. As we staggered out of the meeting and made for the car, Edith Morrison gestured towards the miners streaming out of the school and stretching their legs. 'Ee, 'erbert,' she said, 'That were a bit above their 'eads.'

I was a spellbound spectator of the wild scenes in the House as Eden's premiership crashed on the rocks of the Suez fiasco in 1956. The crisis caused by the nationalisation by President Nasser of the Suez Canal, gave rise to bouts of tumultuous behaviour among MPs, much more so than the docile mood of the Commons in the run-up to Bush and Blair's war on Iraq in 2003. In the Suez debates the Speaker frequently had to suspend sittings as tempers boiled over amid strenuous but untruthful denials by the government of British duplicity in conspiring with France and Israel to attack Egypt. Ostensibly the action was to protect the sovereignty of Israel, but its secret real purpose had always been to wrest back international control of the Suez Canal.

Oddly, because I was doing many other things in the intervening quarter of a century, I attended the only two Commons debates ever held on a Saturday in modern times: the first was the Suez debate on 3rd November 1956, and the second on 3rd April 1982 at the outset of the Falklands War, when I happened to be in the press gallery on behalf of BBC radio. On the first occasion, the government was hammered by an angry and self-righteous opposition; the second saw a near-united House of Commons expressing a national mood of patriotic resolve to oust the Argentine invaders from the Falkland Islands. The Cassandra at the feast was Enoch Powell, with his sombre warning to Mrs Thatcher that the war would 'test the mettle' of the Iron Lady.

The frenetic mood surrounding the Suez debate, I remember, was slightly relieved just as the foreign secretary, Selwyn Lloyd, was rising to his feet to present the government's case, by an altercation in the press gallery between Randolph Churchill and the wife of the proprietor of the *Daily Telegraph*, Lady Pamela Berry: the former had apparently patted the latter's bottom and commended her on the luxuriousness of her moustache as she squeezed past him to reach her seat.

l to r: Nicholas Garland, Peter Paterson, Ivan Rowen, Richard Bennett

Chapter 12

THE first national newspaper I worked for was the *Daily Telegraph*, which I joined in January 1958: the second was its running mate, the *Sunday Telegraph*, within months of its foundation in 1961, though sometimes while on the *Daily* I would sacrifice my weekends for reporting assignments all over Britain for the *Observer*, having been taken up by the Sunday newspaper's then news editor, Mark Arnold-Foster, one of the shrewdest and kindest executives I ever met in Fleet Street. He'd been a torpedo boat captain in the war, and encouraged the *Observer's* reputation for uninhibited writing - known as 'colour pieces', a style not much liked in those days by the *Telegraph* – thus turning these weekends for me into a welcome escape from routine.

Both *Telegraphs* shared the same offices in the centre of Fleet Street, the building bearing a distinctly fascistic façade redolent of its period, the 1930s. Its most distinctive feature, apart from a magnificent clock, was a bas relief over the entrance depicting two winged messengers running in opposite directions with, at first glance and because of the soot covering the sculptor's work, their ankles bound together.

The *Telegraph* building is now occupied by a merchant bank, but even when I joined the paper its imposing foyer distinctly resembled a banking hall, with a substitute for a teller sitting behind a glass screen in one corner dispensing advances on expenses, in cash, to those journalists in receipt of the appropriate form signed by their immediate boss. The object was eventually, many months later, to claim for expenses disbursed, from which the advances would then be deducted: more often than not, the total of the former would exceed the latter.

Among many tales of this expenses credit line, one of the best concerned a sportswriter, the amiable Lainson Wood, who specialised in tennis and boxing. A man of considerable girth, Wood collected a cash advance late one morning to meet the cost of covering a tennis tournament next day in Brighton.

Reaching Victoria station to take the Brighton train, he ran into various drinking friends, until all of a sudden it was evening and his pockets were empty. Returning to the office, he presented another expenses form but the clerk on duty refused to give him any more money, on the grounds that he had already received his advance.

An indignant Lainson went up to his office and typed out a complaint to the then-proprietor of the *Telegraph*, Lord Camrose, employing a quotation from the Bible. It was a verse from Deuteronomy, chapter 25: 'Thou shalt not muzzle the ox when he treadeth out the corn', but it was too late for Lainson to use anything other than his own resources to get to the tennis. Nevertheless, he received a handwritten reply from his lordship which he would proudly fish out from the back of his wallet from that day on – he showed it to me the first time we met - for it read: 'Mr Lainson Wood is to be allowed an advance on his expenses whenever he requires'. I have since used Deuteronomy myself when seeking a pay rise, but without the charmed response he received.

Wood was by no means the only eccentric on the *Telegraph*. On the day I joined the paper I was taken round the building to meet my new colleagues, and it was like entering the still-far-in-the-future bar scene in the first *Star Wars* movie. Everywhere I went I quite literally met the halt, the maimed and the blind.

There was the property correspondent, John Armstrong, who had lost both hands during the war and tapped away on his typewriter with a metal hook. Peter Utley, a leader writer with whom I was to become great friends, had been blind from childhood: he scorned to learn braille or carry a white stick, and wore a patch which constantly slipped out of place, revealing a hazy blue eye that appeared to float rather crazily within its socket. He was also rumoured once to have mistaken the radiator in the office of Lieutenant General Martin, the defence correspondent, for a urinal, after edging unaccompanied along the corridor from his own office searching for the required facilities, and believing, erroneously, he had found them, sending the general's elderly lady secretary into hysterics.

As I made my tour of the office it seemed that the *Telegraph* could easily have fielded a one-eyed and one-legged cricket team, for the handicapped filled various jobs, both important and menial: clearly, in keeping with its consistently patriotic editorial line, the paper staunchly kept faith with employees who had been wounded in the war.

I arrived at 135 Fleet Street among an influx of new blood – three reporters arriving at the same time. I was the youngest at the age of 27, and my companions were John Bullock, whose father, a merchant navy captain, had been killed when his ship was bombed during the Spanish civil war, and Harry Miller, who was to become a much-loved 'Limey' correspondent in America with a small but telling role in Hunter S. Thompson and Timothy Crouse's best-seller, The Boys on the Bus, their story of the 1972 presidential election.

The news room of the *Telegraph* was sometimes likened to the House of Commons, not because it was the home of debate - though a typewriter at least once, was hurled into Fleet Street from the windows at a particularly heated moment - but because if every reporter on the staff, like members of the Commons, were to turn up at the same time there would be neither desks nor chairs to accommodate them all.

There was a convention that newly arrived reporters were ignored for a while, perhaps until the established denizens became accustomed to their appearance and habits. So Bullock, Miller and I would sit silently reading the papers, wandering up to the library to check press cuttings on stories we, frustratingly, were not sent out to cover, and slipping out to the pub to complain to each other of the boredom of our situation. Before my time, one famous Fleet Street character, Rene McColl, was sitting in this fashion, newly-installed, isolated and ignored, when the door opened and in came the Rev. Canon Mortlock – inevitably known as Deadlock – pastor of a City church and the *Telegraph's* ecclesiastical correspondent. 'Christ,' said McColl loudly, 'Now it's time for prayers!'

Although the working hours were nowhere near as onerous as those on the *Extel*, *Telegraph* reporters seldom went home early. The paper nurtured a Falstaffian drinking culture in the pubs around the office, and between six and seven in the evening we would congregate in the Kings & Keys next door, or across the road, appropriately in the Falstaff, to commence a solid drinking session. The Kings & Keys was run by an Irishman bitterly opposed to the IRA who kept a baseball bat under the bar in case they ever came calling. In the basement loo there were two chromium air fresheners above the privy, looking like microphones, one marked 'BBC' and the other 'ITN', while a scabrous graffito was signed 'E.W. Swanton', taking the name of the paper's dignified and gentlemanly chief cricket writer's name in vain.

One valid reason for hanging about drinking when the day's work was done, apart from the sheer entertainment provided by the company of one's fellow hacks, was to await the arrival of the early editions of rival papers to see if they carried stories that the *Telegraph* had missed, and would need to catch up with. The phone in the pub would start ringing, with the news editor or one of his assistants requiring a reporter to return to the office, or for a piece to be hastily scribbled at the bar and phoned in: the reasoning was that it was better voluntarily to be on the spot ready to deal with such exigencies than to be interrupted at home just as the wife was putting the supper on the table.

En masse, the *Telegraph* crowd were fractious, quarrelsome, learned and very funny. On most evenings the demon furioso was the whisky-drinking Michael Hilton, a man usually at the epicentre of any dispute and the occupant of a surprising post, considering his temperament – he was the paper's diplomatic correspondent. His tempestuousness may have run in the family, for he was the brother of the well-known artist, Roger Hilton, who was reputed to have kicked a hole through his own canvas at a civic reception given by the city of Liverpool to celebrate his award of a lucrative art prize. The younger Michael's favourite target was John Armstrong, the handless war veteran. 'If I were you,' Hilton would jeer, 'I would cut my own miserable throat. But you can't, can you? You can't even hold the bloody razor!' John would show remarkable restraint, for his hook and artificial left hand, covered in a tough leather glove, could have done considerable damage to his tormentor.

Michael Hilton, however, was not the sole cause of acrimony and dissent, and was often himself goaded by Brian Harvey, the features editor, aided and abetted by his wife, Sheila, the local government correspondent. As the evening wore on, disputes over the facts of a past news story, or the size, weight, speed or age of some object, institution or person would suddenly flare up – this was in the age before pub quizzes – and extravagant bets would be made on the correct answer. As a new arrival I soon learned that it was best not to act as a boy scout in these matters by rushing back to the office to consult the library for the answers. Left alone, the quarrels would evaporate on their own, awarding one side the satisfaction of knowing they were right and propelling the losers into a prolonged sulk, divesting the saloon bar of half of its custom as the aggrieved temporarily migrated to a different pub.

Telegraph readers, I sometimes reflect, would have been astonished had they known how the journalists, behind the slabs of grey type in the paper that adorned their tables at breakfast time, behaved around Fleet Street bars at lunchtime and of an evening.

My arrival at the paper roughly coincided with a vastly more important event - the creation of the partnership between Colin Welch and Michael Wharton in writing the paper's satirical Way of the World column, under the pseudonym, Peter Simple. I became and remained friends with both Welch and Wharton for nearly forty years. Both were extraordinarily learned and witty, Wharton quietly-spoken, reserved and calm even amid the tumult of the *Telegraph's* finest gathered in the bar. Welch was more outgoing, a wonderful writer inclined to get drunk before riding off on his motorbike into the night. It was he who gave the column its political edge, alongside Wharton's cast of fantastical characters representing a biting satire on the modern world, particularly the Left and politically-correct elements he so hated and despised.

Whatever mayhem it may have caused in their private lives, the fact of Wharton's journalist wife, Kate, becoming Welch's lover appeared to make little outward difference to their working partnership, and the three frequently socialised together in the pub.

Almost from the moment in 1966 when he joined the *Daily Telegraph* as the paper's first cartoonist – not first as in senior, but, amazingly, the first since its foundation one hundred and one years earlier – Nicholas Garland and I became close and firm friends. His background was in art – he'd trained at the Slade, been involved in the Sixties' satire boom with Beyond the Fringe, and scored a great success with Barry Humphries in drawing their *Private Eye* cartoon strip, Barry McKenzie, the adventures of a wide-eyed and foul-mouthed Australian in England.

I had always longed to be able to draw. I spent hours as a child meticulously but incompetently copying the covers of John Bull magazine and attempting to paint watercolours of flowers and country cottages during art lessons at Spurgeon's. But I had absolutely no talent for it.

I was overjoyed, therefore, occasionally to sit alongside Nick at his drawing board as his daily cartoon emerged, offering my advice and suggestions on the political scene. At the beginning, it was all a question of confidence: nonsensically fearing that people might not recognise his political caricatures he would tend to append unnecessary explanatory labels. My job was simply to convince him that his cartoons were first class and would be better still without the labels. Like the stabilisers on the wheels of a child's bicycle, they soon disappeared, and one of the greatest political cartoonists since Vicky and Low was speeding confidently along. I'm pleased I had my uses: once, I returned to the office to find on my desk a self-portrait by a worried-looking Garland, captioned 'When are you getting back from lunch, Patterson?', the misspelling indicating that it must have been drawn quite early in our relationship.

Despite its reputation for conservatism with both a capital and lower case 'c', the *Daily Telegraph* was as innovative as any other national paper, even if changes had to be surreptitiously introduced to disguise from the readership that anything had altered at all. I had long gone from the paper when, under the aegis of Hugh Montgomery-Massingberd (who to my disappointment later made the world a little less colourful by dropping the first clause of his surname) the *Telegraph* pioneered the modern, no-holds-barred style of obituary-writing.

The layout of the page remained the same, but gone were the studied euphemisms that previously protected rather than exposing a deceased drunk ('sociable'), a homosexual ('confirmed bachelor'), a notorious womaniser ('man about town'), or an ill-tempered bully ('possessing a gruff manner'). Humour also became a feature of the obits column, along with the celebration of the lives of a wider circle of mankind than respectful valedictories to the high-born and the mighty. It was through Hugh (who was later to join me among the lost league of TV critics) and his successor, David Jones, that I started writing obituaries for the *Telegraph* and, later, *The Times*.

One of the early obits I wrote was for my close friend and colleague on the *Sunday Telegraph*, Ian Waller, who fell sick but happily recovered swiftly, so my assessment of his life and work was filed away by the obituaries department for later use. Ian was the paper's political correspondent, a sweet man whose idealism was never swamped by the rough trade he was in. He was constantly under pressure to deliver by Friday evening his weekly 'think piece'. A big, handsome man in a hurry, his huge fingers would sometimes relocate themselves one letter to the left or right on the typewriter keyboard, producing whole paragraphs of what looked on the page like Serbo-Croat. The chief sub-editor in the features department, Ralph Thackeray, had the skill to translate these wayward sentences back into English.

On press day, Saturday, Ian had a mutually defensive arrangement with James Margach, his opposite number on the *Sunday Times*, when each would divulge to the other the stories they would be writing, thus avoiding any nasty surprises later in the day. I shared an office with Ian so I was perfectly aware of this arrangement, and they both knew I was in on their secret. At around 11 o'clock Ian would telephone the *Sunday Times* and guardedly ask for Margach, announcing himself as 'Mr Munro': if the call was in the other direction – even if I answered the phone - James would call himself 'Mr Scott'.

Both papers, of course, were in pursuit of scoops, but it was hard to find exclusive news stories in a field like politics, where the journalists of nine or ten daily newspapers and three serious Sundays were all in pursuit of the same thing. This also applied to my own specialisation - I was industrial correspondent of the *Sunday Telegraph*. There were two occasions early in the life of the Sunday when I made it my business to think up ideas for him sensational enough to occupy the prime front page position of lead story.

The first joint came from something I gleaned from a short paragraph in an obscure aviation publication I happened to be skimming through amid a pile of magazines on the desk of the temporarily absent defence correspondent, Ivan Rowan. The item pointed out that, with the purchase of some US-built Starfighters (an unsafe aircraft known to pilots as the Widowmaker), the Netherlands air force now had more front-line fighters than the RAF.

This proved impossible to confirm on a Saturday morning and, unelaborated, was not quite strong enough to bear the weight of a front-page lead. But with the inclusion of another element we realised it would make headline news. I knew that the chief of staff of the armed services was entitled to direct access to the Prime Minister over the head of the Secretary of State for Defence, if he was worried about some crucial aspect involving the defence of the realm. And what, we thought, could be more alarming for the country's safety than a critical shortage of fighter planes? I decided, and Ian agreed, to credit the chief of staff with the patriotism and the right degree of anxiety to go straight to the top, reasoning that if he hadn't fulfilled this obligation, he should certainly have done so. I've no idea whether this resulted in a large order for new aeroplanes, but it certainly produced a Page One story.

Another creative lead story occurred to me dangerously close to deadline one Saturday. Lord Halifax, then chairman of the National Savings movement, had made a speech a few days earlier that could have been – indeed had been thus interpreted by various political commentators - as a criticism of Denis Healy, then Chancellor of the Exchequer. My suggestion that we go for the story was certainly unethical but this was a desperate moment, and we convinced ourselves that the Chancellor – a tough politician - would certainly not put up with public criticism from someone whose job was in his own gift: we could therefore assume that Halifax's days in the post must be numbered. Ian wrote the story with some trepidation, a short time later, Halifax's departure was announced.

A legitimate reason for this dubious kind of activity was the sheer newness of the *Sunday Telegraph*: we were the new kid on the block and it took time for the political class to become accustomed to our presence and start channelling, or leaking, stories to us.

Our correspondence editor was in a similar plight. Richard Bennett, a former editor of the magazine *Lilliput*, a publication famous among teenagers in the 1950s and 1960s for its mixture of culture, humour and tasteful nude photographs, found it was a long time before his page attracted enough publishable letters to fill the available space.

He would solicit contributions from well-known names with a point of view on topics in the news and induce his colleagues, for a nominal payment, to concoct letters under false names, a state of affairs that gradually became unnecessary as more letters started to arrive. Bennett also initiated the idea of illustrating the letters page with tiny cartoons, drawn by James Boswell, a well-known painter, war artist and former Art Editor of *Lilliput*, who was now editing the Sainsbury supermarket chain's house magazine. On Friday evenings, Boswell and I would link up with another artist friend, Paul Hogarth, for a drink at El Vino. It gave me a particular frisson to be socialising with Boswell and Hogarth, imagining that they were their nominal predecessors in art and journalism.

I am not sure whether Donald McLachlan, the first editor of the *Sunday Telegraph*, was aware of any deceit in the news pages and the letters department, though I suspect he was. I should also point out that, adding to the pressure on all of us to produce exclusives, was the advertising slogan borrowed by the *Sunday Telegraph* from Kit Kat, the chocolate bar, that this new Sunday newspaper 'filled the gap', meaning the gap between Saturday and Monday, rather than the readers' appetites.

A former schoolmaster, McLachlan had been a wartime naval intelligence officer of some renown, and deputy editor of the *Daily Telegraph*, where at the time of Suez he had written a famous leader – now an established cliché - criticising the Tory government for the absence from their thinking of 'the smack of firm government'.

He was a Prodnose of an editor, prying, pedantic and interfering in every aspect of the paper, which is better than a cold, distant and detached editor. He would engage in loud arguments with his staff in the corridors. Sometimes these were spillovers from discussions in his office, with Donald, having refused his permission to a writer to use, say, the word 'shit', and trying to mollify him - usually it was Alan Brien, who at different times was film and theatre critic - by shouting for all to hear, 'You can't have "shit", but "crap" might be acceptable!'

More than thirty years after my adventures in creative writing under McLachlan's editorship, my son telephoned me at home early one morning in 2003 to give me the sad news that my dear friend Ian Waller had died, and that I should read the obituary in that morning's *Daily Telegraph*. When I did so I was amazed at the inside knowledge the piece displayed of the subject's life and career, even including the covert Scott-Munro relationship (James Margach had already passed away). I phoned the *Telegraph* to ask who had written the obit, to be told, 'You did.' I had entirely forgotten having done so.

l to r: Peter Paterson, Nicholas Garland, Philip Hope-Wallace

Chapter 13

THE first mark I made at the *Daily Telegraph* was the result of the kind of serendipity born of the freedom of movement that once provided the newspapers with many stories, but today has diminished following the journalistic diaspora from their old Fleet Street home. Scattered to Docklands in the East, Kensington High Street in the West, and Victoria in between, reporters are nowadays more often confined to the office, on the end of a phone or staring at a computer screen.

It was 1959, long before all these changes, when one morning I was sent to cover a press conference which produced nothing worth reporting. So after phoning the office to say I was on my way back, I wandered off to find a pub and ordered a beer.

The place was empty, apart from two men at the far end of the bar. As I drank my pint, it was impossible not to overhear their conversation, and I soon gathered they were connected with the Courtauld Institute. The Institute was not only an art gallery but a centre for art research and restoration, led by a renowned expert, Sir Anthony Blunt who, wearing another hat, was Surveyor of the Queen's Pictures and in his spare time, we later learned, a spy for the Soviet Union.

I've no reason to believe that either of the men was Blunt, a reserved and chilly individual by all accounts, and an establishment-figure remotely unlikely to be found refreshing himself in a pub at any time of day. I listened idly to the pair talking about a painting by Titian in the Queen's collection. In the course of cleaning the picture at the Courtauld, a work hitherto presenting two figures had apparently disclosed the existence of a third who for some unknown reason had been painted out: the men speculated that the trio might have been a pair of friends or members of a club, one of whom, following some quarrel, had been spectacularly expelled by having his portrait extinguished.

Although I knew little or nothing about art, the royal connection struck me as a pretty good story, and I hastened back to the office. Before-and-after pictures of the painting were somehow obtained. The story made the front page.

Partly as a result of my little scoop, the *Telegraph's* managing editor (and subsequently editor of the *Sunday Telegraph*), Brian Roberts, known as Scruffy, offered me a promotion - not, I hasten to make clear, to become art critic, but to join the industrial staff as No.3 to its formidable leader, Hugh Chevins, a fine reporter who, during the First World War, had the unusual experience of serving with a Chinese labour battalion in France. Unlike me, Chevins was an art connoisseur, acquiring a portrait by Augustus John of the former *Telegraph* art critic, W.T. Earp, who was his friend as well as the artist's. Travelling with Chevins in a taxi through Smith Square, Westminster, one day, Earp learned that they were passing Transport House, the headquarters of the Labour Party, and sighed, 'Transport House – what a wonderful name for a brothel!' The same building also then housed the Trades Union Congress, which failed to avoid a similar interpretation when it subsequently chose a name for its own separate new premises in Bloomsbury: it was called Congress House.

So life changed a little for me after the Titian story, but the altered state of the Queen's picture remained in my mind if only because the *Sunday Times* subsequently seemed to specialise in this genre of before-and-after comparisons of scrubbed-up classic paintings, perhaps because in the Sixties, when everything had to be bright and fresh and new, picture-cleaning – sometimes badly botched - became something of a fetish among gallery directors.

But, of course, when I wrote my story I never dreamed that there might be a connection to be drawn between the cleaning of the Queen's Titian (or, should I say, one of the Queen's Titians) and the Cambridge upper crust ring of spies who had been busily transmitting national secrets to the Soviet Union during and after World War Two. Guy Burgess and Donald Maclean, the first and second of the traitors to defect to Russia, had fled to Moscow in 1951 apparently after being tipped off by the third member of their coterie, Kim Philby, that they were about to be arrested. Philby also took refuge in Moscow, but not for another twelve years. Anthony Blunt – the fourth man – was firmly in the frame, suspected not only of being part of the spy ring, but like Philby, of assisting Burgess and Maclean to escape.

But Blunt was not outed publicly as a Soviet agent until Mrs Thatcher named him in the House of Commons in 1979 - presumably granted immunity from prosecution back in the Sixties in exchange for 'assisting' the authorities. So for some years we had the peculiar situation of a known spy acting as a close advisor to the monarch on her art collection. Might she have been aware from reading state papers, of her courtier's treachery?

I was tremendously interested when this ironic situation was seized upon by the great Alan Bennett, who took up the subject of the Cambridge spies in two brilliant one-act plays under the joint title, Single Spies, with both parts, An Englishman Abroad and A Question of Attribution shown on television. The first play, written nearly thirty years after the event, was of an encounter in Moscow in 1958 between the visiting West End actress Coral Browne and the disgraced Guy Burgess, the latter languishing in bitter and dreary exile, longing for the news Ms Browne brought from London and missing his drunken, gossipy, homosexual former life dreadfully.

The second play, A Question of Attribution, however, brought the picture that I still thought of as my Titian into focus once more. As suggested by the title of Bennett's play, its legitimacy as a work by Titian was doubted by Blunt: in the drama, he informs Her Majesty that its provenance cannot be proved and that it might well be a fake. But the overhanging question is how far the Queen is aware as they converse that her Surveyor of Pictures is a traitor – in short, that Blunt might be just as much, perhaps more, of a fake than the dubious Titian. And at the fade-out, Bennett reveals that the picture, under the brushes and chemicals of the cleaning process, had revealed not just a third man, but subsequently, exactly in line with the Cambridge spy scandal, a fourth and fifth man as well.

We don't know, of course, if the tale of quite so many revelations emerging from the cleaning is true, for while Bennett described his plays as 'an inquiry in which the circumstances are imaginary', he tantalisingly added, 'but the pictures are real'. If that really means that the cleaning of the alleged Titian did indeed eventually yield up five figures (and the intriguing possibility has been raised that one of the figures might have been of Titian himself, and another his son), then photographs of the work in its various stages of cleaning would one day make an interesting exhibition.

Once I had switched to the industrial beat I soon managed to repeat my feat of securing an exclusive ('scoop' is a word not universally liked in the trade), and once again it was hatched in a public house – this time in Fleet Street itself. In October 1960 I was having a quiet drink in the Falstaff when I was approached by a journalist from the News Chronicle, now, of course, a defunct title. This was unusual, for cliquey reporters usually drank in pubs close to their own offices so that they could easily be found and summoned back – besides, why should someone from a rival paper like the Chronicle wish to give me an exclusive story?

The tale he had to impart was that his newspaper, together with its companion London evening paper, the *Star*, were both about to be closed down by the owners, the Cadbury family. But before proffering this information my informant required a promise that he would, in exchange, be given a job on the *Telegraph*. I explained that this was beyond my power to grant, but I would approach my bosses to see whether it might be possible.

My news editor's response was entirely non-committal, but extraordinarily, when I conveyed this to the *Chronicle* man he seemed blissfully unworried. It was as if he had become so excited over having a hand in a story that would amaze the rest of Fleet Street, one that he was obviously unable to write for his own paper, that the fears he had for his own future became quite secondary. Or perhaps he already had another job lined up.

The circulation of the *News Chronicle* was declining, but it was still selling close to one million copies a day, more than enough with today's printing technology to prosper, but seen at that time as close to unviable. It boasted some excellent contributors in a long liberal tradition, including most notably James Cameron, Vernon Bartlett, Arthur Koestler and, earlier in its history, Sir Arthur Conan Doyle and H.G. Wells. Although the title dated only from 1930, its antecedents were the *Daily News*, founded in 1846 by Charles Dickens, and the *Daily Chronicle*, which went back to 1872.

Morale within the *Chronicle* had been at a low ebb, partly due to indiscipline – for which read activities by its print workers amounting to industrial sabotage, a malaise that afflicted the whole of Fleet Street - and partly as a result of the departure three years before the paper's closure of an inspirational editor, Michael Curtis, whose suggestions for radical change were rejected by the owners. In its last days, consultants were brought in, with one, it's said, claiming that the fortunes of the paper would improve if only it would introduce, like some of its competitors, a slogan for display on its front-page masthead and sales boards: e.g. 'The Paper You Can Trust' (used by the *Daily Telegraph*; the eponymous 'Forward with the People,' and the *News of the World's* 'World's Highest Circulation', which of course would not have been true of the *Chronicle*, nor, taking Japan and China into account, of the NoW). A competition among the staff, with a modest cash prize to meet this perceived requirement for the paper's survival, sadly attracted no entries apart from one necessarily anonymous contribution: *'News Chronicle,'* it ran, 'Fewest Pages, Lowest Wages'.

My tipster on the *Chronicle* staff had fortuitously exercised a reporter's disgraceful compulsion to read any letter left lying on an unoccupied desk, or even one that was occupied, so long as he was adept at reading upside down: in this case the desk was his editor's. (Leaving important documents open on a desk is also, of course, a means of covertly leaking information. It was practised in by the notorious John Stonehouse, the MP who faked his own death in Miami in 1974, was discovered soon afterwards living in Australia where the police mistook him for Lord Lucan, and was eventually imprisoned for seven years. As Postmaster General for a few months in 1969/70, he would casually stroll out of his office, leaving me and any other reporter who might be visiting him, to study anything he'd 'casually' left lying on his desk.)

My contact's discovered letter contained the information that both the *Chronicle* and the *Star* would cease publication the following week on Tuesday 18th October 1960, with the papers being 'merged' instantly with those of the purchasers, Associated Newspapers, owners of the right wing *Daily Mail* and one of the then three extant London evening papers, the Evening News.

I wrote the story and on Monday 17th it went into the first edition of the *Telegraph* on the front page. But on the BBC's 9 p.m. radio news, a statement by the *Chronicle's* chairman, Lawrence Cadbury, introduced some doubt into the closure plan, insisting that the future of the papers had 'yet to be decided' and 'a further announcement would be made shortly'. Michael Berry, proprietor of the *Telegraph*, lost his nerve, insisting (after I had left the office) that various ifs, buts and maybes should be introduced into my story in case Cadbury's statement was true. The consequence was that among the few people who read the perfectly accurate first edition story were foreign correspondents of the national newspapers, including *Chronicle* journalists in faraway places discovering rather brutally that they had lost their jobs.

When both the doomed papers duly failed to appear, I walked into the *Telegraph* newsroom to a cheer from my colleagues. A repentant Berry wrote to me explaining that he had been influenced to modify the story by the doubt instilled by Cadbury's statement (but omitting to note the first syllable of the vendor's family name). I was certain that their fork-tongued statement was designed simply to ensure that the *Mail* was able to grab the *Chronicle's* readership, though Berry seemed to be sticking to some gentlemen's code between newspaper proprietors: 'Unfortunately,' he wrote to me, 'I have more confidence in human nature than you', and enclosing 'a material token of your achievement' – the one bonus I ever received in fifty nine years in the newspaper business. I can't now recall if the cheque was for £25 or £50 – at a guess I would say it was the former - but had Berry had the nous to print extra copies to thus ensure that every *Chronicle* reader was handed a free copy of the *Telegraph* that morning, my employers might have profited by the advance knowledge I gave them.

If there is one lesson to be learned, not just from the story of the Queen's dodgy Titian or the sudden demise of the *News Chronicle*, but a host of other exclusive stories that have hit the newspapers over the years, it is that reporters need to be given the freedom to get out and about, get to know as many people as possible, and mingle with the public they write for. Today most of them spend far too many hours at their desks in front of computer screens, pursuing stories electronically, with wistful and distracting pictures of their wives and children framed on their desks. And after work, they proceed not to the pub to await the first editions of rival newspapers, but to the gym (now part of the facilities of many newspaper offices) before going straight home. Since I retired, the additional burden has been laid on them of returning to their computers to write a slightly different version of their story as a blog on their paper's website.

Of course, reporters are still allowed out of the office to cover events, but mostly these are guaranteed to deliver in terms of column inches and front-page headlines such as natural disasters, terrorist outrages, court stories, Royal occasions, West End film premieres, and the like, all of which are covered simultaneously by all their rivals. For the most part, on these set-piece occasions reporters meet no-one but public relations people or other reporters – the latter not a source entirely to be sneezed at, for reporters tend in conversation to give their confreres good ideas – but nowhere near as good as finding exclusive and fascinating stories through the mysterious workings of serendipity.

What has now almost disappeared is the freedom to mooch around, waiting for something to turn up, listening and talking to people, even indulging in a three-hour lunch, without constantly being summoned back to the office by a call on the pesky mobile phone.

News editors, who once indulged a degree of bad behaviour in their reporters because they knew that the perpetrators were also great story-finders, have now become like cautious generals unwilling to commit their forces to battle until utterly certain of victory, short-sightedly keeping their staff tethered to the office in reserve. I regret that the consequence is that much of the fun has gone disappeared from the reporting game.

Chapter 14

A general reporter is expected to become an instant expert in almost any topic he or she is asked to write about, analagous to a barrister studying his brief for a forthcoming trial, before moving on to another case.

On the *Daily Telegraph*, thanks to my suddenly acquired interest in Italian Renaissance art, I was turned into a specialist reporter on industrial relations, and for a newspaper still at that time preferring to call the Labour Party, 'the Socialists', it may have seemed on the surface that I would have to abandon my then generally leftist views.

Fortunately, the 'straight' reporting style demanded in those days didn't require me to take a Tory or any other particular line in what I wrote – comment, however biased, was left to the leader writers and the editor, Sir Colin Coote. (Incidentally, Coote was the only editor of any paper I worked for but never met, though I was acquainted with his son, a sportswriter on the *Telegraph* - another example of Fleet Street's traditional, and to my mind highly practical horses-for-courses nepotism.)

Michael Berry (later Lord Hartwell) the proprietor of the *Telegraph* papers, was increasingly apprehensive as union power and influence grew, not only in the country at large, but in his own industry. After I had moved from the *Daily* to the *Sunday Telegraph*, at one of the lunches he held for his senior journalists (I had now somehow reached this category), we were sipping the lethal dry martinis customarily served by his butler on these occasions when I asked Berry, for want of anything else to say – he was a painfully shy and reserved man – where he would be spending his holiday that summer. 'We're going down to my boat in the south of France,' he replied, then realising that he was addressing his tame expert on the unions, added defensively, 'It's not a yacht, you know, just a small sailing dinghy!'

I had the distinct feeling that in his mind was a nightmare vision of newspaper proprietors being hanged from the lamp posts of Fleet Street by communistic workers, no doubt egged on by me. He did not publicly flaunt his wealth, possibly another protection against the advancing revolutionaries, and would arrive at the office each morning in a humble Ford Cortina, though a *Telegraph* commissionaire was always on hand to hold up the Fleet Street traffic while 'the owner' turned into his private parking space. Granted, there was a certain opulence about his private eyrie on the fifth floor at 135 Fleet Street, with a Venetian scene Canaletto or a Guardi (I couldn't decide which, and never asked) on the wall, the revolver carried by H.M. Stanley in his quest for Livingstone (later stolen in a burglary) nearby, and an original *Telegraph* street placard announcing the relief of Mafeking.

And outside on his balcony, high above Fleet Street, was this tiny, well-kept lawn with a small mower parked to one side, presumably for the use of the butler when he was not serving dry martinis. A fellow labour reporter, Keith MacDowell, told me that when he was an office boy at the *Telegraph* he and fellow malcontents would go up to the sixth floor and throw their cigarette ends down on to the grass.

Along with everyone else in Britain in the sixties, I naturally knew something about trade unions, strikes, working-to-rule and overtime bans before the *Daily Telegraph's* managing editor, Brian Roberts, decided that I should specialise in industry and its discontents. I had been a union member myself from my time on the *Fulham Gazette*, subscribing to the fairly useless National Union of Journalists, whose minimum-wage mentality helped the staff of struggling weekly and provincial papers but was less relevant at the payment-by-results system operated in Fleet Street: the union eventually fell into the hands of what was known at the time as the loony-left, a number of them members of a coven of Trotskyites on the *Sunday Times*, one of whom, having abandoned his revolutionary beliefs, now occupies a high position in Scottish society. Along with many others, I eventually allowed my membership to lapse.

There may have been an element of predestination in my specialising in the up-and-coming field of industrial relations. Back in my days in Fulham I remember hanging around a bus repair depot at Parsons Green during a strike, talking to pickets at the gates and writing sympathetic stories about their cause. And when I was with the *Exchange Telegraph* I often worked alongside their industrial correspondent, Mike Edwards.

He was a war veteran, and like my poor old Uncle Bill who acquired his during the First World War, had a metal plate in his head, the consequence of being thrown or blown out of a jeep somewhere in the Far East. Mike had ended the war leading an army unit rounding up Nazi war criminals in Norway, many of whom were duly hanged: he would reflect (jokingly, I think) that the work came naturally to him as descendant of a long line of East Anglian butchers.

Mike had more contacts than any other journalist I've ever encountered, ranging from the staff rooms and pantries of Buckingham Palace to followers of the most obscure political sects. He used to talk mysteriously of a regular and productive assignation he made on his way to work in London from his home at Fetcham in Surrey, saying, 'Sorry I'm late, but I've been meeting Mr Plod at The Rat'. I found this meant that he was eliciting stories from a police officer at a pub in Guildford which, before a recent name-change, was called The Rat's Castle.

Sometimes, when called back from the pub on a Saturday night to the office of the Sunday Pictorial (later called the *Sunday Mirror*), where for many years he moonlighted – he would be at the Red Lion pub off Fleet Street, distinguished from its two nearby namesakes by the Chinese restaurant on the upper floor - he would cheerfully pour the remains of his chop suey into his half-depleted pint of beer and down them together, perkily assuring us 'It all goes down the same way.'

In our days on the *Exchange Telegraph* agency, Mike and I included among our regular drinking companions journalists from the British Communist Party's organ, the *Daily Worker* (later re-named *Morning Star*), among them Alan Hutt, a typographer and the foremost newspaper designer of his day, the *Worker's* veteran industrial correspondent, George Sinfield, Frank Gullett, its exuberant news editor and Peter Fryer, who would resign from the paper over the censoring of his reports on the Hungarian uprising in 1956.

I was at the Communist Party's congress in Hammersmith Town Hall in 1957 when disillusioned members walked out en masse after listening restlessly to the Stalinist general secretary, John Gollen – one of those gangling men whose most prominent physical characteristic was his Adam's apple - vainly trying to defend the Hungarian debacle. One after another, disillusioned defectors stuffed their membership cards into the pockets of the stewards at the doors as they left. (I was awarded a leading article of my own in the *Worker* after writing a story for the *Sunday Telegraph* about a subsequent visit to Moscow by Gollen, speculating on the nature of his discussions – or receipt of orders from – Khruschev. The editorial sarcastically suggested, 'Paterson must have been hiding under the table in the Kremlin'.)

But in my line of trade, with the Party's activist membership concentrated in the trade union movement, communist contacts were always extremely useful. Some of those who defected never strayed far from the Party, instead joining Trotskyite factions and attempting to organise the workers just as they had always done. And many were good friends, too, and remained so long after I had left both *Extel* and the *Telegraph*.

One particularly close friend – is there any finer token of friendship than someone who volunteers to look after one's dog while one is away on holiday? - was Reg Birch, a senior official of the Engineering Union and chief negotiator with the Ford Motor company. On one occasion, with the unions (Ford recognised 23 unions in those days) trying to secure an improvement in the pensions scheme, a union-management meeting was interrupted by a loud tapping emerging from beneath the conference table. The noise was discovered to be from the rapping of Birch's knuckles: 'It's the retired workers banging on the sides of their coffins, having been driven to an early grave by the company's meanness,' he explained.

Reg attracted a great deal of criticism when he agreed to be elected to the national executive of the Communist Party after the Hungarian uprising. When I asked him how he could possibly have sided with the 'tankies', so called because of the use of Russian army tanks to quell the revolt, he said, 'They wanted a trade unionist who could stomach Hungary, and I fitted the bill.' Later, he would leave the Party anyway, going off to create his own breakaway communist movement, but one that looked for inspiration to Maoist China and, extraordinarily, Enver Hoxha's backward and autocratic Albania rather than Russia. His new political group unsurprisingly attracted little support and very few members. I tend to think that he mainly formed it in the great cause of cheering us all up, and at the same time raising two fingers to his enemies in the Communist Party of Great Britain.

Under the tutelage of Mike Edwards I covered a long-running strike at Smithfield Meat Market in the 1950s that offered an interesting insight into my mentor's approach. Instead of awaiting the usual daily statement of defiance and demands issued by the strike committee, Mike would take me along to a public house where we would, by pre-arrangement, meet the branch chairman and secretary, both of whom were among his old acquaintances. Over a few drinks he and I would scribble out a draft for the statement presenting the strikers' case cunningly fashioned to capture headlines. The signatories might amend our script slightly but in essence we would decide most of what went into the communiqué, Mike ensuring that via the *Extel* teleprinters it was distributed to the rest of the media.

Such episodes, and the scandalous injustices inflicted on junior hospital doctors in the 1960s, emphasised an important aspect of the coverage of industrial relations, certainly in the early years I was involved. The fact was that correspondents on this beat had easier access to trade union members and officials than we ever did to the other half of the equation, the employers, which ensured that the newspapers invariably gave more space to union grievances than to the bosses' side of the story.

Later on, employers wised up a little and started to employ public relations officers to speak to the press on their behalf, but it was a very long time before chairmen or managing directors felt able, or were even expected, to brief reporters when their companies were involved in an industrial dispute – probably not before the two great miners' strikes in the Seventies and mid-Eighties, I would say, did we enjoy equal time and access to both the warring parties in a major dispute.

This bias towards the unions obviously resulted in a chronic imbalance in the media coverage of industrial relations. A union leader with whom we were on personal terms could get his case across more swiftly and effectively than the remote chief executive of a national company disseminating his point of view through the filter of a lowly PR employee or a hired-gun communications company uninvolved in making the firm's policy.

I rapidly got to know the leader of almost every union because, among other encounters, I attended their annual conferences. A week at the seaside listening to their debates, staying at the same hotels and socialising round the clock made for the establishment of close relationships.

Union conferences varied widely – in those days the biggest railway union, the NUR, held its annual meeting of branch delegates entirely in private, leaving reporters to wait on the general secretary each afternoon for his resumé of the debates. Then we would scamper around to buttonhole individual delegates in the bar for the real story. Most unions, however, were glad to have the reporters inside their conferences.

By far the most gentlemanly of the union conferences were the annual gatherings of the National Union of Mineworkers before their in-house Sampson, Arthur Scargill, toppled the pillars of the union's structure by ignoring its own rule book on strike ballots. Before the doleful strike of 1985 the miners would take the press along on the annual outing that provided a rest day during their conferences - I remember one all-day cruise in beautiful weather up the River Clyde to the Kyles of Bute on a hired steamer, getting to know Will Paynter, leader of the Welsh miners and a hero to my coal miner foster father, Dai Tom Evans, in wartime Wales.

The miners also went in for social evenings with everyone mistily singing English, Scottish, Welsh, and Irish folk songs, plus American union ballads, after dinner – even mysterious visitors from behind the Iron Curtain, present as 'observers', would join in. An intriguing (in both senses of the word) foreign 'friend' at union conferences was Boris Averyanov, an exceedingly affable official of the Soviet Union's state-controlled trade unions, enormously fat and with a constant stream of perspiration sending his glasses sliding down his tiny nose, he could have signed up for a Hollywood film career as a sinister agent of SMERSH, the forerunner of the KGB, to which he undoubtedly belonged. Boris spoke English extremely well, only becoming aware of occasional shortcomings when attending a trade union dinner on his first visit to Britain: the person sitting next to him kept repeating a word he'd never heard before, but which he felt bound eventually to respond to because it clearly occurred as part of a seemingly urgent question. Sign language established that it was 'ashtray' that was missing from his vocabulary.

Assuming that we might possess useful information, some of these Iron Curtain visitors, and diplomatic residents, targeted journalists throughout the Cold War. I found myself being invited out to lunch quite frequently by Hungarian, Czech or other eastern European diplomats. My strategy, over the first drink, was to offer to provide them with every possible assistance should they decide during their service in London to defect. Our own security services were also busy: during one strike I followed a picket into a phone box he'd just vacated, and realised when I lifted the receiver that the line was still connected to MI.5.

In sharp contrast to the miners and other unions of manual workers, notoriously badly behaved conference delegates were those from white collar and civil service unions. They were the most liable to be arrested by the police for being drunk and disorderly in the streets, but seldom landed up in court because seaside resorts valued the business the unions brought in. In most cases the local police chief would simply have a quiet word with the union's general secretary, and an offender would be sent home.

The annual conference of the TUC was the highlight of the union conference season, and was always hard and grinding work for industrial reporters, with entire pages devoted to the debates, speculation about union attitudes to various government policies, and analysis of voting patterns. The trade union version of democracy was complicated by the tendency of William Carron of the Amalgamated Engineering Union on occasion to cast his union's 'card vote' on behalf of his one million members both for and against the proposition in ballots on contentious issues, thus frequently plunging the TUC into squabbling confusion (Carron's role was acknowledged by the establishment, first with a knighthood and then a seat in the Lords). It was easy to forget when union leaders behaved in a Jesuitical fashion that the universally accepted book of rules for the conduct of public meetings (of any variety) was written by Walter Citrine, a onetime general secretary of the TUC, who would hardly have approved of a chairman yelling, 'Shut your gob!' at a delegate trying to make himself heard over constant interruptions by political opponents. Admittedly, that particular ruffianly intervention occurred at a Labour Party conference.

Weather permitting, before the annual TUC conference proceedings began each September, there was a beery cricket match between the industrial correspondents and the governing general council. The only outing of the week, however, was a mystery coach-tour organised for the wives of council members. I recall the indignation of Clive Jenkins, as a newly-elected member of the general council, on discovering that his promotion to the ruling body meant that his wife, Moira, in line with her husband's lack of seniority, would be expected by the other TUC wives to board the bus last: Jenkins's gesture of protest was to hire a chauffeured Rolls Royce to convey his wife to the bus stop.

A rigid public morality governed the behaviour of union leaders in those days, perhaps inherited from the evangelical Christianity that helped to build the movement in its early days, and sustained for some time after traditional attitudes to marriage elsewhere in society began to crumble in the 1960s. So disapproving eyebrows were raised when one prominent trade unionist, Lord (Fred) Cooper of the General & Municipal Workers, left his wife for another lady shortly before a grand banquet marking the anniversary of the founding of the Transport & General Workers Union was due to be held at one of the large hotels in London's Park Lane. Lord and Lady Cooper had naturally been invited, but Cooper insisted that he should be accompanied by his new love rather than his wife, forcing the hosts to torture the rules of etiquette by hastily amending the guest list on the souvenir menu to read: 'Lord Cooper and Mrs Cooper', perhaps hoping that Mrs Cooper would be taken for Fred's mother.

Specialist reporters, whether covering parliament, the unions, motoring, medical matters, or the City and financial scene, tended to spend a great deal of time in each other's company. This produced some odd alliances, particularly where speculative stories were involved. Thus, anyone reading more than one newspaper might sometimes have been surprised to notice that a front page story claimed by, say, *The Times*, to be exclusive to that paper, also appeared as a 'first' in the *Daily Mirror*.

This indicated that whichever reporter came up with the story was anxious to lay off any risk involved in running it by reassuring his own perhaps slightly nervous news desk that even if it did appear elsewhere, it would not be in the columns of a close competitor. Since this practice continues to this day, it helps to answer the question, when is a scoop not a scoop?

For the same reasons, a reporter in possession of an 'exclusive' – might offer it around to his friends on other papers on condition that they withheld the story until after the story-donor's first edition had gone to press. He would thus preserve his achievement in securing the story first in the eyes of his own newspaper, while placing his colleagues in a position to produce a swift follow-up. Meaningless to the readers, perhaps, but a classic restraint of trade.

I swiftly came to appreciate the experience and the helpfulness of the most senior of the industrial correspondents. Looking back, I can see that I was searching for father figures in my admiration for men like Eric Wigham of *The Times* and Trevor Evans of the *Daily Express*, both unstinting in their help and advice. Leslie Randall of the *Mail*, played a different role, that of the weary and cynical old journalist who had been everywhere and seen everything: he had originally been appointed shipping correspondent of the *Mail*, promising worldwide travel on luxurious ocean liners, until some seamen went on strike in London and he had to cover the story and was stuck from then on as a labour correspondent. I was with him one morning when we learned that his front page headline story confidently forecasting that a major transport strike would be called off that very day was about to be sharply denied at a press conference by the leader of the union concerned. Leslie's story – perfectly accurate when he wrote it - had enraged the union into prolonging the strike by asserting that the workers concerned were 'surrendering'. I walked into the press conference alongside him as he shrank under his battered trilby, apparently on the point of a nervous breakdown and muttering to himself, 'The f***ing bastards! The f***ing bastards!'

One of my greatest friends was Eric Jacobs, whom I had known slightly when he was on the *Guardian*, but first struck up a warm and long-lasting friendship with when we were both covering the troubled birth pangs of the liner, Queen Elizabeth II, Eric for the *Sunday Times* and I for the *Sunday Telegraph*.

We found ourselves, on a raw autumn day in 1968, staying at the same hotel in Glasgow. The QE2's fitting-out phase at the John Brown shipyard on Clydeside, ready for handing over to its owners, Cunard, for its already long-delayed maiden voyage, was now long overdue and was to be finished at sea.

Glasgow may have been the ancestral home of the Patersons, but I had never, out of the womb, been to the city before. Eric was born a Glaswegian, his urologist surgeon father the doyen of the city's medical profession, sending young Eric to one of Scotland's top public schools, Loretto. Inevitably we teamed up on the QE2 story.

We visited the shipyard together, sought out individuals who were working on the ship, and quickly discovered a delicate side to our enquiry: that one of the biggest problems causing the over-run in the construction of the ship was the constant pilfering, known in Glasgow as 'squirrelling', of the liner's contents. We heard tales of fixtures and fittings being delivered to the ship in the morning, only to be carried off again by thieves in the labour force at the end of the shift.

We visited the home of a bailie, or mayor, of one town on the Clyde, whose council flat quite unashamedly was furnished entirely from the QE2, including the carpet on the floor bearing the ship's monogram. He also had a splendid cocktail bar built from the ship's materials, complete with rows of purloined bottles of wines and spirits marked with the ship's insignia. He was proud of his acquisitions, making no attempt to hide them from his visitors.

Our chief interest, however, was the fact that the ship was about to set sail over the weekend for its maiden voyage carrying no passengers but a full complement of plumbers, carpenters, electricians and other tradesmen busy trying to complete the job that should have been finished months before.

As we wandered from place to place, we encountered – inevitably in a bar – an unusual shipbuilding worker from the QE2. He was hospitable, informative and talkative, with an ability to quote from Shakespeare and the Bible, a love for politics, and a compendious knowledge of shipbuilding trades. He was keen, besides briefing us on the story we were covering, to take us off to a football match. After watching the game he invited us back to his home on a distant council estate.

When we arrived there seemed to be nobody else about until our host opened the door to the living room, in darkness save for the glow from the largest TV set Eric and I had ever seen. As our eyes adjusted, we could make out a woman and a small child crouched before the screen. Our renaissance man then barked at his wife, 'Get us some food, woman!' at which, without a word, she went to the kitchen and fried up egg and chips for us. On our return to London, 'Get us some food, woman!' became a catchword we used to our wives – after cravenly making it clear that we were only joking.

My friendship with Eric continued until his death in 2003. A highly intelligent man with a sweet disposition, amicable, easy-going, and with an attractive dry wit, he became, towards the end of his career, in the words of our mutual friend, Ian Aitken of the *Guardian*, a Boswell to the novelist Kingsley Amis's Johnson, a relationship that resulted in a fine biography of the author, much of it the result of their almost daily meetings over three years in the Garrick Club, where I would occasionally join them.

Eric became a great support to Kingsley in his final illness. He had finished writing his book, but continued the biographer's habit by keeping a diary during his subject's dying months when he spent much time with him. It was unfortunate that he acceded – as he told me, it was against his better judgement - to a pressing request by his employers, the *Sunday Times*, to publish his account of Kingsley's often distressing last illness. The fact that he did this without consulting the Amis family, and that the diary contained intimate details of private familial relationships, angered Kingsley's son and fellow-novelist, Martin Amis, who decided that as a consequence of this perceived betrayal of trust Eric should be cast into outer darkness. And although there had been a verbal undertaking on Kingsley's part that Eric should edit Amis pére's collected correspondence, this arrangement was cancelled.

My own difficulty in all this was that I was friends with Martin as well as Eric, and since the latter had admitted to me that he had been guilty of a ghastly misjudgement, I hardly felt I could take up the cudgels on his behalf with Martin, even had he wanted me to. Remembering Randolph Churchill's remark, that it is precisely when you are in the wrong that you most need your friends to support you, I felt additionally guilty. After the memorial service to Kingsley, I was standing among the throng on the portico of the church of St Martin-in-the Fields when I spotted Eric, for once the outsider, standing disconsolately on the pavement. I had been invited by Martin to attend the wake that followed the church service but was moved by Eric's dejection, so to cheer him up I took him to lunch elsewhere instead.

In a eulogy at St Bride's church in Fleet Street on Eric's death, I recalled, among other aspects of his life and career, his experience of National Service, when he had been a tank instructor attached to the Iraqi army, with which Britain and America were now at war. 'If Eric's pupils are now generals,' I observed, 'they're bound to win,' which I hope made him laugh.

Chapter 15

I was fortunate to be an industrial correspondent when a new wave of more militant trade union leaders emerged in the 1970s, people I had already come to know from my years of slogging around the seaside conferences while they were climbing to the top of their unions.

Union leaders seldom got a good press, particularly in the leader columns, because they were seen as a political threat, an alternative focus of power to elected governments – or so both sides in this argument believed. But they did have twelve million members, so it was an act of folly for one-term Tory prime minister Edward Heath, forced by a miners' strike to impose a three-day working week on the country because of energy shortages, to call an election in 1974 under the slogan 'Who runs the country?' To which a frightened electorate's response was to return Labour to power, believing that Harold Wilson would be better placed to rein in his party's union 'partners'.

There were many reasons for the decline of British industry (including the coal industry, which at the time was chiefly on Heath's mind) apart from strikes, among them the beginnings of a shift from coal to oil and gas and a longer-term transition in the national economy from production (making things) to services (finance, telecoms, leisure). But it was the wrecking tactics of militants, particularly in the car factories with their televised car-park mob parliaments chanting 'One out, all out' as they embarked on their bewilderingly frequent unofficial strikes that most people would have identified as the prime, if not the only cause for the increasing exasperation towards the trade union movement in the Seventies – and on into the Eighties - by public and politicians alike.

There was little, however, that union leaders could do to stem the anarchy in the car plants, and easy for militant spokesmen, often of a communist or Trotskyist persuasion, to use antiquated union rule books, often written in the late 19th and early 20th century, to do much as they pleased. The reality was that the union bosses did not possess the overweening power popularly attributed to them.

The TUC was supposed to be the liaison body overseeing the trade union movement, but either lacked the levers of control over individual unions to call them to order, or was anyway loathe to intervene in their internal affairs. So the unions looked from the outside like a rudderless juggernaut fast propelling the country towards post-industrial ruination. The chief sufferer from this widely-held impression was, ironically, the Labour Party, which in or out of power was as helpless as the TUC and the national leaders of the unions to curb excesses. The political parties did their best with Barbara Castle's timid In Place of Strife reforms, but Britain would have to await the arrival of Mrs Thatcher for a more radical reform of union power.

Labour suffered because the TUC appeared weak and the individual unions overmighty, a situation the media firmly blamed on the party. Individual unions, after all, were nearly all affiliated to the Labour Party and provided the bulk of the party's finances. What people did not realise was that the TUC itself was not formally linked, or, in the terminology, 'affiliated', to the Labour Party, even if most individual unions were. So by tradition, and because individual unions wanted it so, the annual conference of the TUC was routinely allowed to become a cockpit for internal Labour Party disputes on such matters as unilateral nuclear disarmament, often mischievously stoked up by Labour MPs with a foot in all three camps, unions, TUC and party. What everyone wanted, by contrast, was that industrial relations problems should be sorted out rationally, with less resort to strikes, particularly those of the unofficial variety.

What often struck me, in the midst of all the confusion, was the essential likeability of most of the union leaders I came to know, their genuine commitment to their members, and – this was the downside – in many cases, their lack of schooling. And, compounding this initial disadvantage in life, few had received anything much in the way of training for the complex roles they were occupying.

A union leader's job demanded a range of skills, including negotiating ability, oratory, public relations, and a grasp of law, finance, and psychology. But most of them emerged as paid officials while still quite young, after a brief experience of their own industries as apprentices or low-paid, unskilled workers, with little organisational experience beyond the level of shop steward - part-time workplace union reps. The TUC did its best to offer advice and education, and some individuals benefited from adult degree courses at university, but there was always a gulf between a TUC headquarters stuffed full of bright-eyed and bushy-tailed graduate officials, many with political ambitions of their own, and the command structures of individual unions.

I had first known Frank Cousins, a particular bogeyman to the *Daily Telegraph*, long before he became leader of what then was Britain's biggest union, the Transport & General Workers (he had about 1.3 million members, roughly the same as the circulation at the time of the *Telegraph*). In the mid-1950s he was a relatively junior official in charge of the London busmen, engaging in a punishing strike that incidentally forced Londoners for the first time in the modern age to look to the River Thames as a useful highway for commuters trying to get to work: there's a bright side to everything.

Frank had left school at fourteen to become a miner and then a lorry driver, and was a full-time union organiser in his early thirties.

A large and powerfully-built man, he reacted badly to criticism or perceived slights, not least from within the union, where he often clashed with its tyrannical right-wing boss, Arthur Deakin. I and other reporters were often on the receiving end of his ire. He would steam up to one, whatever the occasion, to unleash a rebuke in a very loud, harshly-metallic Yorkshire voice: it was like being barked at by an aggressive guard dog. But his anger quickly passed.

Cousins's combativeness, and his inability to accept any rule book other than that of the T & G, doomed his foray into elective politics as MP for Nuneaton - he almost gagged at having to address his Tory political enemies in the House of Commons as 'Honourable' Members. He gave up his seat, after serving unhappily as a minister, after only a year.

His successor in the union, Jack Jones, was less well-known to most of us when he arrived as boss of the T & G, since his climb up the ladder had been mostly in the Midlands He was keen to get the press on side when he first became general secretary, and I remember sitting with him in his car during a rainstorm in Scarborough while he outlined his hopes and aspirations for the union as I peered out at an angry sea, clearing the rain-spattered, steamed-up car windows with my elbow, and thinking that the waters were to prove even choppier for the T & G, and the trade union movement as a whole before Jack retired to try to instil the idea of standing up for their rights, union-style, into Britain's old age pensioners: thanks to their high drop-out rate, they were not to be organised like shop floor workers. While it was widely known that his wife was a communist, it came as a shock to me, after his death, when evidence emerged that Jack not only provided information to the Soviet Union, but accepted money for his services as well.

For years I would meet and talk almost daily to people like Joe Gormley of the miners, a strange mixture of slyness and music hall jollity; David Basnett of the General & Municipal Workers (a flying boat pilot during the war); Clive Jenkins, whose ego, ideas, and brilliant instinct for publicity, made up for his union's lack of numbers; papal knight William Carron of the Engineers and his successor Hugh Scanlon; Frank Foulkes, subsequently disgraced over a huge ballot-rigging scandal in the Electricians' union, and his successors, Frank Chapple and Les Cannon; and the gentlemanly Sid Greene of the Railwaymen, who went about his business not by train but in his exclusive Bristol motor car. Their company was by no means boring, and most of them were motivated by idealism, believing – whatever the leader writers said to the contrary – that their aim was to improve the lives of working people. They may be forgotten now, but in their lifetimes they destroyed as many forests turned into newsprint as vacuous modern here-today-gone-tomorrow celebrities.

Some were great characters and I remember them with huge affection. Ted Hill of the Boilermakers' Union had a sparkling cockney wit. He would freely acknowledge that to keep his members' wages high – in competition with other shipbuilding unions - he deliberately limited the number of apprentices entering the boiler-making trade. This tactic, he once boasted to me, had been so successful that 'there ain't a boilermaker in Gateshead under the age of 58'. On another occasion I was asking him about the serious problem of absenteeism among shipyard workers. 'It's the same as it always was,' he said, 'On Monday morning the lads go out into the back yard and chuck a stone up in the air. If it stays up, they go to work…'

But he was naively susceptible to the tricks played by Fleet Street photographers: I watched, fascinated, one night at the Pindar of Wakefield pub in Greys Inn Road, while the snappers, excited by something derogatory Hill had said about royalty, gradually manoeuvred him with calls to move inch by inch to the right, on the pretence that he wasn't quite in focus, until they got the picture they wanted – Ted Hill standing directly beneath a large reproduction of Annigoni's famous portrait of the Queen.

The train drivers' union, produced an individual and quirky series of leaders. The union occupied a mansion in Hampstead that had once belonged to the Beecham family, where its most famous scion, the conductor Sir Thomas Beecham, had built a large and elegant music room now used by the union for meetings and receptions. At the foot of the grand staircase was an elaborately carved wooden tabernacle containing a large ball of white marble – one was always told it represented the foundation of the original owners' fortune, the Beecham Pill.

When Jim Batty, the first leader I knew, arrived in office and was almost immediately plunged into a prolonged strike, he was given the standard treatment by the Fleet Street tabloids: his picture, taken while he was out shopping with his wife on a Saturday morning during the strike, sprawled over the entire front page, under the headline, 'Why is this man laughing?' This earned him much sympathy from his fellow union leaders, most of whom had been around longer and were accustomed to press hostility, blamed not the reporters they knew, so much as the evil and manipulative newspaper owners.

Ray Buckton, perhaps the best known of union leader and Clive Jenkins's closest pal in the fraternity of union bosses, was an immensely friendly and outgoing individual with a background far removed from the dark satanic mills of trade union legend, though he did have the cachet of having been an engine driver during the last days of the age of steam. He had been brought up in rural Yorkshire where his father worked on an estate owned by Princess Alice, daughter of King George V and sister of Edward, Prince of Wales (I remember during my upbringing in the orphanage being given a tin of toffees and a commemorative mug for Edward's never-to-be coronation as Edward VIII). Buckton once told me that as a small boy he witnessed a quarrel between the Prince and his brother-in-law, Princess Alice's husband, the 6th Earl of Harewood, while the pair were out riding: the Prince ordered Buckton to hold their horses while the Royals dismounted to engage briefly in fisticuffs. History might have taken a somewhat different course had they fought a duel.

The Electricians' union, the ETU, was a troubled outfit, its influence reduced by a long-running internecine quarrel between the communists who ran the union and their opponents – all the more bitter because the opponents were themselves more often than not ex-communists. Unlike many other unions, before they were all forced by Thatcherite legislation to hold individual votes of their members on key decisions, the ETU had always been ruled by the ballot box: regrettably, however, the ballots were blatantly rigged. My *Daily Telegraph* colleague Bob Garner, visiting a provincial office of the union, was astonished to find that in place of toilet paper the lavatory was furnished with thick bundles of undistributed ballot papers.

The president of the union was Frank Foulkes, a louche, easy-going Liverpudlian who seemed to pay little attention to corruption in the union nor the inclination to deal with it, leaving the running of the union to his tough communist general secretary, Frank Haxell. In later life, after his retirement, Foulkes once showed me his refrigerator, packed with eastern European sparkling wine, brandy, and caviare. 'I get all these invitations to Iron Curtain embassies, but I rarely go nowadays,' he said wistfully. 'But it's nice of them to send me round this stuff.'

The opposition to Foulkes and Haxell was led by two ambitious men, Frank (later Lord) Chapple and Les Cannon, who exposed the ballot rigging with a great deal of help from the press and the Labour MP Woodrow Wyatt, but little from the TUC, which was supposed to deal with such image-destroying matters. However, those campaigning against corruption were not completely immune from sharp practice themselves. In due course Chapple and Cannon won their battle for control and became president and general secretary, respectively, of the union, but immediately began manipulating the timing of a further election in what looked like an effort to prevent their opponents from challenging for one of these posts. Chapple threatened me with a libel action when I somewhat facetiously wrote that he and Cannon had borrowed the rules of the unreformed game of billiards, where 'the red ball and cue (spot) ball could be jammed in the mouth of a pocket and endless cannons scored off them'. The complaint was finally settled a year later when the *New Statesman* published an apology of such recondite complexity that no-one, including myself, could understand it, any more, I suppose, than most of my readers appreciated my punning.

I always found Cannon, in contrast to the cheeky-chappy Chapple, a difficult man to deal with, chippy, suspicious and unforthcoming, though on one occasion I may have misjudged him when I went round to his house, at his invitation, to talk about the anti-corruption campaign. As we spoke together the television set blared out in his living room, and I was annoyed by what I saw as an example of bad manners. Only subsequently did I wonder whether the TV was left on because he feared his room was being bugged.

My fellow labour reporter, Peter Jenkins of the *Guardian*, during the time of unrest when Harold Wilson's government was threatening to introduce restrictive rules on trade union activity (enshrined in the optimistically titled, In Place of Strife) invented the conceit that the prime minister had warned Hugh Scanlon, president of the engineering union, 'Hughie - get your tanks off my lawn!'

We all liked Scanlon, the last man one could imagine threatening anyone with violence. He was the only union leader I ever met who had learned shorthand specifically because he mistrusted the employers to produce accurate minutes of negotiations. He was also a champion swimmer in his youth. I interviewed him for the *Oldie* magazine after he'd just returned, in retirement, from a holiday in the Canaries where, out for a swim, the tide turned against him, sweeping him far out to sea. He was rescued by a windsurfer who deposited him safely back on land but modestly disappeared without leaving his name. Next morning, Scanlon and his wife went to look for their rescuer to thank him, discovering that he was called Jesus, a common enough name in Iberian countries. 'You see,' Scanlon told me delightedly, 'Jesus saves'.

Another interesting thing about union leaders was that they were a rich repository of British regional speech, which sometimes led to problems of interpretation. In the run-up to the 1984-85 miners' strike, Mick McGahey, the leader of the Scottish miners, and a fine orator, addressed several meetings of the Welsh miners, who were led by Dai Francis (the union had a federal regional structure, destroyed by Scargill's refusal to hold a national ballot to authorise the 1985 strike, thus justifying the Nottinghamshire miners' refusal to withhold their support). One evening over drinks following a meeting in South Wales, McGahey expressed his irritation at Francis for invariably introducing him to audiences as Mick 'McGee'. The Welshman was forced, apologetically, to explain that 'Gahey', following the same root as 'khaki', was inappropriate because it sounded exactly the same as the Welsh word for shit.

The devotion of McGahey, along with his communist brother, Alex, to the cause of the workers was never in doubt: it was said that when their mother died in her nineties, the hearse was decorated with a sign declaring, 'Murdered by capitalism'.

Before the creation of the Advisory, Conciliation and Arbitration Service (ACAS) to offer disinterested advice to the participants in industrial disputes, more acute strikes were tackled by officials of the Ministry of Labour known as industrial commissioners, who would get the parties together around a table and, with a minimum of sustenance beyond the occasional cup of tea and a sandwich, keep them there for many hours until hunger and exhaustion inclined them towards a peace agreement.

In a big strike, not only the unions and the employers, but we journalistic hangers-on might find ourselves spending days on end and long into the night at the Ministry's offices in St James's Square – or, more truthfully, at the Red Lion pub around the corner, awaiting an outcome. Then someone, usually a brilliant civil servant, Charles Birdsall, would emerge from the ministry to tell us that industrial peace had been achieved and providing us with the settlement details. When Harold Wilson was prime minister, he liked to take the credit for himself, so the warring parties would announce a settlement not at St James's Square but in his beaming presence at 10 Downing Street, with due acknowledgement paid to the Prime Minister's beer and sandwiches.

Usually, however, wherever peace was proclaimed, the dear old *Telegraph* newspapers – and most of the rest of Fleet Street – would run yet another leading article bemoaning a surrender to union power and predicting the onset of ruinous inflation for which the Labour government's economic mismanagement had to have been the underlying cause. Because of weak management, or weak government intervention, the unions in the Seventies experienced surprisingly few reversals. One exception was a strike by the postmen's union, the Union of Post Office Workers, led by Tom Jackson, who sported a marvellous set of whiskers and eventually retired early to run a shop specialising in second-hand books for children. Poor Jackson's strike was roundly defeated in 1971, a victim of the myth of trade union solidarity. After all, the other unions had noisily promised their fervent financial support for the postmen at the 1970 TUC conference. However, when Jackson's members stopped work, 'the brothers' signally failed to deliver. Isolated and bitterly disillusioned, and with his union close to bankruptcy, Tom was forced to call off the strike after seven weeks.

The first long-running strike I covered was the month-long Fleet Street newspaper strike in 1955, which blacked out the news of Winston Churchill's retirement as Prime Minister and the Queen's farewell dinner date with Winston at Number 10 (as a news agency man I was unaffected by the strike), I was standing in Downing Street late at night, shivering in a bitterly cold wind as the aged Prime Minister and the youthful Queen emerged and stood for a moment for the photographers, pictures that had to await the end of the strike before they would be published. But the real question was whether the Queen and Prince Philip, Winston and Clementine, would die of pneumonia.

This was in the days before unions dominated the political scene in quite the way they would in the following decades; there were plenty of strikes but the idea had not yet developed that the unions were becoming too big for their political boots. That realisation arrived when first Barbara Castle for Labour, and then the Conservatives under Thatcher, introduced legislation aimed at curbing union power.

However selfish and parochial the point may seem, the battles to curb the unions, and their fight-back between 1969 and the end of the miners strike in 1985, gave industrial correspondents a status above that of the hitherto top dogs, the political correspondents. We would lead the coverage of Labour Party conferences, where the unions had the bloc vote and the biggest say, and consistently overtook the politicos in securing front page lead stories and headlines.

Once, in the late Seventies, when I was freelancing, there was another sign that political and industrial correspondents were allotted a similar status. James Margach, the political editor of the *Sunday Times*, had fallen sick just before a Labour Party conference in Blackpool. It was far too late to cancel the half-page advertisements in the dailies on the Saturday morning prior to the conference, which announced, alongside a large photograph of James, that this 'experienced, sagacious' political reporter would be covering the event for the *Sunday Times*. At the last moment I was asked to deputise for him and had to withstand a great deal of ribaldry from the press corps to the effect that the great Margach was being replaced by such an inexperienced and callow substitute.

Before the Thatcher reforms that eventually reduced the power of the unions – today their strength is half the 12 million they had before the Thatcher reforms and largely concentrated in the public sector - people had become deeply frightened of industrial militancy, believing the unions were driving the country into a downhill spiral of anarchy. This fear reached its climax in the 1978-79 Winter of Discontent during the last pre-Blair Labour government, saddling forever the prime minister, James Callaghan, with the remark, 'Crisis – what crisis?' on his return at the height of the unrest from a conference in the sunny West Indies: at home the weather was appalling. I didn't hear him utter this remark, but whether it was invented by a *Sun* headline writer or not, it captured Callaghan's apparent insouciance on returning to find mountains of rubbish piling up in the streets, most damagingly in the heart of London, bodies left unburied by municipal gravediggers, and hospital and schools staffs on strike.

It was the largest prolonged mass strike since the General Strike of 1926, and was followed by a further six years of industrial unrest before legal shackles were finally attached to union power and what proved to be a final union surge - the year-long miners' strike of 1984-85. Miners' leader Arthur Scargill, foolishly motivated by revolutionary rather than industrial ambitions, made a number of serious errors in his management of the strike. Not the least was to unleash the stoppage following a winter in which the government had built up massive strategic coal stocks while the union was refusing to allow its members to work overtime, thus diminishing any cushion of savings they might have. His worst blunder, however, was to refuse to hold a strike ballot, irrevocably splitting the union between the productive Nottinghamshire miners, who insisted on their right within the rules of the union to a vote, and in its absence to continue to work during the stoppage: unwisely, Scargill's supporters were allowed to rampage across Nottinghamshire attacking working miners.

An unhappy and divided public watched Mrs Thatcher, deploying an aggressive police force, and Mr Scargill, often leading violent mass picketing himself, slugging it out – almost, it seemed at some moments, to the death. In the end, it was the coal industry, which had employed 500,000 people when it was nationalised in 1948, that was almost wiped out, mocking Aneurin Bevan's famous remark that as an island built on coal and surrounded by fish (he couldn't foresee the arrival of the redoubtable Thatcher or the European Fisheries Policy), Britain need never lack for warmth, nor starve.

While I was on the *Daily* and then the *Sunday Telegraph*, the whole of Fleet Street was afflicted by numerous wildcat strikes constantly halting production, with the management becoming so fearful of union reactions to anything written about them that my boss, Hugh Chevins, along with his deputies, Bob Garner and I, were forbidden to write about strikes in the printing industry. If they had to be mentioned in the paper at all, only reports distributed by the national news agency, the *Press Association*, could be used. Yet night after night circulation was being lost as the print run was sabotaged, often by the simple expedient of a printer literally gumming up the works by surreptitiously applying a bit of chewing gum or a coin to the edge of the continuous stream of paper going through the presses, bringing them to a shuddering and extremely messy halt.

On a Saturday night, when the first edition of the Sunday was on the presses, I would walk into a pub close to the office to watch the entry of a stream of casual, non-staff print workers nominated by the unions for the work and paid by Hartwell for doing little or nothing at all (and signing for the money under such tax-evading soubriquets as 'Mickey Mouse' and 'Clark Gable', the entire system known, for some curious reason, as 'Spanish practices'). One by one, the casuals approached union officials sitting at a table like New York mafiosi, to hand over a proportion of their earnings. Such corruption – forcing the papers to employ more workers than they needed, and then extorting a slice of their pay, either for the union or the personal enrichment of its officials - went on at all the other national Sundays as well.

Such excesses continued on and off until Rupert Murdoch finally exploded his bomb beneath Fleet Street thirty years later by moving the *Sun* out of Fleet Street to Docklands under cover of darkness to a secretly-prepared printing works, to be quickly followed, once his battle had been won, by the departure from Fleet Street of most of the other papers. The decades-long struggle to introduce modern production methods to the newspaper industry had at last been won, heralding a period when profits (and I'm pleased to say, journalists' wages) soared.

It was a great irony that Fleet Street's most favoured new home, in the old London docks, was the site of another ancient industry whose viability had been destroyed by a strike-happy labour force and new technology – in the dockers' case the new technology was containerisation. Back in the 1950s I had often covered strikes in the docks, reporting the violent wars between the Blues and the Whites – activists from the Stevedores Union, the Blues, and the Transport and General Workers, the Whites. Men in London and Liverpool, the original home of the Blues, fought each other on the quaysides, and it was not unknown for men to be hurled into the empty holds of cargo ships.

The old licensing laws then still in force ensured that at markets like Covent Garden and Smithfield, together with the docks, where workers had to turn up at dawn, the pubs were permitted to open early. We reporters were therefore sustained by bacon sandwiches from tiny market and dockside cafés, and a pint of beer from the pubs next door.

Conditions were appalling in the London docks before the reforms were introduced in the 1960s. In the cause of research, I once had to put on my oldest clothes and hitch a lift on the back of a docker's motorbike to get myself smuggled into the docks to observe the workings of the old system of casual labour. Men started to line up before dawn to see if they would be selected for a day's work by gangmasters, many of whom were more accurately described as nepotistic and corrupt gangsters. Grown men had to raise their hands excitedly, like children trying to attract the attention of the teacher, in the hiring process, known as the 'call-on'. Those who secured regular work – the so-called 'blue-eyed boys' - had to belong to the right union, the right religion, the right family, or be prepared to offer kick-backs to the gangmasters. Those whose faces did not fit scrabbled around for the irregular, menial and ill-paid work that was left over once the call-on was concluded, or were simply sent home.

Now, under the trendy title of Docklands, the old warehouses have been transformed into apartment blocks for yuppies, the docks have been turned into yacht basins or concreted over to make room for office blocks in the modernist style that became known as Docklands Light Architecture. This is where many of the national newspapers re-located, quitting their old Fleet Street home after 200 years. And to rub salt into seeping wounds, one found on taking a taxi out to Docklands that often the cabbie had been a Fleet Street printer in an earlier life.

The reality, as anyone who had a close-up view of the unions in their years of pomp knew well, was that they were always a disunited guerrilla force capable of pressurising individual employers or even entire industries over a short period of time for short-term aims. Whatever I contributed as an industrial correspondent to building up their image, time showed that unions, in the often-repeated phrase of those times, did not make Britain ungovernable.

Much as I liked the old union bosses, they were mostly poor leaders and administrators, quite incapable of uniting to achieve anything so grand as bringing down governments. Some of them liked to boast that it was the unions that destroyed the Heath government in 1974. Perhaps they nurtured some kind of syndicalist ambition to rule the country, but it was hardly exemplified by the disrespect of a delegation from the National Union of Mineworkers invited to meet Prime Minister Heath in Downing Street, and responding to his Good Morning greeting with cries of 'Hullo, sailor!' – an allusion to his rumoured homosexuality as much as his prowess as a yachtsman.

In reality, union 'bosses' demonstrated little that could be construed as initiative, except perhaps, at the dawn of the 20th century, in their creation of the Labour Party – and even then many of them, including the miners, had been reluctant to leave go of the hand of their first nurse, the old Liberal Party.

The unions have always been utterly dependent on governments, even for things they might, perhaps should, have fought for themselves and been better off as a result: health and safety at work, equal pay for women – especially equal pay - and the minimum wage, to name a few, were all government initiatives, however slowly they were implemented. Unions needed government more than governments needed unions, yet outside the public sector, hardly anyone, it would seem, needs them any more at all, a reality that Mrs Thatcher latched onto with reforms that even the Labour Party, supposedly the unions' firmest ally, refused materially to alter or abolish during three terms in office.

Chapter 16

MUCH as I enjoyed covering the trade union scene for the *Sunday Telegraph*, and freelancing on the side, I started to become restless, hoping for a change, or even a temporary break, to do something different.

After a conversation with an official of the Australian High Commission I became excited over a tentative all-expenses-paid offer to visit Australia for a few weeks to research a book on how British migrants fared when they settled there. In our union agreement there was a newly installed provision for sabbatical leave (I was on the committee that negotiated it), so I asked the then editor, Donald McLachlan, whether I might take this opportunity. He refused, on the grounds that I was busy doing what I was doing, and he couldn't – or wouldn't - spare me.

I'm grateful that, years later, the *Daily Mail* enabled me to go to Australia, thus curing me of a slight obsession I'd had since I was around fifteen years old to settle in that country, for a while thinking I might go as an emigrant '£10 Pom', but I seethed over McLachlan's decision, deciding to bide my time while looking out for another job. Then the *Telegraph* announced that it was to launch a colour magazine, under the editorship of John Anstey, who had been the launch editor of the tremendously successful *Sunday Times* magazine.

While the *Telegraph's* magazine was still on the drawing board, a plan formed in my head. I had never been to the United States, and longed, beyond reason, to do so. It was the heady time of John F. Kennedy's Camelot presidency, and his brother, Bobby, as JFK's attorney general, was engaged in a knockdown, drag-out fight with Jimmy Hoffa, leader of the mighty American lorry drivers' union, the Teamsters, over corruption, racketeering, Mafia-connections, and the misuse or outright theft of the members' pension money. In the

American way, just as the climax to the baseball season is inflatedly known as the World Series, Hoffa held the title of President of the International Brotherhood of Teamsters, though the union organised only in the United States and Puerto Rico.

Following the ETU ballot-rigging scandal, what a splendid moment, I thought, to interview Hoffa and write a contrast-and-compare piece for the magazine on union corruption in Britain and America. I put up the idea and was almost casually given the go-ahead, though with many other projects starting to pile up in the magazine's in-tray it would be some time before I would be able to go. So by the time I boarded the plane, John Kennedy had been assassinated in Dallas.

Before I was able to leave for the USA, however, as is often the way, another exciting opportunity suddenly arose, this time to go to China. The Pakistan government at that time was close to Mao Tse-Tung's regime and the country's airline, (Pakistan International Airways), was about to open a new route from Karachi, via East Pakistan, to a newly-constructed airport south of Shanghai.

The *Sunday Telegraph* allowed me, at the paper's expense, to go ahead on this 'proving flight', despite the fact that I would first have to go to Karachi to obtain a visa to enter China, where I would be masquerading as an aviation correspondent. On our way, the Pakistanis gave us a stopover in the country's eastern province, now the independent country of Bangladesh, but my confidence in PIA – slogan: Great People to Fly With - was slightly dented as we landed in the capital, Dhaka, during a mighty thunderstorm. Our pilot dropped down through the clouds to find that he was not aligned to the runway, and performed an adroit side-slip with his Boeing 707, putting the plane down with a bump that shook loose the oxygen masks and terrified his passengers. An amended slogan came to mind: Great People to Die With. But aboard the plane was the head of PIA, Air Commodore Nur Khan, who instantly sacked the pilot, whose exuberance was explained by the fact that he had started his career flying Spitfires.

Once safely in China we moved in easy stages by train, plane and car along the east coast, taking in the sights on the way: in Shanghai the Chinese made great play of a sign that had appeared on the riverside parkway, the Bund, in colonial days, reading, 'No Dogs or Chinese Allowed'. Very bad - but this unpleasant glimpse of the past was offset by a visit to another, more acceptable and therefore surviving showpiece from those days – the still-extant bar claimed by merchant sailors to be the longest in the world, even if its atmosphere had changed from a den of iniquity into that of a puritanical youth club.

Rural China impressed with its tranquillity and beauty immediately before Mao's iniquitous Cultural Revolution was unleashed. Ninety-nine per cent of the population seemed to ride bicycles, and honesty, or a deep fear of the law, was so pervasive that if one left a sixpenny ballpoint pen in a hotel, a messenger would arrive hotfoot further along the route to return it (something I'd only previously experienced in Spain under General Franco).

One of my British companions was Ian Coulter of the *Sunday Times*, a close friend who had been taken prisoner when his Fleet Air Arm plane was shot down in the Korean war: he was later exchanged for a Chinese captive. From birth he had suffered from vegetarianism, his parents having adopted the diet for ideological reasons and subsequently abandoned it. But by then Ian was unable to change, suffering all kinds of side effects when he was obliged as a prisoner-of-war to eat meat.

Throughout our time in China he was to endure the consequences of the complete inability of our hosts to comprehend vegetarianism. We attended any number of banquets, always carefully explaining to our hosts that Ian was unable to eat meat: his meal would invariably be served with the pork or chicken cut up into tiny pieces and hidden among the rice or noodles. A bulky individual, he started to lose weight fast, while I gained pounds from eating his share.

We eventually arrived in Beijing in time for May Day, 1964, flying up there in one of a fleet of recently imported, made-in-Britain Vickers Viscount turbo-prop airliners, its seats, like those of a brand new Ford Prefect outside the home of a proud new British owner who'd never had it so good, still covered in clear plastic from the factory.

In the capital on May Day we were invited to watch a magnificent fireworks display from the vantage point of the Forbidden City, and boggle at the sight of more than a million people gathered in Tiananmen Square. Later, we were summoned to meet and drink green tea with foreign minister General Chen Yi, one of Mao's early companions on the Long March, along with a dozen more members of the Politburo, but Mao himself was unwell and we were sent an extraordinarily polite, even florid, apology for his inability to grant us an audience.

A couple of days later, we interviewed Chou-en-Lai, the prime minister, who unlike any of the other notables we encountered, spoke reasonably good English and, having once been a waiter in Paris, better French. It would be ridiculous to say that he let it slip, for the story was beginning to leak out elsewhere, but we were excited when he told us officially, but almost casually, that China was about to explode its first atomic bomb. The story provided a good news peg for the *Sunday Telegraph*, but I was still smarting from having been awakened in the middle of the night to be handed a cable from Brian Roberts, later to become editor of the Sunday but at the time managing editor of the *Daily Telegraph*, to whom I had sent a short piece on the fireworks display. The message read: 'Why only 200 words May Day Pekin?' The fact was that it was impossible to find any way of sending a story without the Chinese providing the means (and countries where one is unable even to read the word for 'toilets' always present difficulties). On this occasion they gave us only five minutes to pound out our pieces on a teleprinter before whisking us away: and, anyway, I have to admit that my first loyalty was naturally to the Sunday, not the *Daily Telegraph*.

Chou en-Lai chain-smoked throughout our conversation, on his desk cartons of Craven-A, a once popular brand of English cigarettes. Like the gleaming black American limousines in which chauffeured government ministers weaved their perilous way through the hordes of bicycles on the streets of the city, the cigarettes were imported from the then-British colony of Hong Kong. As a lifelong smoker myself, when Chou died of cancer in 1976, eight months before Mao departed this life, I recalled that the advertising slogan of Chou's preferred brand proclaimed, 'Craven-A do not affect the throat'.

The office had loaned me a camera for the trip, and for the first week or so I took a number of pictures before throwing it back into my suitcase: I realised that thinking about camera angles, settings and picture opportunities prevented one from actually seeing what was going on. However, on my return – to the disgust of one or two of the staff photographers who thought reporters taking pictures threatened their jobs - it was the *Daily Telegraph* that published a double-page spread of my snaps of China, which had a novelty value, the country having been virtually closed to visitors for some years after Mao fell out with Stalin and sent the Soviet military and industrial experts back home. My China portfolio remains the only picture credit I ever received.

One thing I did notice while still armed with the camera was that among the crowds that gathered to watch our little group wherever we went, I could distinguish one phrase uttered alike by curious young people and old ladies, often leftovers from the ancien régime, still hobbling around on bound feet. I busily clicked away as party activists shooed the people away, scolding them for their rudeness in staring at foreigners. The phrase sounded like 'da beeza', and our woman translator shyly admitted that it meant 'big noses', but I was thinking back to Mr Beazer, the old sergeant major back at Spurgeon's Orphanage who marched us up and down like little Victorian soldiers, and wondering whether he had acquired his name while soldiering in China in his young days, for he did have a particularly large nose.

At this time, Robert Kennedy was about to quit as Attorney General in order to run for the Senate in New York, but first, he was determined to complete his legal pursuit of the man I wanted to interview, James Riddle Hoffa, who Kennedy frequently and publicly vowed would be sent to prison.

I flew first to New York, where the place looked reassuringly as it did in the hundreds of films I had watched all my life, except that the yellow cabs on the streets were not immaculately polished as in the movies but dirty and full of dents and scratches. At pavement level the vaunted skyscrapers set up swirling wind storms which – it was October - blew waste paper, dust and other detritus around, stinging the eyes. I also made the mistake, having become momentarily lost in Greenwich Village, of asking a policeman for directions: 'Go buy a map, buddy,' he snarled, making me realise now, after many more visits to the city, that at least the manners of New Yorkers have improved over time.

Arriving in Washington DC, I lost little time in finding the headquarters of the International Brotherhood of Teamsters, 'the marble palace' as it was confusingly known, for this is a city jam-packed with marble palaces. I was a little nervous, walking past the building two or three times before going in, despite an abiding faith that Hoffa would not dream of refusing to see me.

I stated my business to a tough-looking functionary behind a desk in the entrance hall and was told to wait while he phoned someone within the building. In a few minutes a man came down to see me, introducing himself as from public relations, to tell me, 'Mr Hoffa doesn't do interviews,' and adding, 'You'll have to leave.' The toughie, as he heard this, was already coming round from behind his desk in a slightly menacing way to usher me out of the building.

Standing outside on the pavement in bright autumn sunshine I was deeply bewildered by this rebuff. This wasn't how it was in the movies. Wasn't every door open to reporters in America? Would reporter Hildy Johnson in The Front Page have accepted such treatment? And how was I to tell the office that the interview I had so confidently promised to deliver was not to be had? Should I go home and face the sack, or just disappear among the huddled masses, turning my back on the old Europe?

Disconsolately, I went to the *Telegraph's* office in the National Press Building and sought the advice of Stephen Barber, the Sunday's *Telegraph's* resident Washington correspondent. Stephen was one of three journalists on the paper who, curiously, were entitled, had they wished to use it on their headed notepaper, to the Egyptian honorific of Bey, since their fathers were all Pashas - high-ranking civil servants in the British colonial administration in Egypt (our other Beys were letters editor Richard Bennett and columnist Lionel 'Bobby' Birch, who had the additional distinction that one of his five ex-wives, Inge Morath, succeeded Marilyn Monroe as spouse to Arthur Miller).

Barber, as usual, offered sound advice, suggesting that I send Hoffa a telegram via Western Union – telegrams had not yet quite been abolished in Britain but were in steep decline and not used much any more by newsrooms. Before the arrival of the telex machine, foreign correspondents filing stories, or forced to explain why their expenses claims were excessive, would reply in staccato words designed to reduce the expensive per-word cost of telegraphing (one Fleet Street hack, taking offence at being accused of exaggerating his excess while reporting from some remote spot indignantly and economically responded, 'Upstick job arsewards'.

I adopted a slightly aggrieved tone in my message to Hoffa, pointing out that I had come 3,000 miles to see him and then been more or less ejected by one of his underlings. To my astonishment, within an hour, he was on the phone inviting me to come and see him right away.

This time, I received a much friendlier reception, with my public relations friend waiting by the front desk to greet me, leading me into the lift and up to Hoffa's office, as the receptionist glared like a dinnerless Rottweiler deprived of biting a juicy chunk out of my leg.

A thickset, smartly-dressed, fit looking man of fifty-two years, with a head of thick black hair gleaming like patent leather, and no more than 5 ft 6 inches tall (all calling to mind the film star Edward G. Robinson in one of his celebrated gangster roles) the Teamsters' leader shook my hand warmly, inviting me to share the wonderful view from his window across the parkland to the towering dome of the Capitol, the United States Congress. 'You should'a told me you were coming,' he said in explanation for my original difficulty in penetrating what was clearly his fortress.

Pausing to boast about the table where his many union vice-presidents met – the largest table in the world fashioned from a single piece of wood, he claimed - he was soon launched on a denunciation of Robert Kennedy, gesturing threateningly towards the Senate as though expecting the attorney general to be sitting with his window open listening to this diatribe.

I was a little shocked to hear Hoffa describing his adversary, a member of the closest thing the Americans had to a royal family, and one so recently bereaved, as 'Booby' Kennedy: in the context, it was obvious that this was no slip of the tongue. And I received another earful when I asked why the AFL-CIO – the American equivalent of the TUC – had expelled the Teamsters within days of Hoffa becoming the union's president on the grounds that it was 'corruptly' controlled: i.e. that Hoffa was in thrall to the Mafia.

Hoffa insisted, playing to a British audience, that it was the AFL-CIO that was corrupt, since it had done nothing about Dave Beck, his immediate predecessor as Teamsters' leader, who had embezzled union funds to build a lavish house for his son, and, eventually, been sent to prison (albeit in a case brought not by the government but by reforming elements within the Teamsters). Moreover, Hoffa went on, Robert Kennedy's campaign to clean up the union was nothing less than a ruthless attack on the working class on behalf of employers who resented the first-class deals the union secured for its members: I'd heard similar paranoid rhetoric from British union leaders over and over again. As to his alleged Mafia links, he retaliated by saying it was the employers who used crooks and racketeers to attack and injure workers on strike, adding, 'The American working man is short-changed every day.'

I hardly got a word in during this lecture, but to my surprise, on dismissing me on the grounds that he was too busy to be interviewed any more, he invited me to return early the next day. This time, I was able to ask him more personal questions, after first accompanying him to his office gym, where he showed off his ability to perform a startling series of press-ups without, I must say, persuading me to accept his invitation to join him in his exercises. Back in his office, his answers to my questions revealed the paradox behind Hoffa's public attitudes. On the one hand were his aggressive claims that the Teamsters concentrated solely on fighting for truck drivers' wages and conditions, on the other, Kennedy's allegation that he was a crook using the Teamsters' gigantic pension fund as a private bank to finance casino-building and other projects controlled by the Mafia, were backed by a vigorous opposition inside the union.

He appeared to have no taste for the high life, and no apparent vices that would make him susceptible to blackmail by the Mafia. It seemed to me the rumour that as a young union organiser he sought the help of the Mafia in a strike, and thereafter could never escape their clutches might have some truth in it yet he remained married to his first and only wife, neither drank nor smoked, and lived in the same modest house in Detroit he'd bought when he got married.

Next, Hoffa invited me to sit in on a meeting with two or three trucking employers – I suppose we would call them hauliers, though this might underrate the size and importance of their companies – accompanied by their lawyers. No doubt showing off to me, the

Teamsters' boss treated his negotiating partners with an exaggerated contempt, constantly interrupting and talking over them. Then with a barked 'Gedouta here!' he dismissed them: they filed out with their shiny blue suits and slim briefcases, clearly angry over the contemptuous way they had been treated. Hoffa continued bragging to me of the mighty power of the Teamsters, their monster trucks transporting food, clothing, medicine, raw materials and fuel all over the country – everything that America needed to live and survive. He assured me with an undisguised lip-smacking excitement that a nationwide strike by his Teamsters would close down the nation and result in starvation and death. It was almost as though he was anticipating such a disaster, though the record shows that he never embarked on a national strike.

Later, we shared a sandwich lunch at his desk while he enlarged on his achievements, particularly the establishment of the pension fund and the compulsory dollar-an-hour contributions he had forced the bosses to pay into it for every employee. But he was unforthcoming when I asked about the soft loans he'd allegedly approved towards the development of casinos owned and run by Mafia figures, and vehemently denied that he had ever received under-the-table 'points' – a percentage on loans advanced by the pension fund. Indeed, whenever the conversation turned to money, it was like talking to the confident chief executive of a well-run bank rather than a rough-hewn union boss in league with the Cosa Nostra and determined to concede nothing of the charges piling up against him.

He escorted me around the well-appointed Teamster building, introducing me to various officers of the union, ducking out to see to some office business and leaving me to spend time alone with his deputy, Frank Fitzsimmons, who at once told me with some pride that he had been born in Cornwall. Of the two men, it struck me that

Fitzsimmons appeared the shiftier, and there was something insincere in his lavish praise for his boss (whom he would, not to my surprise, eventually replace). I half expected him to wink when he declared that Hoffa possessed 'true greatness'.

When I sat down to write my *Telegraph* magazine piece I made the mistake of relying too heavily on my skimpy knowledge of American trade union history in trying to chart the way in which I predicted Hoffa's career might develop. I took as a model John L. Lewis, leader of the American Mine Workers Union who, like the Teamster's leader, antagonised the US Congress and frightened the country's commercial establishment, but ended up as a greatly admired figure and adviser to Presidents.

I was not to realise that eleven years after I met him, much of which time he spent in the courts or in prison, Jimmy Hoffa would suddenly disappear off the face of the earth, creating a mystery still not satisfactorily solved to this day. I blush when I remember – referring to his domination of his union – that I even wrote of his 'astonishing powers of survival'.

Yet because of a bizarre mishap, my reputation as a supposed expert on trade unions and their leaders, let alone their foreign counterparts, would not suffer as a result of my gross misreading of Jimmy Hoffa's prospects. As a consequence of a shortage of printing capacity in Britain, or an industrial dispute – I can't remember the precise cause – the edition of the *Telegraph Weekly* containing the article was printed in Germany, and then moved to a warehouse before distribution, where the entire run was destroyed in a fire. No wonder they say it's better to be born lucky than rich.

Chapter 17

MY love affair with America – like most people I mean that part of the continent between Mexico and Canada once occupied by the cowboys and Indians whose adventures enthralled my childhood – began long before my first visit to the country.

Fascination was developed essentially by the movies, which from my teenage years constituted my favourite entertainment – I would often visit the cinema twice a day. An earlier influence, however, was the arrival, among the desultory gifts that people tend to donate to charities, of old copies of American magazines Life and the Saturday Evening Post.

I was impressed by *Life's* vivid photojournalism and can still remember one entire issue devoted to the Australian and US armies' campaign against the Japanese in New Guinea, a theatre of the war little publicised, so far as I recall, in Britain. But it was not this far-off military sideshow that I found arresting so much as the stunning shots of the dramatic topography, mountains, ravines, wild rivers, waterfalls and jungles captured by the magazine's photographers, and which I longed to visit (and never have).

In the *Post*, Norman Rockwell's superb Americana-fostering covers delighted me, and I spent hours trying to copy them in a bid to teach myself drawing. But hand and eye sadly failed to co-ordinate.

What fascinated me most about these American magazines, however, were the advertisements which, in grey, wartime Britain presented an image of unimaginable prosperity and happiness. Here were smiling, neatly-permed young housewives in gingham aprons carrying steaming turkeys to the table ready for their handsome husbands and contented children's Thanksgiving dinners. Then there were gleaming, streamlined cars in dazzling colours, their lines enhanced by opulent chromium fittings. Nor has anyone made booze look more enticing, with lifesize bottles of honey-gold bourbon and rye whiskey filling entire pages from top to bottom. The ads offered an unsubtle picture of American wealth and wellbeing that proved ineradicable before, much later, I witnessed first-hand the poverty still to be found, in US cities and the countryside of the South.

My interest in American politics had been boosted by my 1964 trip to Washington to interview Jimmy Hoffa, but the spark had been struck long before when I saw a cinema newsreel showing what must have been the 1948 convention of the Republican Party, held in Philadelphia. Here was all the now-familiar razzamatazz of an American political convention with seemingly hysterical supporters of the candidates in silly hats waving placards amid innumerable balloons and streamers descending from the ceiling, and oompah music pumping from perspiring bands.

A wildly overexcited chairman was introducing one of the contenders for the party's presidential nomination, shouting at the top of his voice into the microphone, 'Ladies and gentlemen, I give you...' before raising his voice to an impossible further pitch to make himself heard above the din, 'I give you Mi-ster Republican, Mi-ster America – Sena-tor Bob Taft!'

Whatever happened at the convention – in fact, the isolationist Taft would be defeated for the nomination by New York Governor Thomas Dewey - was buried by what occurred at the general election later that year. Dewey, having eliminated Taft, had been hailed as a racing certainty to defeat incumbent President Harry S. Truman, whose poll ratings were sagging - such a certainty that some newspapers printed early edition headlines on election night hailing a Dewey victory before the vote had been declared. However, it was the unfancied

Truman who won, a setback that scarred the polling industry for years.

The movies – ah, the movies, what pleasure they used to bring me - told different stories about American politics. In the upbeat Mr Smith Goes to Washington – made in 1939 but which I saw just after the war - James Stewart, as the purest of the pure and the youngest senator in the US, exposes corruption in high places. By contrast, there was All the King's Men (1948), a thinly disguised biopic of the corrupt but wonderfully colourful 1930s Governor of Louisiana, Huey Long, brilliantly played by Broderick Crawford. So one could take one's choice - Stewart imparting a warm feeling of idealism as he triumphs over the prevailing cynicism, and Crawford, perhaps telling more of the truth.

By the Sixties, with several years' experience of British politics as a parliamentary reporter, through my friendship with Tommy Ives and Len Maynard, both full-time Labour Party agents in what had become my home town of Fulham, I decided to write a book on what my friend and future editor, Anthony Howard, called the 'secret garden' of British politics – the selection of candidates for the House of Commons. The title I chose was The Selectorate.

It soon struck me that the British candidate selection system was riddled with croneyism, secrecy, obfuscation and various forms of corruption, not formally criminal, maybe, but certainly involving undisclosed private wealth or access to trade union funds, as well as horse trading, deceit, and the exploitation of family and business connections, all to further the cause of particular would-be MPs. Looking at what people would do to secure safe Labour or Tory seats for themselves or their protégés – and the vast majority of seats were 'safe' for one party or the other - Dickens's picture in Pickwick

Papers of an election in the fictional town of Eatanswill, and the rotten boroughs of the House of Commons prior to the great 19th century electoral law reforms, seemed not quite so dead-and-gone as people might have imagined.

But writing a book of that kind also binds one at least to try to present an answer to alleged shortcomings, always bearing in mind Dr Johnson's observation that most schemes of political improvement are very laughable things. The solution I presented emerged from my slight knowledge of American politics, and was summed up in the subtitle I chose for the book - The Case for Primary Elections in Britain. I'd read somewhere that the first primary election in which all the voters had a hand in choosing a candidate took place in Pennsylvania in 1842, a mere ten years after Britain's first limited Reform Bill reached the statute book.

I also noted that, in the late 1960s, media markets, particularly television, previously the monopoly of a politically timid BBC, were expanding with the arrival of a regionally-based commercial TV system, thus enabling, along with local newspapers and independent radio, the publicity vital for primary elections to take root. (When the Conservatives, in the wake of the parliamentary expenses scandal, ran a primary election in the Totnes, Devon, constituency in the summer of 2009, more than 20 per cent of eligible voters participated, but there's no sign that the idea will be taken further any time soon.)

Although only mild interest was evinced by the publication of The Selectorate in 1967 – in its wake I was invited to address some university societies and even to try to explain my ideas to readers of the Daily Mirror – I can't say that the political world took much notice. Sales failed to cover the extremely modest advance I received from the publishers which, come to think of it, has similarly applied to my occasional subsequent exercises in authorship.

My greatest disappointment, however was that, at the time The Selectorate was published, I was again in America and thus deprived not only of the opportunity to publicise my book on radio or TV, but also missing out on the modest wine and nibbles party usually paid for by the publisher on the arrival of a new book. What had happened was that Stephen Barber decided to take some accumulated leave and I was sent to Washington to fill in for him for four or five weeks. Circumstances intervened, and I found my time in Washington extending to several months.

Like other Fleet Street exiles, I soon discovered that practising journalism in the US was refreshingly different from what we were accustomed to at home. But combing through American newspapers each morning to learn what was going on, I found them extraordinarily tedious, since they contained little of the clever design or the entertainment element that even our most serious newspapers inject into their offerings. As well as being visually unattractive they were complicated to read, usually forcing the reader breathlessly to pursue a story from a single-column introduction on the front page, through the back pages, and even on to other sections of the newspaper before completion was achieved. 'Rivulets of news running between banks of advertisements' was how Cecil King, boss of the *Mirror*, accurately described US newspapers.

On the other hand, access to information was very much easier. Early on in my time in Washington, I found that following up stories relating to national defence were, simply by picking up the phone, discussed in an open, remarkably easy and friendly fashion by staff members and politicians on congressional committees dealing with defence and foreign affairs. It was, and still is, a far more difficult task in uptight Britain, where we now have a Freedom of Information Act that needs to be easier and cheaper to access than it has proved to be so far.

Although I was amused for years by newspapers like the *Mail* and the *Express* treating America, in dedicated daily columns, less as a serious superpower than a circus act, displaying the country as the home of the bizarre, eccentric, and outlandish, I was quite unprepared for what happened when I arrived in Washington DC as Barber's stand-in. On my first evening, just hours off the plane, I found a note from him bidding me to take his place on a Meet the Press TV programme he'd agreed to appear on.

I found my way to the TV studio only just in time, where, with two or three other non-American reporters, I was to interview Congressman Ogden Reid, known to his friends, apparently, as 'Brownie'. He was the scion of the family that owned the *Herald Tribune*, in those days a major daily in New York but today exiled to Paris as the *International Herald Tribune*, a newspaper for American expatriates and tourists. As well as being the Herald Trib's editor-in-chief, Reid was a New York congressman who could boast more Jewish constituents in his electoral district of New York than the entire population of Israel, where he had previously served as US ambassador.

We were in the immediate aftermath of the June 1967 Six Day War, in which the Israelis had smashed the numerically superior armed forces of Egypt, Jordan and Syria combined. The effect of Israel's victory was hailed by ordinary people in London and in the US (one particularly noticed the special pride evinced by Jewish taxi drivers) as a stunning achievement. There was also disquiet, however, over the behaviour of the Israelis in the Golan Heights, the West Bank and East Jerusalem – the so-called occupied territories. And I felt it was a good idea to raise this question with Ogden Reid.

As a foreigner and a guest on the programme, I did not want to treat the gentlemanly Mr Reid as being responsible for whatever had gone right or wrong in the recent war, still less for the behaviour of Israeli soldiers. But I quite forcefully asked him for his views on reports of Israeli troops in East Jerusalem identifying the homes of supposed Palestinian 'troublemakers', by marking their doors with red paint, and then sending in bulldozers to destroy the houses so marked. Wasn't this a very tragic irony, I asked, given that only two decades earlier, treatment of this kind was handed out to European Jews by the Nazis?

Mr Reid shied away from the subject, delivering a series of reassuring sentences on the prospects of Israel and its enemies engaging in negotiations, each phrase or assertion beginning with the undermining word 'Hopefully'. My colleagues on the panel changed the subject and the programme meandered towards its end. I just wondered, with the plethora of TV channels available to American viewers, whether anyone at all would have bothered to watch this one.

Next morning, I went to the office in the National Press Building for my first working day and the office secretary came in to tell me that a group of people had arrived to see me. I was astonished: how could anyone have been aware of my presence in so short a time? She made it clear that the visitors would wait for as long as it took.

The group of half a dozen men who entered the room were clearly of the Jewish faith, some in long black coats and Homberg hats, heavily bearded and with dangling ringlets, others in yamulke skull caps. Their leader stepped forward, and to my amazement, declared that they had come to congratulate me on my TV appearance of the previous evening. 'Mr Paterson,' he said, 'we belong to an organisation called Jews Against Israel,' before launching into a lecture on their clearly deeply-felt anti-Zionist beliefs.

As they left, I remember thinking to myself, 'Only in America!' and grudgingly admitting that those British newspaper columns itemising day by day the strange ways and happenings of America had probably got it right.

My stay in the Washington of the Sixties became a wonderful explosion of sensations and adventures. Each morning I would drive downtown from Stephen's smart North-West suburban house, my journey taking me through Rock Creek Park and Foggy Bottom and the yet-to-become-notorious Watergate building.

The city centre was full of vast car parks mostly serving the great white public buildings. These car parks were run by agile, exuberant black youths who spoke their own patois, incomprehensible to most of their customers. I used to fantasise that when no-one was looking they would dance, as in a Busby Berkeley routine, on top of the massed cars, hopping from bonnet to boot, somersaulting and cartwheeling from one car park to another, gathering in their hundreds to yell their strange imprecations pointedly at the FBI building as they gyrated along the street.

Stephen Barber's pride and joy was the car he left behind for my use, a two-tone – blue and white - Dodge Dart convertible, unlike anything I'd seen before, with all the important controls, including the electrically elevating roof, operated by an array of push buttons. To me, the Dart was one of those Saturday Evening Post advertisements from my wartime childhood come to life. It was in this car that I explored the countryside around Washington, visited George Washington and

Thomas Jefferson's homes, one day stopping on a whim to hire a ride in a tiny helicopter parked in a farmer's front yard to view the site of the Civil War Battle of Manassas, as the Northerners called it, or Bull Run, as it is known in the South. The farmer at the controls gave me a running commentary as we swooped and wheeled over the groups of old cannons and trench lines marking the places where the battle had been fiercest.

Often I would fly somewhere in the States to dig up material to write a feature article for the paper, experiencing the scenery of this beautiful country, the local accents and customs, wincing over displays of racism (one internationally renowned medical scientist in Mississippi showed me around his newly-built house, bemoaning the necessity to make measuring sticks to help his illiterate black labourers standardise the height of the door handles) and learning that you can't judge America simply by the standards imposed by New York, Hollywood, or its host-state California: the West always seems a foreign country to me, far less familiar and, in my experience, less welcoming than the East.

I also went to Chicago for the first time – a wonderful feeling for a film or music fan, to stand at the junction of State Street and Wabash Avenue - for the foundation of the ill-starred New Party, an anti-Vietnam War, anti-nuclear weapons movement, one of whose founders was Dr Benjamin Spock. Over the Labor Day weekend, at the Palmer House hotel, the New Party's adherents attempted to produce a joint programme to present to the country: it was not difficult to see that they would fail when I saw a notice outside the (closed) door of the black caucus warning fellow-delegates, 'Whitey, Keep Out!'. The New Party, like most efforts to form a viable third party in opposition to the Democrats and Republicans, quickly petered out, though its name has occasionally been revived, briefly, by others.

The Eastern Airways round-the-clock shuttle flights made it easy to commute from Washington to New York, a city, awake or sleeping, full of stories. In the torrid riot-torn summer of 1967, having already witnessed the destructive upheavals of discontented black people in Detroit, I did a story on the surprising absence of street riots in Bedford-Stuyvesant, an almost entirely black suburb of Brooklyn. Walking its streets was like being in an African country, where all the patrolmen and the chief of police, as well as the ordinary inhabitants, were black. There had been forebodings of riots during the long summer school break, when subsidies paid by the city to 'young leaders' – i.e. potential troublemakers – ran out, and the authorities economised by locking up the fire hydrants that normally provided cool relief from the heat for kids playing in the streets. The police commander persuaded the city to continue the payments and open up the hydrants: for that summer at least, with full-scale riots breaking out elsewhere, Bedford-Stuyvesant remained peaceful.

I was also in New York to report on the rise of an exciting young heavyweight boxer, Joe Frazier, who was on a winning streak. I had been to Philadelphia to meet the future three-times holder of the world championship, discovering that he was 'owned' by a syndicate of no fewer than twenty-one people, their number including a minister of religion. Frazier's latest opponent was George Chuvalo, a Canadian with a reputation for a level of toughness unusual even in his profession. I had a ringside seat for the last fight-night at the old Madison Square Garden, scene of many of Joe Louis's great triumphs, before it was replaced by the present Garden, built over Pennsylvania Station. The contest turned into a bloodbath, with the Canadian staggering about in the fourth round, unable to see through the mush that remained of his right eye, exhausted by Frazier's unrelenting body punching and vicious left hooks, but still amazingly game. Mercifully, the referee stopped the fight.

I found my short course in Americana immensely beguiling. I had instantly acquired a social life with a set of new best friends. I also learned something of American women, one of whom, an academic teaching Shakespeare at a provincial university whom I had met through some Americans I'd known in London, invited me to dinner at the Greenwich Village flat she had borrowed from a friend while doing some research in New York. I awoke in the night with fearful abdominal pains causing me to roll around on the floor in agony. Far from showing concern or sympathy, my hostess screamed, 'You can't stay here! How can I explain a dead guy in an apartment that doesn't belong to me?' I found a late-cruising taxi to take me to my hotel at the other end of Manhattan, realising just how many pain-inducing potholes are disguised by the slow-moving daytime traffic of New York. I called the hotel doctor who, in a strong Hungarian accent, diagnosed infectious hepatitis and told me that I should promptly remove myself to a hospital. Feeling slightly persecuted, the anti-inflammatory tablets he gave me banished the pain and sent me to sleep: I subsequently discovered on my return to Washington that I had been suffering colic from a kidney stone. The incident did not deter the lady concerned from writing to me in London a year later, not to enquire as to my wellbeing but to see whether I could find holiday employment for two of her students studying in the UK.

These few months in Washington were the forerunner of many visits I would make to the US over the following years, private trips to stay with friends, as well as on assignment, several for BBC Radio 4. And before such things were more closely supervised, some of my children and stepchildren would make the journey to Washington to work as interns for a charity or in a congressional office, made possible by my new acquaintances in the city.

Chapter 18

MY sojourn in Washington DC resulted in the creation of a lifelong friendship with two remarkable men and the renewal of an acquaintance with others I had met previously in London. My new friends were my fellow residents at Stephen Barber's fine house near the city's Episcopal Cathedral and the British Embassy.

Like so many people in Washington, Donald Anderson and Wyche Fowler toiled in the city's main industry – politics. Anderson, a black man with green eyes whose antecedents possessed American Indian and Jewish as well as slave blood, was a lawyer and, at the time, counsel to the congressional Government Affairs Committee.

He was familiar with London, having studied transport policy for a master's degree at the London School of Economics. His previous experience in Washington was as an aide to Adam Clayton Powell, the stormy African-American politician (black, negro or coloured were the terms then in use: one of Powell's achievements was to end the use by congressmen of the word 'nigger' in debates). But when he interviewed Donald for the job, having invited him on the basis of his CV, he confessed he had expected to see a white man. Donald loathed the modern usage of African-American – 'I'm an American, not an African', he used to say, but until the end of his life he would, in jest, call himself 'just a poor old nigger'. There were traces of bitterness, too, exemplified by his description of the Washington Monument in Washington DC as 'a Klu Klux Klansman with red eyes (the navigation lights at the top of the figure) glowering out over the South'.

No-one has ever beaten Powell's record of steering fifty bills through Congress, many of them helping to implement President Kennedy's New Frontier programme and, subsequently, President Johnson's Great Society. But during the late Sixties, his zeal in the cause of black people's rights appeared to wane as he spent more of his time as a playboy than at work in New York or Washington, having discovered the Bahamian island of Bimini as a place of recreation and respite from his cares.

A serious threat hung over him in 1967 when the House of Representatives investigated allegations of dereliction of duty and corruption against him. He was expelled from the House, subsequently winning back his seat but still seldom attending Congress, living on his island paradise until his death in 1972, at the age of 64.

I soon learned that there had been a falling-out between Donald Anderson and his old boss, but I never knew the details. Perhaps Powell's arrogance was a factor: members of Powell's team were paraded one Sunday morning at New York's Abyssinian Baptist Church - Powell had inherited the pastorship from his father - while their charismatic chief delivered a sermon on the theme that 'green power is greater than black power', a notion he illustrated by taking out his wallet and scattering a fat wad of greenbacks over the worshippers. He then exhorted Donald and the others to step up one by one to tell the congregation how many dollars a year they were each paid to be working for Adam Clayton Powell.

A year after my stay in Washington, Anderson would abandon his congressional career to launch a charity, the National Association for the Southern Poor (now called the National Community Development Organisation). NASP was virtually a one-man band - for Donald always found it difficult to the point of impossibility to delegate. He worked among a largely forgotten population in rural parts of the South among impoverished people left behind in the huge post war black migration to the great cities of the north. The outlawing of discrimination in state-run schools by the Supreme Court in 1954 had led to Southern whites pulling their children out of the system, with the county governments simultaneously choking off funding to the already cash-starved black schools. Donald was to spend the rest of his life encouraging, first in Surry County, Virginia, and then more widely across the South, the inhabitants of these rural spots of extreme deprivation to take their destiny into their own hands, and to organise themselves socially and politically, sometimes with remarkable success, and, it must be said, sometimes less so. And all the while he was driving thousands of miles tirelessly teaching and inspiring people, approaching wealthy individuals, church organisations, charitable trusts and foundations for the money needed to finance the work.

Wyche Fowler was the other member of our household. Like Donald, a lawyer and postgraduate student of the LSE, at the time we met he was working for the Democratic Party youth organisation – he was a decade younger than Donald and me – at an address later to become notorious for a certain burglary: the Watergate.

A Southerner from Georgia, Wyche was on the brink of engaging in elective politics, becoming a member of the Atlanta city council and cheekily securing a late-night radio programme on which he presented himself as Atlanta's 'night mayor' helping to solve voters' grievances, and providing a nightmare to the city's elected mayor. He also worked for Congressman Charles Weltner of Atlanta, who resigned his congressional seat rather than sign the required loyalty oath to the Democratic Party nominee for the governorship of Georgia, the segregationist Lester Maddox. Maddox was the man who built a political career on threatening a posse of black church ministers with a pickaxe-handle when they protested against his ban on black customers setting foot in the café he and his family were running.

Wyche was later elected to the House of Representatives for Weltner's old 5th District of Atlanta, and then to the Senate, before becoming US ambassador to Saudi Arabia. During my stay in Washington he would sneak me into seminars held for young Democrats at the Watergate, where members of Lyndon Johnson's cabinet briefed us on the issues of the day. What I heard sometimes made useful copy for my despatches to the *Sunday Telegraph* in London. One lecture I recall concerned the urge on the part of young people to participate in the Sixties zeitgeist by taking drugs. The Secretary for Health offered a reassuring angle to the prevailing parental anxiety that the youth of the nation were shooting up and turning on, and imbibing illicit substances in an orgy of mind-bending escape from the reality of the increasingly unpopular Vietnam war. The truth was, he said, that most young Americans hadn't any access to LSD, heroin or cannabis, so were unable to emulate the beats and swingers of the day. Instead, they looked around for readily available substitutes, which included allowing oranges pierced with toothpicks to rot, in the naïve hope that some kind of fermentation process would occur so that sniffing them would magically produce a mind-altering experience. More dangerously, boys and girls had been found lying on their backs at the end of the runways at regional airports and inhaling the fumes of jet engines in the belief that this would offer the transcendental experience they pined.

Whenever we could get the time the three of us would drive out of Washington to a spot called Daniel's Mountain, close to the small railway town of Clifton Forge, Virginia, in the Allegheny Highlands. The drive, in the days before the interstate highway system had reached western Virginia, could take up to five hours. Girls, who outnumbered males in Washington's political corridors, were sometimes invited, and we would pitch tents on the highest point, a magnificent view stretching before us over the mountains while we drank Famous Grouse whisky, now a leading brand but in those days almost unknown. Donald liked to boast that only three people in the world drank the Grouse – the Queen of England, Adam Clayton Powell and himself – and now Wyche and I were added to this exclusive list. Slightly undermining his claim, however, was the fact that we could buy it at any good liquor store in DC.

Daniel's Mountain was one of a number of fifty-acre lots of poor grade land in the Alleghenies given to their freed labour by the slave-owners in the aftermath of the Civil War, and had been in Donald's family ever since. His father, a medical practitioner who owned and ran a hospital in Florida, had sent him to survey the land, unvisited for many years, with a view to selling it. Donald was captivated by its beauty and isolation, and over the next few years would buy one of the neighbouring tracts, building two timber houses, one for himself and one for the family that looked after his Tennessee Walking horses – bred for riding long distances at a smooth rather than undulating gait - and various other animals, including goats, pot-bellied pigs, a succession of Weimaraner dogs, cats and peacocks.

The place had acquired its name when, on one of Donald's early visits, he and Wyche uncovered in the undergrowth a tiny graveyard of slaves who had once worked the land. Surrounded by an ornamental iron railing, one of the few still-legible headstones commemorated a 'Daniel', hence, Daniel's Mountain. Over subsequent years, Donald's father and mother, my colleague Stephen Barber, and Donald himself, were all to be buried at this spot.

Anderson's father, Russell, merits a footnote to this story as a man who apparently died twice. In September 1939 he was a promising young scientist in the field of genetics, and assistant to a Nobel prizewinner who had been invited to an international conference in

Edinburgh but, unable to attend, sent Russell in his stead. The outbreak of World War II ended the conference prematurely, with the twenty-eight American participants hastening to Liverpool to catch the next available ship back across the Atlantic, the SS Athenia. The travellers were advised by the shipping company that because so many people needed places, cabins would have to be shared. One of the three-hundred American passengers objected to taking accommodation with a coloured man, so Russell was left on the quayside. The ship was sunk on 3rd September, the opening day of the war, by a German submarine, its torpedoes the first shots to be fired in the Battle of the Atlantic. Donald would recall, 'My father owed his life to some unknown person's racism.'

What made Anderson such a constantly fascinating friend was the breadth of his interests, which often verged on obsessions. He loved the opera but Shakespeare took first place with him, his everyday speech often culling phrases verbatim from the Bard: 'Allons, ensemble,' he would echo Henry V whenever we left the house, 'While we tarry here our royal battle's lost or won'. But tarrying was in his nature: he was an excellent cook, but the food for a dinner party with an 8 o'clock start seldom reached the table before 11.

Once a year at Daniel's Mountain he would hold an open day for family and friends, which he called a Usufruct (after the concept in Mosaic law that we hold property only as caretakers for future generations). The centrepiece of the Usufruct was the production of a Shakespeare play, invariably with Donald, an actor manqué, in one of the lead roles, followed by a magnificent barbecue which took seven or eight hours to cook in what looked like the boiler and chimney from George Stephenson's locomotive, Rocket. I remember, for my fiftieth birthday, Donald presenting me with an audio tape of Macbeth. When I played it on my return to London I found that he had spoken every part in the drama from the Porter, the Witches, Banquo and King Duncan, to Lord and Lady Macbeth themselves.

So carried away did I become with Anderson's facility with Shakespearean quotations that it contributed to my making a fool of myself. Donald and I had been invited to the golden wedding celebrations of Wyche Fowler's parents in Atlanta. Unexpectedly asked to say a few words, and trying to be a little too clever, I remarked that I could not recall Shakespeare ever giving any of his characters the ancient English surname of Fowler – except that, in Act One, Scene One of Macbeth, Macbeth observes to Banquo before they meet the Witches, 'So fair and foul a day I have not seen.' This pun earned me a polite round of applause which two weeks later I realised was entirely undeserved when I saw a Broadway production of the play with Macbeth, played by Christopher Plummer, saying to Banquo, 'So foul and fair a day I have not seen.' A pity, really, that Wyche's family name was not Faraday.

On his first visit to Britain after we made each other's acquaintance, Donald joined me for a family holiday in the Scottish Highlands, north of Inverness. Two things he saw and heard were to influence him for the rest of his life. First, he was captivated by the sound of the bagpipes, and secondly, he was intrigued by some mink-coloured hounds he saw: as soon as he returned to Virginia he acquired one of these dogs, calling him Victor, the first in a series of Weimaraners, all given the same name, including one with only three legs which, nevertheless, gamely followed him when he rode out on one of his string of horses.

As to the bagpipes, Donald insisted, the day after he first heard their tones, on my driving him to Inverness where he bought a second-hand but extremely expensive set of pipes. From then on, having signed up with an émigré Scottish pipe major as tutor, he played the pipes almost daily even inside his Washington house (and once, to my horror, in my London flat). Otherwise, on his travels he practised on a chanter, a small instrument that kept the bagpipe reeds in condition and allowed him to rehearse his finger movements without creating excessive noise. On holiday in France, we walked to the edge of a village called Descartes, where we were staying, so he could practise on the full set of pipes. In no time at all, the sight of a black man in a kilt making an extraordinary wailing noise attracted an appreciable crowd, some of the locals throwing coins at Donald's feet.

At Daniel's Mountain he would play in the evening, marching up and down the terrace outside his cabin. While he preferred the traditional, intricate Scottish pipe music, the pioabaireachd, he would good-naturedly concede to his audiences' incessant demands for more familiar tunes, such as Amazing Grace and The Skye Boat Song as we waited, and waited, for our dinner.

In the years following our lodging together in 1967, the three of us met with remarkable frequency, either in London or in America. I took part in several of Wyche Fowler's election campaigns, sometimes forced to address high school children on behalf of the candidate and take part in local radio programmes during his three campaigns for the House of Representatives.

In Wyche's black majority 5th district, the churches played an important role in political campaigning. Once, my friend Eric Jacobs of the *Sunday Times* and I accompanied him to the huge Beak Street Baptist church in Atlanta, where we found seats right at the back of the congregation while the candidate joined the pastor, Rev. Borders, on his podium. As a former boy preacher, Wyche was quite at home in the pulpit, but the charismatic Borders was determined not to be outshone by a mere politician, tugging at his guest's microphone lead when he suspected he was getting too much applause from his flock. Seeing us as a ready diversion, Rev Borders greeted Eric and me: 'Hey, you little white boys, stand up and be recognised by church.' We got to our feet and stood self-consciously, gazing at the predominately female, hat-wearing, middle-aged Afro-American congregation. 'I want you to look around you,' said the preacher, 'You may be looking at the woman you're gonna marry!'

In Wyche's 5th District was unassailable Democratic territory, so it was the primary rather than the general election that provided political excitement. Time after time, having won the congressional seat of Andrew Young, America's first black United Nation's ambassador, Fowler's opponents in the primaries determined to unseat him were prominent figures from the circle around Martin Luther King, including John Lewis and the Rev. Ralph Abernathy (Young was also a clergyman, once telling me he chose the calling because, in his impoverished childhood, 'preachers were fat men who ate chicken and drove big cars'.) I think it was in Wyche's third term that a reporter from the Atlanta Constitution told him that an aspiring young black politician called Clint De Veau was intent on running against. 'I'm not sure,' said Wyche, 'that Atlanta is yet ready to elect a Frenchman to Congress.' As the election duly proved.

My services as a voluntary campaign worker did not always please him. At a reception in Atlanta one evening, I felt him clutching urgently at my sleeve a couple of times before I could drag myself away from the fathomless depths of the big brown eyes of the singer Dionne Warwick: Wyche rushed me to the other side of the room to meet a small, predominately grey man with slightly bulging blue eyes who was talking about his experience in the US Navy's nuclear submarine fleet. When I was introduced to him he uttered the words that were about to become a nationwide catch-phrase in the bid for high political office he was about to launch, 'Hi, my name's Jimmy Carter and I'm running for President.'

At another election, I was stationed one morning at the entrance to a large suburban supermarket, while Wyche glad-handed the shoppers. It was a tricky time for the political class with the Abscam scandal, an FBI sting operation in which agents disguised themselves as Arabs, had resulted in one senator and five congressmen being found guilty of accepting bribes in exchange for political favours. When Fowler walked over to tell me that we could now suspend our efforts and adjourn to the bar, he was flabbergasted to find me placing one of his leaflets in the trolley of each arriving customer, with the words, 'Add a congressman to your shopping list – everyone's buying them these days.' In fact, Wyche was a squeaky-clean politician, demonstrating his rectitude the moment he was elected to congress for his first term by ordering the removal from his offices of a Coca Cola machine dispensing free refreshment to his staff: Atlanta, of course, is the headquarters of Coca Cola. Nor could he resist a joke: after President Clinton's much ridiculed admission that he had smoked marijuana but never inhaled, Wyche – in common with nearly every other legislator – was questioned by reporters on whether he had ever indulged in the weed, responding, 'Only while committing adultery'.

In the autumn of 2003, we both went to Daniel's Mountain to see Donald, who by then was desperately ill, spending several days with him almost forty years after the three of us had first met. He was unable to walk more than a few paces, but we took him outside to enjoy the sunshine and drink beer as we talked over old, happy times. In January 2004 he died in hospital, aged 71, and we listened misty-eyed as his pipe major played laments over our old friend's coffin as it was lowered into the slaves' graveyard on Daniel's Mountain.

I made another close American friendship in the early 1970s but decided to keep it separate from Donald and Wyche, particularly Wyche, making no attempt, as one is normally inclined to do with new friends, to introduce them to each other. Although I gossiped freely to all three about each other, I made sure that they never met under my auspices. The reason, unashamedly, was the shadow of McCarthyism that still overhung American politics, a shadow which, twenty or thirty years on, still had the power to damage political careers.

Long before I met him in the early Seventies, I had known quite a lot about Alger Hiss, first learning of the cause célèbre that resulted in his imprisonment from a book defending him by Lord Jowett, Attorney General and lord chancellor in Labour's 1945 government. I became a close friend of the man who had been an advisor to President Roosevelt at the Yalta conference and executive secretary of the founding conference of the United Nations before his career crashed when he was denounced as having been a communist in the late 1930s and a spy for the Soviet Union – both charges he always vehemently denied.

His accuser was the unstable Whittaker Chambers, who denounced Hiss at a 1948 hearing of the House Committee on Un-American Activities (HUAC). Hiss initially denied knowing Chambers but it emerged that he had sold him an old car and lent him money in the Thirties, having met him as a hard-up freelance journalist under the name of Crossley. My own belief is that the homosexual Chambers, an admitted communist, had developed an unrequited obsession for the handsome and successful Hiss, seizing on the publicity surrounding Senator Joe McCarthy's campaign against communist infiltration in the 1940s and 50s, to destroy the man who had unwittingly helped him. The statute of limitations made it impossible for McCarthy and

Richard Nixon, then a young congressman on the HUAC committee, to bring the more dramatic charge of treason against Hiss, but the case raised the profile of the ambitious Nixon, leading him to the Senate in 1952 and eventually, in 1968, the Presidency.

Hiss unsuccessfully sued Chambers for libel and was indicted by a grand jury for perjury. 'I was tried for treason under the rubric of perjury,' he said to me on one of the occasions we discussed his precipitous fall from success and high office to a four year-sentence in Lewisburg Federal Penitentiary: on his release prisoners cheered and applauded him for the educational and welfare work he had undertaken on their behalf.

Searches through the Soviet archives and the records of the American communist party have produced thin pickings for those trying to prove that Hiss was indeed a Soviet spy. I do not regard myself as an expert on his case, but I am certain that had he been tried in a British court he would never have been found guilty, if only because of disgraceful abuses in the trial process. The first hearing ended in a mistrial when the jury failed to agree. The second could be called a scandal because of the misbehaviour of the prosecution, in cahoots with the FBI, infiltrating a spy into Hiss's defence team to report back on their deliberations and courtroom strategy. They also arranged for a shaky witness to view Hiss through a spy-hole in the courtroom during a pre-trial hearing so that she could confidently 'recognise' him when she later went into the witness box.

Alger Hiss ruefully noted the effects of celebrity in American life when he left prison in 1954, telling me how, before his right to practice law had been restored by the New York bar, he had been anxious that his notoriety might have unpleasant side effects. But, embarking on a lecture tour soon after his release, he booked into a hotel in the Mid

West, immediately receiving a call from the manager. Apprehensive that he would probably be asked to leave, he was surprised instead to be told, 'Mr Hiss, we're absolutely honoured and delighted to have such a famous person as yourself to stay in our hotel and in our city!'

I invariably visited Alger Hiss when I was in New York and he reciprocated when in London, extending his friendship to my wife and three stepdaughters, his warm personality enchanting all of us. I once took him to a *Spectator* lunch, where, according to the magazine's historian, Simon Courtauld, this 'caused some consternation', though I cannot think why, since he was – unlike some others – a perfectly polite, well-behaved and interesting guest. To me, he was a good friend, a wise advisor, a fascinating embodiment of an unhappy period of history - and an American Dreyfus.

It may be that my love affair with America contributed to the breakdown of my first marriage, not to my credit, and I have been married and divorced several times since – an aspect of my life and that of others concerned which I do not have the right to explore in these pages. What I can say however, is that the most meaningless advice I have received on the subject came from someone who profited from the process – a divorce lawyer, 'Peter,' he said, 'the way of the transgressor is hard.'

l to r: Peter Paterson, John Moynihan, Philip Hope-Wallace, Nicholas Garland

Chapter 19

As Fleet Street moved from the Sixties into the even harder-drinking Seventies I swiftly discovered its best-known hostelry, El Vino, with its pseudo-club atmosphere of petty rules and restrictions, the absence from its shelves of beer and its propensity for inducing Ray Milland-style lost lunchtimes.

It is difficult with today's more puritanical attitude towards big lunches and drinking during working time to appreciate just how extraordinarily bibulous Fleet Street was in those days. The alcoholic intake of the average journalist was of quite epic proportions, as it had been, by all accounts, among previous generations in the trade. One of the reasons was probably because wages, even in the higher reaches, were comparatively low, while expenses, which were easy to massage, were high. The largest element of most expenses claims was for 'entertainment', an ill-defined category that required little elaboration of the identity of the individual or individuals ostensibly receiving a newspaper's hospitality.

The amazing thing was how inebriated reporters still managed – sometimes with a little help from their friends – to perform their duties. Teetotal reporters were virtually unknown: I once knew one, and his life was made miserable by his colleagues' untrue accusations that, consuming nothing but designer water, he listened to their stories as they rehearsed them to admiring friends while drunk, retiring to the loo to write a plagiarised version.

El Vino had another role in addition to dispenser of cheap champagne to quench the thirst of journalists and lawyers. It was also a central player in Fleet Street's highly efficient labour market, at a time when most vacancies for writing journalists were advertised by word-of-mouth and filled on personal knowledge of qualified individuals acquired in the watering holes up and down what was in effect a village street.

As well as a labour exchange, El Vino, in the days before credit cards, was also a cash-on-the-nail business, which entailed a good deal of temporary lending and borrowing among its customers. Such transactions were underwritten less by a superior sense of honour among journalists than the fact that most of the money they spent there came from their expenses, their consciences eased by the justification that they often found more stories, and columnists more ideas for their columns, from talking to each other than to outsiders.

Around 1968, I got to know the great Australian entertainer Barry Humphries through my friendship with *Daily Telegraph* cartoonist Nicholas Garland. Nick illustrated Humphries' comic strip, Barry McKenzie, the adventures of an Ozzie ocker in London, then running in *Private Eye*. Over a drink, Barry asked me one day whether I might lend him a rather larger sum than would normally be required to buy a round of drinks: I can't remember precisely how much it was - £100 or £150, perhaps – but in those days it represented quite a strain on my resources.

I expected the loan to be repaid in a few days anyway, but Barry suddenly disappeared from the scene, and by the time I heard that he'd returned to Australia, in my mind I had written the money off. It must have been almost a year later, however, when I was drinking in the Red Lion, a Saturday night haunt of Sunday paper reporters, that he dashed into the pub and thrust the money into my hand, explaining that he had suddenly been obliged to return to Australia without time to settle his affairs before he caught the plane. Having repaid me, he didn't stay for a drink, because he had his wife and children waiting in the car outside – I walked him to the car to say hello - and as I subsequently gathered, while he was away in Australia he had signed the pledge to foreswear the booze.

An actor and budding comedian in those days, Barry Humphries has since, of course, justifiably become an international star, the creator of that exemplar of Australian womanhood, Dame Edna Everage. We've never met since that night at the Red Lion, but I have sometimes wondered uneasily whether he might have borrowed not just my money but my name, slightly misspelled as often happens, for another of his great stage characters, the disgusting, belching, dribbling, food-stained and wildly funny Australian diplomatic attaché, Sir Les Patterson. There were moments of over-indulgence that I can recall from those days, but few, I swear, that would really have qualified me for such a high honour.

I talked earlier about being 'introduced' to El Vino because there was a convention that one didn't go there before reaching a certain status in what people knew as the Street of Shame, the Street of Adventure, or Grub Street - take your pick. Entitlement was something you determined for yourself but for a first visit it was best to be accompanied by someone of higher rank and reputation already familiar with the place, otherwise you would be regarded with suspicion by the establishment's stern, frock-coated patron, Mr Frank Bower, who might simply make you burn with embarrassment and slink away by declining to serve you.

In the end I went in with Ronald Payne, an old chum who divided his time between the Crillon bar in Paris, where he represented the *Daily Telegraph*, and in London, El Vino. We circumnavigated 'the Beef Trust', a group of very large men who customarily gathered most lunchtimes just inside the front door. The Trust included Derek Marks, a one-time foreign correspondent and editor of the *Daily Express*, Roly Herman, a defector from the *Daily Mail* to the *Daily*

Mirror, Peter Vane, foreign editor of the *Sunday Express*, political writer Vic Patrick, Tom Tullett of the *Mirror* and his fellow crime correspondent from the *Daily Express*, Percy Hoskins, the latter making up in girth what he lacked in height. Not one of them would have weighed less than sixteen stone.

Moving further along the bar I chose to drink whisky – I've always thought wine was better taken with food than as a bar-room or pub beverage – and quickly discovered that El Vino's own brand of scotch, imported from Scotland and diluted in-house to the then statutory 40 per cent proof, seemed unusually powerful as I staggered out with Ronnie after a couple of hours.

Only on my next visit, this time alone, did I discover that I had been watering my whisky from unlabelled, clear glass bottles sitting on the counter with metal spouts protruding from their necks and containing not, as I'd believed, H20, but gin and vodka. (There was also a scurrilous but, I'm assured, authentic story circulated that the tap on the large whisky vat behind the bar, which held two hogsheads, was accidentally left running at closing time one night: opening up in the morning, the floor was swimming in escaped whisky. The management raised the carpet and, undeterred by the heavy foot traffic from generations of bar staff over the years since the floor covering had last been renewed, squeezed out the moisture and returned it to the barrel. All who heard this tale, true or false, would henceforth specifically order branded whisky rather than the in-house variety).

Bower, and after his retirement his successors, the brothers Christopher and David Mitchell (the latter affording much ammunition to *Private Eye* as 'the barman' who was also a Conservative MP) had many grounds on which to exercise high-handedness, the most punitive inevitably visited on women. It was laid down that women could not be admitted unless accompanied by a man, and even in male company they were sent away if wearing trousers. Nor were they permitted to stand at the bar. The rules apparently dated back to the foundation of El Vino, when according to tradition, they were introduced to deter prostitutes from pestering the customers: their retention into the 1960s was therefore not particularly flattering to either sex. (The Fleet Street premises were opened after the original EV, which stood in the appropriate location of Gutter Lane in the City until burned down.)

Men, on the other hand, only had to be 'properly' dressed, preferably in a suit and tie, though barristers, who made up a substantial part of the clientele, were allowed their court dress wing collars and bands (I don't recall ever seeing one carousing in his wig). Ties were available from behind the bar if the individual otherwise passed muster on the dress code.

There were occasions when these house rules were used with cruelty. One widely disseminated story concerned a distinguished journalist, formerly a regular patron of El Vino, who underwent a sex change, experimentally returning for the first time after a prolonged absence, in women's attire. Waitresses at El Vino were mainly recruited from attractive, gap year colonial girls not always familiar with the nuances of English etiquette: as someone ungallantly remarked, they were probably revisiting haunts from which their ancestors had long ago been transported.

On this occasion, the waitress approached the lady, who upon ordering a bottle of Puligny-Montrachet, was told that she could not be served. 'What nonsense,' she replied, 'that old rule about not serving single ladies is years out of date. Besides, I'm waiting for a male friend. 'No,' said the waitress brutally, having, I suspect, been put up to it, 'I can't serve you because you're not wearing a tie, sir.'

Opposite the Beef Trust, on the other side of the aisle, the *Daily Mail* crowd, led by Fergus Cashin, one of the most gregarious and rambunctious men ever to work in Fleet Street, and Nigel Dempster (the leading gossip writer of almost any generation since John Aubrey and Samuel Pepys marked out the territory) drank their expenses-paid champagne along with their firmly seated female companions. Standing along the bar were the regulars, most of whom I already knew, among them veteran reporters Peter Senn, Brian McConnell and Paul Callon, all of the *Daily Mirror*, and Michael Watts, who wrote a column for the *Sunday Express*, offering his readers £1 - 'a crisp oncer' - for each contribution they made towards lightening his weekly workload by sending in their own humorous observations.

McConnell was to achieve fame extending far beyond his own lunchtime in 1974 by going to the rescue of Princess Anne and her new husband, Captain Mark Phillips, when they were attacked in their car outside Buckingham Palace by an armed man attempting to kidnap them. The royal couple's chauffeur and the police bodyguard had already been shot when McConnell, leaping from a passing taxi, confronted the gunman and took a bullet in the chest, to be awarded the Queen's Medal for Gallantry.

Dapper, bow-tied Paul Callon, a gossip writer who turned to broadcasting, and later became theatre critic and all-purpose feature writer for the *Daily Express*, was long dogged by what he insisted was a joking claim to have been educated at Eton, until some spoil-sport consulted the records to prove that he hadn't. Nearby you'd often find Stephen Constant, scion of an exiled Bulgarian aristocratic family whose real name, Danieff, he was obliged to suppress while working for the *Daily Express* because Lord Beaverbrook disliked his reporters to have foreign names. Rather than reverting to his proper name when he moved to the *Telegraph* as a Kremlinologist, he stuck to his slave name.

It was, however, the back room of El Vino that gradually became for me a kind of university, with its frequently brilliant – or so it seemed to me - conversations on books, plays, music, politics and personalities, its disputations between clever men conducted with wit and humour, and occasional bad behaviour, among a constantly revolving company of journalists, lawyers and writers.

On one occasion in 1969 there was even a cultural outing from the back room. Someone reported a new artistic sensation that was on no account to be missed, and four or five of us piled into a taxi bound for a pub in Battersea. When we arrived, two soberly dressed men like City gents slumming it in south London were dancing on a table to a gramophone record of the old Flanagan & Allen music hall favourite, Underneath the Arches. We were witnessing an early performance of what Gilbert and George called their 'living sculptures'. Forty years on, having won the Turner Prize in 1986, they are still at the top of the modern art movement, though their significance, I admit, eluded me at the time, and still does: I just thought that theirs was a very funny act, the novelty of which faded as the dance continued and the same record was played over and over again.

El Vino's back room was a kind of shabby Edwardian saloon, with heavily-figured, nicotine-stained, wallpaper, the walls decorated with framed advertisements featuring the Widow Ponsardin, the 19th century châtelaine of the Veuve Clicquot champagne house. In the Seventies, the facilities were supplemented by the opening of a basement restaurant, reached via a steep set of stairs with male and female lavatories on each side of a landing half way down: inevitably the restaurant became known as the Entre-deux Loos.

Before his death in 1979, the presiding genius of the back room was Philip Hope-Wallace, the *Guardian's* opera, ballet, and sometime theatre critic, who entertained no sentimentality towards his employer: 'Never work for a liberal newspaper,' he used to say, 'they're the only ones who'll sack you just before Christmas.' His table attracted most of the leading figures of what Alan Watkins, one of its best chroniclers, modestly called the 'silver' period of Fleet Street's history.

A tall and burly figure, his massive head evoking the bust of a Roman consul, Hope-Wallace displayed a not exactly Bohemian but nevertheless scruffy style of dress, usually buying his clothes during the sales at Gamages, the old department store in High Holborn, and boasting of how little he had paid. His shirts were usually too tight for his thick neck and distended stomach, his tie askew and collar unbuttoned, vaguely reminiscent of a man in late middle-age re-enacting one of Thomas Henry's illustrations for Richmal Crompton's Just William stories.

Philip was also a notable hypochondriac, particularly after the death of his friend, Michael Wolff, personal assistant to prime minister Edward Heath, who had entered a health spa and died while riding a bicycle in the grounds. Hope-Wallace was devoted to Dr Collis-Browne's Chlorodyne, a remedy that contained opium, at least until modern regulation caught up with it. It was claimed to ease a wide range of disorders, among them influenza, catarrh, asthma, bronchitis, diarrhoea and colic, from some or all of which Philip complained at one time or another, always ready to recommend his vast knowledge of arcane patent medicines to others. Once I'd got to know him well enough for such an impertinence, I would tease him as 'Dr Collis No-Hope Wallace'.

Such a cynosure of El Vino's back room did Hope-Wallace become that several tables often had to be pulled together to accommodate a dozen or more people in an ever-expanding circle around him, the tables laden with bottles of EV's cheaper brand 'cooking' champagne, Baron d'Orville. Philip was inclined to be more fearless in conversation than in print, describing the singing of Maria Callas as 'squawking like a parrot' or 'a tomcat on heat'. He loved theatrical anecdotes, delightedly recalling the occasion (there are several versions of this story) when the actress Gladys Cooper's sister appeared in a small part in one of her plays. In Philip's version, the sibling ran off the stage in tears after delivering her one spoken line, complaining that she had been hissed by the audience. 'No,' she was assured, 'What you heard was the chorus boys telling each other, "That's Gladys Cooper's sister Doris"'. Philip's stories, during cold winter days, were likely to be constantly interrupted by his stentorian roar of 'DOOR!!' as a new arrival let the draught in by using EV's back entrance.

When he died, a brass plaque was erected just where, in life, Philip's chair had been placed: appropriately for a man who suffered for so long from the *Guardian's* renowned plethora of misprints, or 'literals', his Christian name was misspelled on this memorial. It was a piquant error for those of us who had listened to his incessant groans over his paper's lunatic distortions of his copy, which often, because of time constraints, had to be telephoned to the office late at night: among many examples was the review he'd written of Mussorgsky's somehow forgotten opera, 'Doris' Godunov. There was also his account of the inauguration of the UNESCO building in Paris, the opening paragraph reporting, 'Thousands of white gloves were released to mark the occasion'.

Among the company around Hope-Wallace was Henry Fairlie, a brilliant political columnist for the *Spectator* who devised the concept that Britain was ruled by a matrix of cross-party politicians, the church, the law, the ancient universities, members of the aristocracy, and captains of industry, that he termed 'the Establishment'. Fairlie's rackety personal life at one stage led him to flee to America to avoid a libel action, where he died after spending his last days reputedly living as a squatter in the office of the editor of New Republic magazine. I remember, one late night after a riotous dinner in Washington, joining Henry on his knees in the street as we both searched, vainly, for a lost contact lens belonging to one of our companions, Harry Miller, a man I met when we joined the *Telegraph* on the same day.

Other members of the Hope-Wallace circle included Milton Shulman, drama critic of the *Evening Standard*, art collector, military historian, avid student of the turf, and a man of great charm and learning, and Maurice Richardson, a writer who could turn his pen to any subject and took a particular interest in herpetology, on one occasion causing alarm by bringing a small but venomous snake into the bar. When Randolph Churchill, the wayward son of Winston, was reported in several gossip columns to have been expelled by Frank Bower for aggressive behaviour in El Vino, the actual offender was Richardson (it could easily have been the other way round for the pair, both topers, were physically alike: when the confusion was sorted out, Richardson was allowed back).

For a considerable time, Churchill, junior, wrote a weekly political column in the *News of the World*. He was close friends with the editor, Stafford Somerville, who happened to be away one week – possibly attending to his part-time job as editor of a magazine called Our Dogs – when the editor's deputy queried a paragraph in Churchill's column as being 'somewhat obscure'. Pulling himself up to his full height, Randolph responded just as I imagine Dr Johnson would have done: 'Sir – to the obscure, all things are obscure'.

Another evictee from El Vino was the great cartoonist, Vicky, whose crime was to seize Frank Bower's bowler hat and prance around the bar wearing it, a comical sight as Vicky was so tiny. He promptly relocated at lunchtimes to the Clachan, a Younger's Scotch House situated only half a dozen paces outside the back door of El Vino.

John Raymond, a scintillating literary journalist on the *Sunday Times* and close friend of Hope-Wallace, could often be found vehemently defending his corner in an argument he would invariably have started: sometimes he would arrive with cuts, scratches and bruises to his face, which he blamed on his mother, with whom he lived, a tale that caused Philip to raise his eyebrows and shrug, as if to say, 'Who believes that?' Like many another El Vino habitué, Raymond, occasionally called 'J.R.' after the character in the then-popular American TV show, Dynasty, was eventually laid low by alcoholism, dying in his early fifties.

Other frequenters of the back room were Cider with Rosie author Laurie Lee, giving the impression of a farmer just up from the country for a day in London, which wasn't at all the case; reporter turned novelist, Patrick Skeine Caitling, cutting loose like a cowboy at the end of a particularly gruelling cattle round-up after spending a long writing stint incommunicado in the Irish countryside; Arthur Hopcraft, who mixed sports writing with brilliant TV adaptations, including John Le Carré's Tinker, Tailor, Soldier, Spy, and Peregrine Worsthorne, the second man after Kenneth Tynan to use the word 'fuck' on TV, which didn't prevent his becoming a knight after much mocking and dangerously counter-productive agitation on his behalf by Auberon Waugh. Perry, a master of the paradox, liked to stir up debates in El Vino as a way of rehearsing the themes of his forthcoming columns, trying out the aperçus rolling around his brain, often relating to the concept of noblesse oblige he believed the Tories should honour in their dealings with the lower orders.

Another of our companions was Stephen Fay, son of the London editor of the *Manchester Guardian*, whose own writing career embraced investigative reporting, a prize-winning crime novel, cricket reporting, and the theatre. Then there was the tall and dignified Eric Hiscox, a literary agent who, amazingly, as a boy of fourteen fought as a machine gunner in the trenches in World War One, having managed to fool the recruiting officer: even in old age he had the most extraordinarily piercing blue eyes, making it easy to imagine that he must have been a formidable shot. And just occasionally, Hope-Wallace's lover, a policeman, would put in a low-key appearance, naturally in mufti, seldom joining the conversation, and never being introduced.

On Saturday mornings the entire atmosphere of El Vino changed, since it was patronised only by Sunday paper journalists and a small group of regular weekend-only visitors. Among them was Willi Frischauer, a delightful character who, despite living in England since 1935, never lost his rich Viennese accent and reminded me of the Hollywood character actor, S.Z. 'Cuddles' Sakall, who appeared in many musicals and played Carl, head waiter of the bar, Rick's Place, in Casablanca. Willi was to commit suicide, having previously considered achieving this objective by leaping over Beachy Head but changing his mind when the taxi driver taking him from Eastbourne station stopped too far from the precipice: 'I didn't vant to vork that far,' he explained.

Willi's friend, Peter Lawson, director of a Regent Street furnishings shop, would bring quails eggs to El Vino for these Saturday morning sessions, distributing them to everyone in the bar. John Junor, editor of the *Sunday Express* would sometimes drop in – hence Lord Beaverbrook's reported rebuke to him concerning the unlikelihood of his finding stories in this 'public house'.

One resourceful TV producer, Dennis Pitts, used El Vino as a recruiting ground for a daily Granada current affairs programme called Three After Six, collecting journalists whose expertise fitted in with whatever subjects were of interest to the show's producers on a particular day and shepherding them into a taxi - diplomatically not departing before EV's 3 p.m. closing time. He would take us to a satellite TV studio in Chelsea, where, one by one, we would be confronted by a huge TV camera standing in the middle of the room like a menacing piece of artillery. The monster was remotely controlled from two hundred miles away in Manchester, where an unseen presenter would be asking the questions while one sat in a chair addressing the gigantic Orwellian lens.

The old order at El Vino, in perfect conjunction with the spirit of the times, was changed for good by a feminist demonstration demanding equal drinking rights to men. This was accomplished by a mass invasion of the premises one lunchtime in 1969 by a large crowd of women (few of whom had ever been seen there before or would be again). But it was clear to all of us that our original Sixties idea of feminism was adapting more to the spirit of the Suffragettes, even if the objectives seemed less earth-shattering than those of their forebears.

My friend and *Sunday Telegraph* colleague, Ian Waller, a strapping figure with a broken nose, although not forewarned of their arrival (unlike the other male drinkers in the bar to whom the demonstration was an entertaining distraction) instantly took up the women's cause, loudly protesting that the locked front door created a fire risk, and trying, against the combined physical force of the Mitchell brothers, to undo the bolts.

The women, having forcefully made their point, disappeared before the police arrived, but Waller, selected by the management as a scapegoat for the fright they had received, was permanently barred from the establishment. Although he was not a particularly frequent visitor to El Vino – he did most of his drinking at Annie's Bar in the House of Commons – he felt the punishment unjust, as did I, despite my own ignoble role in the affair as a passive bystander. The least I could do, I felt, was to urge the management to accept that they had lost the battle – their rules excluding women from standing at the bar were later adjudged by the City of London magistrates to be unlawful - and to re-admit Ian.

A Twinings teashop a few yards up the road from El Vino, was nominated by Geoffrey Van Hay, the bar's ebullient manager, as neutral ground for a negotiation. It took several afternoons at the teashop for us to thrash out a settlement. Ian promised in future to observe the unwritten rules of the house, soon to be scrapped anyway, while El Vino agreed to lift the ban. I was thus able to hail the signing of what became known as the Tweaty of Twinings.

El Vino today remains Fleet Street's pre-eminent wine bar, frequented as of old by lawyers from the Royal Courts of Justice and the Old Bailey: unlike the journalists, the lawyers' places of work have not migrated elsewhere. But reporters, sub-editors and editors still return for memorial services to their own dead at Wren's St Bride's church just along the street.

In retrospect, I suppose the drunkenness and misogyny of El Vino in the 1960s and 1970s were unpardonable, certainly when seen through the puritanical prism of today's political correctness, but for a young reporter they were exciting times and this was an exciting place. I am unapologetically glad I was there.

l to r: Anthony Howard, Richard Crossman

Chapter 20

THERE are plenty of jobs that pay more, but there is no loftier perch in British journalism in terms of prestige and job satisfaction than working for either of the leading political weeklies, the Leftist *New Statesman* or the Right-leaning *Spectator*. Their market share may be derisory, but given their modest circulations and the non-absorbent paper they are printed on, it's at least uncommon to find anyone eating fish and chips off them.

Over some twenty years, on and off, I worked for both of these weeklies, which was not particularly exceptional since their contributors have always formed a shifting population of writers and cartoonists, not only in the (largely) apolitical arts and book reviews that fill the back pages but the front-end social and political sections as well.

My life up to that point had, I suppose, turned me into something of a left-winger and a regular reader of the *New Statesman* long before I joined it. I suppose I should concede that I read it for the excitement of the hard-hitting politics of the Fifties and the struggles over the decline of the empire, but in truth there was an element of snobbery, too, as I strove to convince myself and others that I was a serious person.

Later on, in the mid-Fifties, when Henry Fairlie and Bernard Levin (neither of them of the Left) were writing their entertainingly scabrous political commentaries in the *Spectator*, I never imagined that I would one day occupy the space they filled so instructively and entertainingly. I felt an almost proprietorial glow towards Levin because my friend, Tommy Ives, secretary of the East Fulham Labour Party, had employed Bernard after he declared himself a conscientious objector to National Service and was required to pursue some socially useful employment during the eighteen months he would otherwise have served in the armed forces: clerking in a Labour Party office apparently filled the bill.

While my fellow-journeymen in the Commons press gallery were making up silly rhymes about our least favourite parliamentarians, such as the Tory attorney general of the day – 'Nothing could be duller/Than Sir Reginald Manningham Buller' - Levin was showing his superior class with his soubriquet for the same gentleman, 'Sir Reginald Bullying Manner', catching a far more important element of the character than his undoubted dullness. But Fairlie and Levin were stars, while we Commons press gallery hacks were only a short step up from stenographers.

Another friend I made in the mid-Sixties was John Morgan, a regular contributor to the *New Statesman* who was becoming famous as a reporter and presenter on the BBC's current affairs programmes, Tonight and Panorama. People would stop him in the street to ask for his autograph, to which he would acquiesce with undisguised satisfaction. A proud Welshman who struggled without much success to learn the Welsh language, John shared his countrymen's love of music, writing the libretti for several operas, earning him the nickname, Dai Ponte.

As more of his time was consumed by his television work he suggested that I should take over his role writing on union matters for the *New Statesman*. The prospect excited and awed me. I was a reporter turning into a commentator: the '*Staggers*', as it was universally known, was an intellectual weekly, and I knew I was not an intellectual. I had not, for a start, been to any university, let alone Oxford or Cambridge, like the majority of its writers, who included professors, dons, authors, MPs, and journalists far better known than I.

I went to see the editor, Paul Johnson, at the office in a corner of Lincolns Inn Fields called Great Turnstile, where he promptly welcomed me as a contributor. Johnson was both eccentric, irritating and loveable, a tremendously kind man, an accomplished artist, and a marvellous journalist of dramatically shifting political views, as he would prove over the years by becoming a fervent supporter, in turn, of Margaret Thatcher and Tony Blair, and the only *Statesman* editor ever to move across to become a regular contributor to the *Spectator*.

At one stage early on in our acquaintance Paul developed a fear that he might be assassinated by Arab terrorists for his enthusiastic support for the state of Israel, his paranoia reaching such a pitch that he would claim that the walking stick he took to carrying around for a while actually hid a sword: he insisted he was quite prepared to use it to defend himself.

Johnson was also the most fecund and diverse journalist I ever encountered, pouring out articles on art, literature and philosophy as well as politics, and over the years writing a series of best-selling (particularly in America) history books: he always struck me as a combination of G.K. Chesterton and Hilaire Belloc, though lacking their ready wit. Because of his huge output, the story was put about that one of his colleagues became lost while driving in the countryside and stumbled on a large factory-like building that proved to be the key to Paul's prodigious output. Entering in search of directions, the traveller saw before him, stretching into the far distance, an array of desks, each furnished with a typewriter pounded by an exact replica of the red-headed Johnson, all churning out articles for the weeklies and doorstep-sized books.

A Roman Catholic, Paul had absorbed the Christian message of forgiveness: I'm afraid I hadn't. I once became enraged with him over an article he wrote for the *Evening Standard* calling for the return of the death penalty, specifically for Irish terrorists. Finding that we had been invited to the same party that evening, I preceded him into every room like an MC or a butler, noisily announcing the arrival of the public hangman, Pierrepoint. He left the party early, but never mentioned my boorish behaviour again. I thought it a great tribute to him that our relationship continued in a harmonious way over a great many subsequent years, thanks in part, I'm sure, to the immense charm of his wife, Marigold (who was present that evening and must have been as fed up with my demonstration as her husband was).

An early problem I had on becoming a *Statesman* contributor was to devise a non-de-plume, since the *Telegraph* papers – I was still a full-time employee of the *Sunday Telegraph* – in those days frowned on moonlighting, which was forbidden by contract unless one could obtain the editor's permission: given the gulf in the political attitudes of the two publications I didn't even ask. Paul had rung me from the printers where he was putting to bed the second or third issue to include one of my anonymous offerings, and pressed me urgently to think up a personal by-line. To my astonishment, for I hadn't given the matter any prior thought, the name 'Arnold Strang' sprang to mind without a second's hesitation. The Strang part probably came from one of the D.C. Thomson comics containing a wild character called Strang the Terrible, who vanquished his enemies with a wire-bound cricket bat he called his 'clicky bar'. Arnold is more difficult to account for, not one of the boys I was brought up with bearing the name, though, of course, I'd heard of the famous Dr Arnold of Rugby

A pseudonym, particularly one your friends know perfectly well but the people you write about do not, produces a great deal of inner pleasure and innocent fun. In the case of Arnold Strang, union officials and employers were constantly asking around among my colleagues, wanting to know who this mysterious figure might be, particularly if I had written anything disobliging about them.

Editorial conferences at the *Statesman*, at which the likely subjects to be dealt with in that week's issue were discussed, took place on Monday mornings – conveniently my day off as a Sunday newspaperman. They were quite entertaining affairs, particularly one day in 1969, when Britain invaded the rebellious colonial island of Anguilla, whose citizens objected to a merger imposed by Britain with its neighbours, St Kitt's and Nevis, and expressed their dissatisfaction by expelling the federation's police force. What made the story so deliciously funny was that the invading force of the colonial power consisted of London's finest, a detachment of the Metropolitan Police. The *Statesman's* regular contributor on Commonwealth matters, the self-important John Hatch, elevated to the House of Lords by Harold Wilson, was quite unable to see the funny side of London bobbies paddling on the beach and enjoying the tropical sunshine. Alan Watkins, political columnist, and I, burst into laughter as we heard his pompous defence of Prime Minister and the Foreign Secretary, and were rebuked by Johnson for refusing to take our lordly contributor seriously.

It was the fashion of the weeklies at the time to carry their leading article on the front page, and it fell to me, first occasionally and subsequently when I joined the staff as assistant editor, more frequently, to write the eight hundred words or so setting out the editorial view on the chosen topic of the week. On the *Statesman* we were automatically anti-colonialist, anti-hanging and anti-censorship, and took a faintly disapproving attitude towards the financial industry. Thus, when I wrote a leader regretting the new opportunities for fecklessness arising from the launch of the first widely distributed credit card, called Access, the argument was perfectly summed up by the headline – ACCESS MEANS EXCESS.

There was a general acknowledgement that we were a little shaky on financial matters, so I was advised to check the article with Harold Lever, a member of the magazine's board and a Labour MP of great wealth (when we visited him at his capacious flat in Eaton Place on one occasion, Watkins whispered to me 'We're guests at the Grand Babylon Hotel'). Lever listened patiently as I read out my little essay to him over the phone, grunted disapprovingly from time to time, finally sighing wearily, 'It's OK – if you really must'.

My opposition to the death penalty was hardly reinforced by finding myself assigned to writing a leader urging a reprieve for a man variously calling himself Michael de Freitas, Abdul Malik, or latterly, Michael X – not to be confused with the American black activist, Malcolm X. In London in the 1950s de Freitas had been a pimp, drug-pusher and strong-arm man for the notorious property racketeer, Peter Rachman. After proclaiming his conversion to Islam in the early 1960s he added Black Power to the mix, transforming himself into a somewhat dubious activist for immigrants' rights and becoming the first person to be prosecuted under the new Race Relations Act for publicly advocating the killing of black women consorting with white men.

Later, having returned to his native country, Trinidad, he was sentenced to death for his involvement in the murder of Joseph Skerritt, a suspect in the murder of Gale Ann Benson, daughter of a Conservative MP and a former lover of de Freitas: his sentence was appealed to the Privy Council in London. Despite urging the overturn of de Freitas's death penalty, I have to acknowledge that I felt not the slightest twinge of regret when the sentence was confirmed and he was hanged in 1975, illustrating, I suppose, that principles – certainly when expressed by unaccountable leader writers - are worth nothing until they are tested.

In spite of the generally pedestrian tone of the *New Statesman* in the late Sixties – not a good time for the weeklies because of sharp increases in costs and the rise of Sunday paper magazine supplements - it was an immensely sociable place in which to work. Like the rest of Fleet Street at the time, the *Statesman*, along with the *Spectator* (the *Speccy*), was fuelled, inspired and propelled by alcohol. Working for the *NS*, there were regular lunchtime sessions in the Bunghole, a drinking establishment around the corner from the office, in addition to our regular longer walk down to El Vino in Fleet Street. At least two members of the magazine's staff were full-blown, certifiable alcoholics, one attempting to disguise his all-day drinking by filling my wastepaper basket – I had an office a floor below his - with empty half-bottles of gin once everyone else had left for the day, a practice to which I was alerted by the office cleaner, anxious for my welfare.

One party, given by Neil Ascherson, then working for the *Observer*, and his first wife, Corinna Adam, who was on the staff of the *Statesman*, gave a new phrase, 'talking about Uganda', to the language, as a neologism for sexual intercourse, thanks to an account of the party that appeared subsequently in *Private Eye*, which from then on employed the phrase incessantly. Corinna, as a gracious hostess, had become concerned at the number of people congregating on the ground floor of her house and was anxious to shoo some of us up to the first floor where only a few were gathered. She urged us all, perhaps the one group of people in London who might be expected to find such a prospect enticing, 'Please go upstairs - there's an interesting man with one leg talking about Uganda.'

Unfortunately, few took up the opportunity and the party – as all good ones do - continued according to its own unregulated dynamic. Much later in the evening, however, our hostess on entering her own bedroom became incensed to find one of her female friends romping naked with the Ugandan, his artificial leg propped against the end of the bed. Those were wild times, but few would have expected so staid a publication as the *Statesman* to produce such a contemporary 'happening'.

Two people I liked and admired on the magazine were unfortunately to die young during this period. Francis Hope, a splendid poet but a reporter with an unhappy knack for being in the right place at the wrong time – revolutions were inclined to break out the moment he'd left a country - was killed in the 1974 Turkish Airlines DC-10 crash in Paris. And Nicholas Tomalin, a brilliant reporter and highly entertaining companion, had died a year earlier while reporting the 1973 Arab-Israel War from the Golan Heights. So achingly trendy was Nick that on buying a new pair of jeans he would wear them into the water at his local municipal swimming baths to allow the chlorine to fade them to the precisely fashionable hue.

A change of editor, more so on a small magazine than on a large newspaper with hundreds of staff, is always unsettling, which is why it happens, so far as possible, only rarely. I was fond of Paul Johnson and disappointed when Richard Crossman, a prominent figure in the recently ousted Labour government, replaced him as the *Statesman's* editor in 1970. Crossman had been disapproved of by the sainted Kingsley Martin, but his links with the magazine went as far back as 1934 when he was assistant editor.

Even so, Crossman's opportunity, as so often happens in life, sprang from disappointment, for he was out of a ministerial job when Labour lost in 1970 to Edward Heath's Tories, and, after a brief reign of two years at the *Staggers* he was obliged to retire because of illness. Death intervened before his ground-breaking diaries of life as a cabinet minister were published, opening the door of cabinet secrecy to a spate of others, with Tony Benn and Barbara Castle first out of the blocks.

Crossman could be quite charming but was inclined to intellectual bullying, impatient of the views of others and difficult to stop when in full flow. He turned editorial conferences into tutorials – as one might expect of a former Oxford don. One regular participant described the editor's method as Socratic. 'That's because nobody else but Socrates can get a bloody word in,' I retorted.

He was also willing to do favours for his political friends, most often for his ally Barbara Castle, thus demonstrating a croneyism that editors, like other public figures, really ought to resist. In the long debate over Castle's white paper on industrial relations, In Place of Strife, she invited me for 'a chat' about her scheme for curbing strikes and democratising trade unions through strike ballots and regulated elections of officers. In her room in the House of Commons, she sat coquettishly, her shoeless feet drawn up beneath her, with the sun through the window behind her shining directly into my eyes. It was like getting the third degree from an attractive but ruthless agent of the KGB. When she disliked what I subsequently wrote she described me in a phone call to Crossman as 'a snake in the grass', a quaintly old-fashioned nugget he eagerly passed on to me, adding that she had also requested, vainly it transpired, that he should sack me.

One regular chore in journalism, particularly on the weeklies, is having to write profiles of well-known people you may never have met, yet you are expected to display an intimate knowledge of the subjects' lives, public and private. Crossman's know-all and mischievous attitude made one disinclined to ask for his advice, so even though he had worked closely with a famous pair of Hungarian economists and advisors to the Wilson administration, Nicholas Kaldor and Thomas Balogh, I simply went ahead boldly as though I knew them as well as he did: which one I was profiling, I do not now remember.

I had briefly met Balogh, whom I identified in my mind as a bulky individual who occasionally visited the *Statesman's* offices, where someone once had to be sent to follow him to the nearby Chancery Lane tube station to ask him for the return of review copies of books he had absent-mindedly removed from the literary department and stuffed into the capacious pockets of his overcoat. Or was that Kaldor? I had seen the latter at some function or other, a leaner, slightly hawk-like figure; but might that, after all, have been Balogh? I really couldn't distinguish between them, so I spent a couple of days writing the profile, utterly unsure whether the characteristics and qualities I was attributing to Kaldor really belonged to Balogh, or the other way around. This was certainly a nightmare assignment, on a par with my confusing first day on the *Fulham Gazette* all those years before, when I had grappled with the story of twin brothers marrying twin sisters. But thankfully the profile when it appeared attracted no complaints, so luck was with me.

During Crossman's reign, the tragedy of Northern Ireland constantly dominated the news. Unusually, he decided to send two of us to Belfast for an account of the ongoing struggle. Such joint reporting ventures as I have experienced elsewhere involves a team of up to half a dozen reporters working on a single project, known in the trade as a 'group grope'. On this occasion I was accompanied by James Fenton, an enchanting young man, aged 21 and a newcomer to the *NS*. He was at the outset of a career that would see him become a heroic traveller and foreign correspondent, a popular poet, Oxford

Professor of Poetry, and a librettist for the English National Opera, as well as achieving riches as the translator of the lyrics of a worldwide hit of the musical theatre, Les Misérables.

In those days, the deceptively languid James, not long down from Oxford, was blood brother to Christopher Hitchens, destined to become a famous controversialist on both sides of the Atlantic, but working then, I think, for *The Times Higher Educational Supplement*. One Saturday morning I encountered them both outside a supermarket not far from my home in Islington, peddling copies of the *Socialist Worker*, the journal of the small Marxist faction they both then belonged to. James was stationed at one corner of the building and Christopher the other; it was bitterly cold, and the pair gradually edged towards each other for a companionable chat. As they met, James pointed to the disappointingly un-dwindling bundles of papers under their arms, the headline story condemning a rise in the price of food, and observed to Christopher in his public school drawl, 'You know, I don't think food really costs that much!'

There was a tangible element of fear in the expedition Fenton and I made to Northern Ireland. I had been to the province a couple of times for the *Telegraph* at an earlier stage of the Troubles and once found myself cowering in a doorway protected only by a British soldier who looked no older than a schoolboy, after women started to hurl rocks at me on the so-called 'front line' in Belfast.

With my supposed nose for news, I suggested to James that a good angle for our joint article would be to track down Unionist farmers I had been told were smuggling arms into the province in light aircraft: this made James laugh uncontrollably, for how, in the couple of days we would be there, were we to find airborne gun-smugglers in the countryside around the 'dreary steeples of Tyrone and Fermanagh' of

Churchill's description?

Once in Belfast, we received a phone call directing us to a particular spot at a particular time of night to await a car. When it arrived we were bundled in and forbidden from looking out of the windows so that we would not identify the route taken or the precise destination. We stopped in one of those nondescript streets of identical Edwardian terraced houses that still occupy large tracts of Belfast: once inside, it was reminiscent of my early childhood home in Manor Park.

We sat in the dimly-lit front room with half a dozen men whose shadowed faces we avoided studying too obviously, awaiting the arrival of an unnamed IRA leader: I deduced later that the man we met was Joseph Cahill, at that time an irreconcilable pillar of republican resistance who would later help steer the Provos towards making peace with Dr Ian Paisley and his Unionists. When he arrived, a lean, stern-looking man around fifty years old, he lectured us on the brutality of the British 'occupation' and justified republican violence as self-defence, before inviting questions. Somewhat nervously, we put a few points to him, but the answers, inevitably, were not particularly informative. Then we were taken back, eyes down, to the centre of the city and dropped off near our hotel.

My first part-time stint at the *Statesman* had lasted three or four years, when later in 1970 I moved, by invitation, to the *Spectator*. There, quite unexpectedly and contrary to the easy flow of journalistic traffic between the two magazines, trouble over my link with the *Statesman* was to rear up - as I explain in my next chapter - before I was offered refuge back at Great Turnstile, before reverting to the *Speccy* once more.

My second stint at the *NS* was at the invitation of an old friend,

Anthony Howard, deputy editor to Crossman, but now in the editorial chair. He proved to be a fine editor, always accessible, full of ideas, and so attuned to the political scene that not a Westminster sparrow fell without his knowing. Today, for radio and TV political programme producers, he has become a latterday Leslie Welch, a musical hall performer known as the Memory Man, who was famous back in the 1950s and 1960s for his ability to answer any question on the subject of sport and, they say, rarely had to pay out the £1 on offer to any questioner who could stump him.

When Tony took over the editorship, the question of columnar names came up once more. Crossman had written the weekly diary under the pseudonym of 'Crux', a Latin play on his own name. Tony followed the same furrow, signing himself as 'Crucifer', the carrier of the cross. It was he who suggested that when I wrote the column I should adopt the more combative signature of 'Lucifer'.

During this second time around at the *Statesman*, I was assistant editor, rather akin to my corporalship in the army. It was a full-time job, for which I had resigned from the *Sunday Telegraph*. A close colleague was the deputy editor, Tom Baistow, a casualty of the *News Chronicle's* demise, a bustling, stocky Scot with Victorian sideburns, who wrote the weekly press column as well as acting as sub-editor and production manager. Tom was the very image of those ultra-reliable Scottish engineers who finally save the sinking ship in boys' stories. He was also a fount of general knowledge, fulfilling a similar role on the paper as Charles Seaton performed as librarian of the *Spectator*: they were very different personalities but both possessed a depth of instantly accessible information that anticipated the role nowadays played by Google.

Both the weeklies – like the rest of the newspaper industry - were in dire straits financially in the mid-Seventies. The *Statesman* was flirting with ideas of industrial democracy then popular in progressive circles. On one memorable occasion we staff members were 'consulted' on whether it was necessary to raise the cover price and what impact an increase would have on circulation. Sir Jock Campbell, Chairman of the Board (and of Booker's, the sugar company that introduced the literary Booker Prize) complained despondently that if matters continued as badly as they currently were the paper would very soon have to raise its price to two shillings: 'It's already half-a-crown,' I gently pointed out to him.

Although I now received a salary of £4,400 a year compared with the £2,000 I received at the *Spectator*, I no longer had my *Sunday Telegraph* income to buttress me. It was not long before I was thinking of extending my freelance activities to improve my financial position and also to provide myself with the time to pursue a crazy scheme I was nurturing to launch a new Fleet Street newspaper (described in Chapter 22). It also occurred to Tony Howard that one fewer mouth to feed on the *Statesman* might help the magazine to survive through the prevailing recession: so off I went. In other words, I was sacked.

Chapter 21

WHEN, in 1970, Nigel Lawson asked me to join the *Spectator* to write the weekly political commentary, it came as a great surprise. We had got to know each other when he was city editor of the *Sunday Telegraph* running the business pages and I was industrial correspondent, and I must say – politics be damned - I was flattered to be asked.

By this time, Donald McLachlan, the eccentric editor of the Sunday had retired, to be replaced by Brian Roberts, known as Scruffy. It was McLachlan who asked the blind political writer, T.E. (Peter) Utley, whether he might care to become the paper's TV critic, a suggestion no more perverse, perhaps, than Richard Ingrams reviewing a TV programme for, I think, the *Observer*, by listening through the wall of his hotel room to a set (and much else besides) switched on in the next-door room.

Roberts was a tough character, preferring to bark out orders rather than reach decisions through debate, which had been his McLachlan's style. When I put Lawson's proposal to him, that I should write for the *Spectator* while continuing as industrial correspondent for the Sunday he readily assented, as I guessed he would, there being no great ideological divide between the *Spectator* and the *Telegraph* – indeed, later on the *Telegraph* group bought the *Spectator*. I had for a long time disguised from my primary employers my part-time role with the *Statesman* by adopting my Arnold Strang by-line, but now there was no such need.

In those days the *Spectator's* offices were at 99 Gower Street, in a soot-blackened Georgian terrace in Bloomsbury that reputedly once housed a brothel. It had a long, uncarpeted stone staircase just inside the front door, creating a safety hazard for anyone getting drunk – as many did - at the magazine's famous parties. Two victims I witnessed, on different occasions, falling from top to bottom of that staircase were Bill Grundy, the TV presenter whose career was to founder on a notorious interview with the Sex Pistols in 1976, and David Leitch, a marvellous reporter who was to become a victim to alcoholism, exacerbated by a Parisian doctor who diagnosed the flu and advised him to drink whisky when he was, in fact, suffering from jaundice. I think Grundy was so baffled by the social nihilism the crude and distasteful Sex Pistols displayed that he found himself goading them into using foul language when such expressions were unacceptable on television: there was a terrible outcry in the newspapers and from then on his career went into decline. Thanks to the heavenly dispensation supposedly offered to drunks, neither he nor Leitch was injured, but out on the street, Grundy had to be hung on the iron railings by the shoulders of his overcoat while concerned friends searched for a taxi driver willing to take him away.

Grundy, a geologist by training and a thoroughly interesting and amusing man, a mainstay of Granada Television, wrote a Press column for the *Spectator*. I was with him one day when his Granada boss, Sidney Bernstein, handed us the latest Granada promotion, little plastic cards listing by year and type the best vintages of wine. Bearing in mind the TV company's northern audience, Grundy told him, 'I would have thought Guinness would be more in Granada's line, Sidney!'

Nor was David Leitch a man to be over-respectful to his bosses. On a journey to Russia with Lord Thomson, proprietor of *The Times* and *Sunday Times* - yet another Canadian attracted to Fleet Street ownership - they found themselves as guests on the Soviet equivalent of the Royal train bearing Nikita Khruschev to some distant part of the country. The dictator took a liking to Leitch's watch and Thomson ordered him to hand it over to their host: David stoutly refused.

Leitch and I had in common our unconventional starts in life, which helped cement our friendship. His origins were more spectacular than mine, for his parents had placed a small ad in the *Daily Express* when he was eight days old, offering him for sale – he always said he'd have preferred it to have been *The Times*. He was purchased by a couple who sent him to public school, from where he won a scholarship to Cambridge, taking a First in English. For years he was troubled by the thought that he was illegitimate, until he wrote a 1973 memoir, God Stand Up for Bastards (he gave me a copy inscribed, 'From one to another'), a work designed, he said, to trace his birth mother. On finally meeting her he discovered that his real parents had been legally married but the people who acquired him had not.

The *Spectator* was now owned by Harry Creighton, a businessman whose interests included selling second-hand machine tools to Third World countries: his hope, never fulfilled, was that owning the magazine might help him get elected to Parliament. Its circulation had fallen to 25,000 and was to descend still further, while its losses, £20,000 a year, left little scope for a promotion budget. To make matters worse, there was a froideur between the new owner and Lawson, the editor he had inherited, who had himself considered putting together a consortium to buy the paper. Creighton was shrewd rather than clever, once boasting to me that he learned more from the notes on the dust jackets of the books that came in for review than bothering to read the contents. And while Lawson, a dashingly handsome and slim figure who became fat after he entered politics and thin again when he retired to the House of Lords, entertained contributors with a glass of whisky in his office upstairs, the owner conducted his own levées in a dining room he had installed in the basement.

I was hired to write the column vacated by Auberon Waugh,

who had just been sacked. Bron and I were already friends, and I knew that, despite the cutting Swiftean wit of his writing, he was a charming, funny and generous individual. I remember a weekend at his house at Combe Florey in Somerset, where I enjoyed observing the rebellious Waugh spirit emerging in the next generation: his daughter, Daisy, then about five years old and nowadays a well-known and successful author, feeling thwarted at being told she must, or must not, do something or other, hurled an apple at her mother, Teresa, who was seated at the opposite end of the dining table. She missed. The next time I was there was for the wake following Bron's funeral on a doleful, squally January day in 2001.

Bron had become preoccupied with the civil war that broke out in Nigeria in 1967 and the part played by Prime Minister Harold Wilson and Foreign Secretary Michael Stewart in providing the arms to the federal government to crush the Biafrans of the Eastern Province attempting to secede. The cause was taken up with huge vigour by Waugh, with Lawson's support, and tended for a while to eclipse domestic political issues in his columns, which Lawson was now anxious to return to.

There is an aspect of British humour that produces a spate of ghoulish jokes in the wake of dreadful tragedies, particularly if they affect foreigners: during the Biafra affair, most examples of this predictable response focused on the emaciated condition of many thousands of the Ibo people who were starving. A more recent instance of the same phenomenon was the circulation of dozens of such jokes after the deaths of twenty Chinese cockle pickers on Morecambe sands in early 2004. Waugh's belief in the Biafran cause was never a joking matter.

Just as the civil war was ending in defeat for the secessionists in January 1970, the *Sunday Telegraph* secured a scoop in the form of leaked documents from the Ministry of Defence outlining incompetence and corruption in the Nigerian use of British military aid. Brian Roberts was prosecuted under the Official Secrets Act, along with Jonathan Aitken, accused of passing on leaked material. On the day the pair were found not guilty on all charges, the *Evening Standard's* front page carried a picture of the tiny Roberts, in a bowler hat, and the lofty Aitken similarly attired, leaving the Old Bailey together. Nicholas Garland, the *Daily Telegraph's* (and the *Spectator's*) cartoonist, superimposed on the photo (for private consumption) a balloon emerging from Aitken's lips telling Roberts, 'You can get off your knees now, Scruffy – we've been acquitted!'

Waugh's mood was deeply gloomy over the defeat of the Biafrans, and a month later his feelings of disaffection and frustration found an outlet that led to his swift departure from the *Spectator* for a prank that neither Lawson nor Harry Creighton could accept, for fear – justified or not - that his behaviour, if repeated, could expose them to possible claims for libel.

It had been Bron's turn to attend the out-of-town jobbing printers for the task of overseeing the production of that week's issue, a tedious chore reading proof pages for printing errors, often delayed until late into the night by the slowness of the printers or their diversion to other orders on their firm's books. On this occasion, having noted a comment in George Gale's column referring to Evelyn Waugh – Bron was always prickly in defence of his father – he mischievously altered the contents table at the front of the magazine so that the offending column was listed as having been written by 'Lunchtime O'Gale', after *Private Eye's* thirsty hack, Lunchtime O'Booze.

Waugh gained revenge when he won a wrongful dismissal case

against the *Spectator* the following year. There were raised eyebrows across Fleet Street over this success. particularly his argument that altering the table of contents was in the tradition of the weeklies. (I remember there had been a similar incident at the *New Statesman* in Paul Johnson's time when Francis Hope, like Bron at the printers, added or deleted the word 'not' in the leading article, penned by Johnson, so that the meaning of its final sentence was completely reversed, reading something like, 'For all these reasons, therefore, we think the country should not continue in membership of the Common Market'. Perhaps it was regarded as a printer's error, for no fuss that I can recall was made of it.)

Soon, George Gale emerged as the successor to Lawson, who embarked on his political career, and Bron was re-hired as a fiction reviewer. When Lawson had invited me to take over the political column I had taken the precaution for friendship's sake, as well as an awareness of Bron's zest for long-running feuds on far slighter grounds than this, to obtain his assurance that he had no objection: he had none.

It was only after I had been doing the job for some months under Gale's editorship that I began to realise I was, as it were, being stalked by someone on the paper seeking to oust me. The background was that George was using his editorship, armed with an instinctive populism honed in his ten years as a columnist on the *Daily Express*, to run a strident no-holds-barred campaign against the European Economic Community, as it then was, and the main proponent of British membership, the new Prime Minister, Edward Heath.

Early on in his editorship he had hired Maurice Cowling, my stalker, as the magazine's literary editor. Cowling was an historian and Fellow of Peterhouse College, Cambridge, an oddball high Tory theorist and unsuccessful journalist (in a year on the *Express* in the 1950s he was fired after only one of his weekly articles was ever published). As an academic, he influenced a number of Right wing commentators from the Sixties onward, all of whom had been with him at Peterhouse, including his then-patron George Gale, as well as my *Telegraph* colleagues (and friends) Colin Welch and Peregrine Worsthorne, and a brilliant but wayward younger journalist, Patrick Cosgrave, who later was to fulfil the dreams of a journalistic Napoleon by spreading himself right across a cash-strapped *Spectator*, front end and back, sometimes filling eight pages an issue.

George and I got on well during Lawson's time as editor, one morning engaging in friendly competition over which of us could write their designated weekly piece the faster (a page in the *Spectator* ran to about 1,000 words). We finished more or less simultaneously, but George had written two dozen more (and I daresay better) words than I had, and was declared the winner, after which almost the entire office adjourned for a lunchtime celebration of the event in the office pub, the Marlborough Arms.

Once he had taken possession of the editorial chair, however, and was pursuing his vendetta against Edward Heath, I had in George's eyes become a wishy-washy liberal – which I concede had some justification. He recalled that back in June and the (1970) general election, I had neither 'pressed for nor predicted' a Conservative victory. The former omission was far from unusual, for a number of my predecessors on the political column had failed to bang the drum for the Tories at elections: besides, I had no monopoly on political comment and the paper carried many voices bearing on the politics. It is true that I did not stick my neck out by making a guess as to the likely winner, which is usually a mug's game, and I saw my approach to politics as objective.

My downfall really came when I observed in my column that Enoch Powell, a sworn enemy of Heath, had no political future, and any prospects he might have had of leading the Conservative party had been 'overtaken, overwhelmed and buried by Mr Heath's election victory'. This comment, which turned out to be reasonably accurate, vastly annoyed the *Spectator's* Peterhouse Mafiosi shop steward, Mr Cowling, a man I scarcely knew. Writing elsewhere in the paper under the pseudonym, 'A Conservative' (borrowing a disguise already used by Powell in *The Times*), he asked rhetorically how Conservative the *Spectator's* political columnist (me) claimed to be. The short answer, of course, was that I had never claimed to be a Conservative and was probably more politically neutral than I had ever been.

Cowling's rant continued, 'We are sure that entry into Europe combined with a further rebuff to Mr Powell would be deeply resented and we doubt very much, speaking for ourselves, whether we would go on supporting a Heath government if Mr Heath allowed this combination of things to happen.' The use of the collective 'we' and the ambiguous 'ourselves' could imply that Cowling was speaking on behalf of the editor in his attack on me. Gale assured me this was not the case.

But George, I believe, felt unable to stand up to his old college friend, understandably preferring to sacrifice me. Either way, I realised my time was up, and I asked him whether he would at least permit me to write a reply to A Conservative in what we both agreed would be my final column the following week. George sportingly agreed, and I had a little fun calling my pseudonymous opponent, 'Mr Enoch Powell's most passionately woolly supporter'.

A note Gale appended to my valedictory column did betray an element of irritation towards Cowling's assumption that it was he, rather than the editor, who set editorial policy. The disagreement between A Conservative and the political commentator, he wrote, 'has nothing to do with [Paterson's] departure, so far as the *Spectator* is concerned'. Mind you, it didn't much feel that way until my successor turned out to be Hugh Macpherson, from *Tribune*, a paper farther to the Left than the *New Statesman* from whence I had come; Hugh's appointment, I like to think, showed Gale finally asserting his authority and causing Cowling to choke on his porridge.

I was not particularly downcast at being sacked – it had been an exciting time in my life, full of fun and laughter, and after a couple of years back on the *New Statesman* I would again return to writing for the *Spectator*. My passion for the weeklies remained unshaken.

Thirty years on, the quarrels of the early Seventies were still echoing. A pamphlet by Thomas Teodorczuk for the anti-EU Bruges Group published in 2009 [Ultimate Vindication: The *Spectator* and Europe 1966-79], trawled over the *Spectator's* long campaign against European integration, disinterring the story of my departure as proof that 'anyone of a pro-Marketeer disposition would not write for the *Spectator* on Europe'. I think he must have meant should not have been allowed to, but his assumption was that I was a Europhile, but I did not have a black and white view of the question (which was yet to be put to a referendum).

Looking back, I would not quarrel with Simon Courtauld, one of my new *Spectator* colleagues in 1970 and a friend ever since, in To Convey Intelligence, his excellent 1999 history of the *Spectator*, asserting that neither I nor my successor, Macpherson, were 'in the top rank of *Spectator* political commentators'. I would certainly not be so daft as to place myself in the Bernard Levin, Henry Fairlie or Auberon Waugh class. Even so, I thoroughly enjoyed writing the column, annoyed only that it was cut short by internal *Spectator* politics, and I continued to be friends with George Gale for long afterwards. I was also pleased, seven years after these events, that one of my *Spectator* essays – ironically, dealing with the European squabble - was chosen by Kingsley Amis for Harold's Years, his selection of writings from the weeklies in the Wilson era: incidentally, Auberon Waugh's characteristic verdict on the book, which included one of his contributions, was that he could see no reason why anyone should buy it.

As to Enoch Powell, I was to meet him a number of times over the years, interviewing him once or twice for the BBC: in life he was a small, hunched-up figure with lank hair, utterly unlike the mesmerisingly powerful image conveyed on the TV screen. I met him again in the late-1980s at a weekend house party hosted by a mutual friend, the journalist Andrew Alexander. In private Enoch could be highly entertaining, almost playful, taking with instant brilliance to the word game Boggle, and still able in his eighties faultlessly to quote yards of his favourite poet and Cambridge tutor, A. E. Housman. And, as I found, invaluable in interpreting Latin texts from memorials on the walls of old churches in rural Kent and East Sussex.

Like it or not, despite the destruction – self-destruction, if you like – of Powell's political career, his 1968 Rivers of Blood speech on Commonwealth immigration has remained in the minds of the majority of the British people, perhaps reawakened by the tidal rise in immigration encouraged by New Labour in the opening years of the 21st century. It was impossible to avoid noticing that even in the depths of the countryside his fame still attracted knots of admiring people. As word of his presence went around, small crowds would gather to cheer him. His loyal wife, Pam, kept a sheaf of small photographs of Enoch in her handbag, which she would hand out to his fans like a PR person attendant on a pop star.

Another moment from that weekend sticks in my memory, when he told me that he had written an obituary of Mrs Thatcher, fourteen years his junior, for *The Times*, with the stipulation that he be allowed to update it every ten years. Powell died in February 1998: as I write, Lady Thatcher is still with us.

After the slight unpleasantness that led to my departure from the *Spectator*, I received a gratifying number of letters from the magazine's readers: one that I retained called the affair 'a sad, sad blow to those of us who value integrity and tolerance in public life', adding that the paper could now 'be written off as the mouthpiece and the refuge of the backwoodsmen – and' (which I thought rather unnecessary) 'their women'. Michael Foot, no friend of European integration, wrote me a note to praise my final column as 'a splendid piece of journalism and a superb kick in the balls' for those responsible for my 'scurvy treatment'. Without my tail anywhere near my legs, I trotted back to the *New Statesman* as assistant editor.

This little kerfuffle was uncharacteristic of the *Speccy*, which normally quite easily accommodates a wide range of views and arose from its temporary capture by individuals, notably Cowling followed by Cosgrave, both indulged by George Gale and Harry Creighton, whose vituperative certainties for a time harmed the paper.

There was a welcome change of atmosphere and mood with the arrival of a new editor in 1975, even if Alexander Chancellor's appointment came in an undisguisedly nepotistic fashion. Creighton had sold the magazine (for £75,000, a price that did not include 99 Gower Street) to Henry Keswick, a millionaire Hong Kong taipan who, like Creighton, hoped that owning it would help ease him into a parliamentary seat: as with Creighton, it failed to do so. The only journalist Keswick apparently knew well was Chancellor, with whom he had been at Eton and Cambridge, and whose father, Sir Christopher, the head of Reuters, was a close family friend: Keswick's mother also happened to be one of Chancellor's godparents. This may not be the approved way that things would be done today – though nepotism, I suspect from the by-lines I see in the newspapers, the voices I hear on the radio, and the faces on TV, still remains a continuing feature of the trade. However it came about, Alexander, who had worked for Reuters and ITN and was charming, witty, outgoing, a good writer himself and a shrewd judge of others, proved in the event to be an inspired choice, pleasing all who wrote for the magazine and boosting its circulation.

Under Chancellor, weekly *Spectator* luncheons began to acquire a celebrity chef atmosphere with Jennifer Paterson presiding in a tiny third-floor kitchen, not afraid to display the temperament, occasionally even the language, of a Gordon Ramsay or a Marco Pierre White. Later she was to achieve fame in her four-year partnership with Clarissa Dickson Wright in the successful TV cookery series, Two Fat Ladies. My immediate impression on first meeting her was of someone from that strange in-between land occupied by the upper-class poor, obliged to live in circumstances greatly reduced from those they were born to. She would talk of looking after 'the Monsignor' – her uncle – and of her brother, the British ambassador in Mongolia: she clearly had connections, but, until her TV success, little money.

Our sharing a surname was the subject of jokes between us – sometimes she would tell people she was my aunt or, more often, that I was her uncle. Once, I drove her to Scotland for a wedding. On the road, she produced a silver jug full of a vodka-based cocktail of her own creation, serving me cupfuls as we headed north. Eventually we drew off the M1 somewhere in Warwickshire and found a woodland glade for our picnic. However, I needed an hour's sleep before I felt safe enough to continue driving.

In August 1999, Jennifer died of cancer, her last days sustained by her delightful sense of humour and her Catholic faith. I arrived ten minutes late at Brompton Oratory for her requiem mass and a few moments later was joined by Marjorie Wise, founder and chief executive of Sane, the mental health charity, both of us standing at the very back of this vast church. I'd known Marjorie from her time as a reporter on the *Sunday Times*, where she first made her name as an investigative reporter.

As neither she nor I was familiar with the ritual of the requiem mass, we took our cue as to when we should sit, stand or kneel from a cluster of fans of Jennifer's TV programmes in the rear pews. A prolonged silence fell over the Oratory at an advanced stage of the long service and Marjorie, assuming that the service was coming to an end, started to gather her briefcase and umbrella (it had been raining that morning). I was more cautious, leaning over to her to whisper, 'Marjorie, it ain't over till the fat lady sings'. And sure enough, a choir in a side gallery burst into voice at just that moment. Jennifer, I know, would have enjoyed the joke.

I found myself reunited with old chums from the *Statesman* as Chancellor engineered the revival of the *Spectator*. The latter included long-term friends like Richard West, Jeffrey Bernard and Jim Higgins, all of whom I'd worked with at the *Statesman*, as well as Simon Courtauld and George Hutchinson, both from Lawson's time at the *Spectator*. I also made a host of new acquaintances, among them the cartoonists – I both love and envy cartoonists – the brilliantly sardonic Michael Heath; the late David Austen, Richard Willson and many others. There was also my Islington neighbour Geoffrey Wheatcroft, Marcus Berkmann, who wrote on a range of topics from cricket to pub quizzes; John McEwan, the art critic, Sam White, the doyen of Paris correspondents, the Washington columnist Nicholas van Hoffman, Timothy Garton Ash, an acute observer of Russia and its European empire, and Shiva Naipaul, younger brother of the Nobel laureate Sir Vidia, and his wife Jenny, who was Chancellor's secretary.

Everyone was stunned by Shiva's death on 13 August, 1985 at the tragically early age of 40. A disappointingly downbeat obituary of Shiva appeared in *The Times*, asserting that he had 'failed to fulfil his early promise'. This seemed to me an outrageous assessment of a young writer who in his short life produced two highly-praised novels, a collection, North of South, of excoriating and, for its time, courageously straight-talking journalism from Africa, and the Whitbread Prize-winning Black and White, a blood-chilling account of the 1979 Jonestown, Guyana, mass suicide of a thousand American followers of a New Age sect. I was in Birmingham, eating breakfast in my hotel and about to leave for Edgbaston to watch England play Australia in that year's Ashes series, when I was alerted by several phone calls expressing outrage over the obituary and suggesting that something should be done.

I called Charles Douglas-Home, editor of *The Times*, whom I knew slightly, and he agreed to my submitting an alternative view to that of Shiva's anonymous obituarist. This reassessment duly appeared a few days later in the same section as its predecessor. I was tremendously touched to receive a note from Shiva's widow, Jenny, hailing me as her 'knight in shining armour', though in truth I was not acting entirely on my own initiative, for it was not only people connected with the *Spectator* who had been upset by the comments in *The Times*.

Sadly, Douglas-Home, who helped to modernise the old Thunderer between 1982 and 1985, himself died, aged 48, less than three months later.

Chapter 22

WITHOUT a full-time job after eight years mainly writing either for the *New Statesman* or the *Spectator*, and parted from the financial lifeline of the *Sunday Telegraph* that for a while made my lifestyle possible, I decided in early 1975 to adopt the life of a jobbing hack, a freelance, hopefully including occasional articles for the weeklies as well as more lucrative assignments from the mainstream press.

I had no doubt that I could easily have joined a national newspaper, for a by-line in the weeklies was an excellent way in those days, and probably still is, to advertise one's wares to Fleet Street.

However, I had acquired a bee in my bonnet, a King Charles's Head, a scheme for a great improvement, that to my mind made it quite impossible to seek full-time employment: if I was to pursue my dream, I would have to rely on occasional freelance life.

For like almost everybody in Fleet Street, apart from print unions pushing up costs with their blackmail, sabotage and strikes, I was sick at heart over the anarchy that for years had been crippling the national press. I recall an executive on the *Telegraph* assuring me that so poor were the returns on their investment that the paper's owners, the Berrys, would be better off putting their money into a savings account at the Post Office than running a newspaper. The *Daily* and the Sunday eventually joined the exodus of the national press to Docklands and elsewhere, but in the end, the family sold out to Conrad Black at what could hardly be regarded as a premium price.

Nor was I the only person to realise that the papers desperately needed to adopt the latest technical advances, notably computer typesetting and the offset press, if they were to survive, but after years of fruitless negotiations this had proved to be unattainable. The pressures the situation imposed on individuals was brought home to me when my friend Sid Holland, who was in charge of trying to modernise production at the *Daily Mirror*, collapsed and died in his mid-forties, partly because of the strain of constant, niggling disputes requiring him to conduct endless negotiations with the print unions far into the night.

Against this anarchic background, I had experienced a eureka moment in 1974 while walking along a beach in Savannah, Georgia, with my American politician friend Wyche Fowler, then a member of the Atlanta city council.

The idea that suddenly occurred to me that morning on the beach was outrageous and, on any rational basis, wildly beyond my reach, but at that moment and for some time afterwards, it appeared to me to be perfectly logical and achievable. My notion was that I could break the deadlock over new technology by creating a brand new Fleet Street newspaper. Wyche, whatever his private thoughts, loyally said nothing to dampen my enthusiasm as we trudged off for a beer and soft-shell crabs.

The concept – though it had not yet qualified as anything quite solid enough to earn that description – raced around in my brain. But before I could properly apply my mind to it there were other distractions, demanding my immediate attention.

Something that could have killed off not only my plans but my life as well came on a short journey on the London Underground on 28th February 1975. The train smashed into a walled-up tunnel at Moorgate station in the City of London, killing forty three and injuring seventy four of my fellow passengers, and the driver, in the worst crash in the history of the Underground.

I was at the front of the second compartment of the six-car train, the only person in the carriage who was standing as the train hit the wall, my back to the direction of travel. I was on my way to the London & Manchester Insurance building in Finsbury Square to interview Tony Benn (then Wedgwood-Benn, the name would be pared down in keeping with his Left-wing populist ambition to lead a Labour Party supposedly frightened by double-barrelled names). At the time he was Industry Secretary, and our encounter was intended as part of a film for an educational programme run by Clive Jenkins's union, the ASTMS, in those days regarded as a very go-ahead outfit.

It was raining hard that morning so my progress along Chapel Street, Islington, around the corner from my home, was at best jerky as I tried to walk briskly while twisting round every few seconds to look over my shoulder in the hope of finding a taxi.

No cab stopped, so I found myself instead going into Highbury & Islington station and boarding a train at 8.30 a.m. on a short, six-station branch line to Moorgate. Despite having lived in London for almost thirty years as a ticket-buying tube traveller - long enough to remember the days when one could happily nip off a train at Sloane Square station for a drink at the bar on the east-bound platform of the District and Circle line platform before resuming one's journey. I hadn't the slightest idea that the Moorgate terminus was a dead-end.

I stood in the first open space (known in the trade, I discovered at the subsequent enquiry into the crash, as a 'vestibule') at the front, my back to the door connecting with the carriage in front, reading *The Times*, my briefcase tucked behind my legs. I scarcely noticed the first leg to Essex Road, except that more passengers boarded and all, in my compartment at least, found seats. Between Old Street and Moorgate, however, I distinctly felt the train was speeding up, noticing a pinging noise as we went round a bend as though the angle of the swaying carriage had touched some wires along the tunnel, perhaps intended to warn the driver to ease up.

As we entered Moorgate station, I glimpsed people on the platform waiting for the return journey (Draycott Park was the other end of the line), but what was alarming was the reaction of the passengers in the two files of seats facing me each side of the central corridor, presumably, unlike me, mostly regular passengers. I could see but not understand the fear and astonishment on their faces as the train, instead of gently decelerating and coming to a halt, continued at speed towards what they all knew to be the walled-up end of a tunnel. There was a swishing noise as the train tore through what I later learned was a twenty-ton heap of sand acting as a drag eighty five feet short of the tunnel wall. There was also a set of buffers on a wooden frame that was swept aside before the train smashed into the wall, the collapsing seats crushing the legs of the regulars I had been facing.

I awoke some time, perhaps forty minutes, perhaps longer, after the crash. It was pitch dark, and as I came round I was lying face up and feeling wonderfully sleepy, relaxed and comfortable, almost as though I was back at home in my bed. I put my hand up and felt metal a few inches above me. Over my left ear was a lump, as though I'd been coshed, but I was feeling no pain. Around me I heard people screaming for help, some moaning or weeping, others silent. A weight across my legs made it impossible for me to move: as I discovered later, it was a body. To my right, a man was mumbling incoherently. I reached out and found his hand, assuring him that he would be all right.

Trying to assess the situation I realised that the conditions – the darkness and the cloying dust – were like one of the many coal mines I had been down, in Britain and in Europe, as well as during my childhood as an evacuee in South Wales. Of course, I had never experienced an accident in a mine, but I knew that in most instances you had to wait to be rescued: with luck you might survive, but it was almost impossible to escape without help.

This realisation may have reinforced my strange feeling of calm, almost detachment. The thought that the wreck might catch fire simply never occurred to me – nor did I think of reaching into my pocket for a cigarette (in those days, smoking was still permitted on the underground). I knew that help must soon be on its way to us, for we were not eight hundred feet down a pit in some rural location, but right in the centre of the City of London, a comparatively few feet below street level. I felt I could wait it out.

Eventually, far behind where I was lying, I heard the voices of the first police and firemen to reach the crash, their bobbing flashlights soon haphazardly illuminating the shattered remains of the carriage for a few seconds at a time. The first carriage was crushed and splintered against the tunnel wall, the driver's cabin reduced from its fifteen feet length to a mere two feet. The second had ploughed into the first and the third into the second, all concertinaed into the space of one, seventy years of accumulated soot and dust smothering the entire scene. The remaining three coaches still stood virtually untouched beside the platform.

When it came to my turn to be pulled out I realised that when the train crashed I had been shot forward and hit something, or somebody, before flying back to lie with my feet towards the front of the train, encased in a kind of recess below the crushed roof of the carriage up against the roof of the tunnel. Doctors were attending to the injured as I was pulled away from the wreckage, but I felt no curiosity towards my fellow passengers: all I wanted was to get out into the fresh air, but strangely, still not in any kind of hurry. Everything was vague and insubstantial. Whether I walked along the platform and up the stairs to the street, or rode in a lift, I cannot recall.

Nor do I remember the ambulance ride to the London Hospital (now the Royal London) in Whitechapel Road. Only when I arrived did my senses start to return, enabling me from my stretcher to ask a hospital volunteer to call my wife and the video studio where I'd been due to meet Mr Benn. As my raincoat and jacket, and then my shirt, were removed, a nurse plucked a piece of glass about three inches long from my navel: it left not a scratch behind. Smaller splinters were embedded in my posterior. My right hand was puffed up from a crack or break in the metacarpal bone behind the index finger, but I had forgotten the bump on my head. Most of the forty three deaths had occurred within a few feet of me: I realised I had had a strikingly lucky escape.

Next morning, Moorgate was the front-page lead story in all the papers, the *Daily Telegraph's* illustrated with a picture of me, with a man in uniform and a younger man in a zip-up cardigan holding on to my arm as I was led out of Moorgate station. The picture bore the caption, 'A soot-blackened survivor emerges from the wreck...' 'Christ,' I thought, 'you'd have thought that someone at the office might have recognised it was me, despite my blackened face. I worked for the bloody paper for enough years.'

Plenty of *Telegraph* readers did, however, recognise the sooty-faced version of me, and at home I was flooded with calls and letters from friends and family congratulating me on escaping unhurt. Allowed home later in the day, I wrote a piece for that week's *New Statesman* headlined, In the Crash, and I was interviewed by the

Evening Standard and BBC radio.

Mr Benn's response – or lack of response - was curious. As a high-ranking government minister one would have thought that he might, as he was on the spot, have made an appearance as the rescue operations continued – the body of the final victim would not be removed until five days later – to offer reassurance, support and encouragement to the rescuers toiling only a few yards away from the London & Manchester. Instead, he raced back to Whitehall in his ministerial car where, according to his published diaries, he had an appointment to keep with the American author, Alvin Toffler and his wife, Heidi, noting that Toffler's book, Future Shock, had 'grossed millions of dollars', and speculating whether the author had CIA connections.

Nor, among the many messages, cards and letters I received over the succeeding days, was there one from Mr Benn, whose diary dealt with the crash in a single short paragraph, quoting the death toll – 'between fifteen and twenty people' - that he must have seen in the early editions of the *Evening Standard*, and regretting 'an appalling tragedy'. What really irritated me, however, was that even seven or eight years afterwards, on the many occasions I met Benn at a party conference or in a radio studio, he invariably asked me whether I had fully recovered from the Moorgate crash. I never, I'm afraid, had the impression that this concern for my post-traumatic welfare was genuine, but simply the one thing he ever remembered about me, an identifying fact tumbling out of his mind as though he had a mental card index entry on everybody he met.

A few weeks before the crash I had been to see him at his ministerial office at the Vickers building on the Embankment to discuss his ideas and plans as the recently-appointed Industry Minister. Suddenly, without prompting, he brought up the then-controversial question of the joint Anglo-French supersonic airliner, the Concorde, which was part of his ministerial remit, abruptly interrupting himself to blurt out, 'Oh, dear – you're not in favour of Concorde, are you?' I was astonished, since I'd written little about the project, but which, as an amateur aviation buff, I rather favoured. But before I could say anything, 'Wedgie' had leapt to his feet, grabbed a duster and wiped off the melamine board on the wall behind him the date he was due to take a proving flight on the aircraft – the board, listing all his diary engagements in coloured chalks was Benn's gesture to 'openness', the forerunner to today's 'transparency'. I thought back to a brilliant cartoon by Norman Thelwell owned by the architect Cedric Price. At first glance, it was simply a skilful portrait sketch of Benn, but on a closer look, the cartoonist, whose subjects were more often Pony Club girls and their mounts than politicians, had drawn propellers in place of his eyes.

Psychologically, I did experience the syndrome known as survivors' guilt following Moorgate, questioning why I should have emerged from the crash relatively unscathed while others alongside me on the train were killed or maimed. This feeling lasted for about a month until that year's early Easter, when a family holiday walking the East Coast beaches around Southwold allowed me to snap out of it.

I was called to give evidence at the official enquiry into the crash, held at the Institution of Civil Engineers building just off Parliament Square, offering my not particularly helpful recollections which were to earn one brief paragraph in the report – I seem to have been the only person who thought the driver might have braked for a split second as the train entered the station, before proceeding inevitably to his and many of his passengers' doom. Perhaps I had imagined, or hoped that he paused, however briefly, before going on to kill and injure so many people.

The outcome of the enquiry was disappointingly indeterminate. The cause of the accident, according to the inspector of railways, Lieutenant Colonel Ian McNaughton, lay entirely in the behaviour of the driver, Leslie Newson, but the inspector found it impossible to determine whether he had deliberately crashed the train, or his action came from 'a suddenly arising physical condition' which had not been revealed by a post mortem. No fault of the train, track or signalling had in any way contributed to the accident.

Laurence Marks, a reporter on the *Sunday Times* (and later, with Maurice Gran, writer of a string of successful TV comedies), carried out an investigation into the Moorgate crash, in which his father was among those killed. He was suspicious of the way the enquiry discounted the presence in Newson's body of 80 milligrams per 100 millilitres of alcohol – the legal limit for motorists. It didn't help that there were conflicts of evidence in the interpretations of four doctors whose opinions were heard by the enquiry: one thought the alcohol level could have impaired Newson's reaction time and made him liable to the risk of automatism from flashing lights; another thought the alcohol was created after the driver's death by the crushing of his body; a third said that if any alcohol had been consumed it must have been a very small amount, and the fourth entirely dismissed the presence of alcohol as a significant factor.

Marks, however, discovered that Newson, who was fifty-six, was in a psychologically anxious state owing to fears of sexual impotence, suggesting that he might, early on the morning of the crash before going to work, have drunk a cocktail from a bar at his home, and was carrying a substantial sum of cash he had intended to give his daughter to buy a car: if suicide was in his mind, Marks speculated, he might, in deliberately crashing, have been reminding his family of what they would be missing by his departure. Marks's findings were angrily disputed by Newson's family, so the final frustrating verdict remained that of Col. McNaughton, when he introduced his report: 'If I am asked what caused the crash, there is only one answer I can give – I just don't know.'

On the morning after I had been summoned to the enquiry, the *Daily Telegraph* made some amends by re-printing the unidentified picture it ran on the day of the crash alongside one of a scrubbed-up Paterson arriving to give evidence. Just before that day's proceedings had properly begun, one of the two assessors assisting Col. McNaughton pointed to my still bandaged right hand, asking whether it had been injured in the crash. I nodded that this was so, and he asked, 'Does it hurt?' Realising that I had been presented with one of those once-in-a-lifetime opportunities, I replied, echoing, I think, one of the Marx Brothers, 'Only when I laugh'.

Not long after the crash, a second distraction focused my attention on matters unconnected with my notion of launching a newspaper. My apprehension by the police and subsequent trial occurred one lunchtime while walking from Fleet Street to Chancery Lane. As I mooched along, a sandwich bar in an alleyway caught my eye. It was a fine day and the pair of plastic tables and chairs under a striped awning outside seemed an enticing place to enjoy a corned beef-with-Branston-pickle sandwich while reading a newspaper. By the time I had ordered, however, the seats were already taken, so I stepped a couple of paces across the alley and sat at a more substantial wooden table outside a pub opposite.

After a couple of minutes a barman came out to inform me brusquely that I was not permitted to sit there without buying food and drink from them. I glanced around in a slightly exaggerated fashion as if looking for a written notice to that effect and could see none, so I told him that I would leave as soon as I had eaten my sandwich. A moment later, a red-faced City of London policeman emerged, hatless, from inside the bar to tell me that I was causing an obstruction. 'I don't think so,' I said, pointing to the tables around me, those across the alleyway, and, further along, a second-hand bookstall taking up half the available walkway.

As I finished my sandwich a police van pulled up on Chancery Lane and three policemen leapt out, seizing me by the arms and frogmarching me to the vehicle. It didn't need a sleuth to connect the arrival of the hit squad with the policeman 'on duty' inside the pub. I protested against my arrest, asking one of the policeman why it was necessary to be so violent when I was willing to come quietly: 'Shut your fucking mouth', he replied civilly. A small crowd had gathered and among the curious bystanders I was relieved to see one face I recognised.

The police van whisked me off to Bow Street police station, where a sergeant told me I would be charged with obstruction of the highway, but in the meantime I was held in a cell. After an hour or so he visited me, this time to tell me that the charge would be changed to one of insulting behaviour, but ignored me when I suggested that the obstruction charge would never have stuck anyway. On my release I continued to my originally intended destination, the *New Statesman's* office, where I told my tale which, gratifyingly, was received with general indignation: V.S. Pritchett, the great literary critic, novelist and short story writer, father of another friend, the humorist Oliver Pritchett and grandfather of Matt, then a schoolboy but now the brilliant front page pocket cartoonist of the *Daily Telegraph*, proposed a demonstration when my case came up, when he would march around defiantly eating a sandwich outside Bow Street.

The solicitor I consulted warned me that without the man I had recognised in the crowd as a witness my chances were slim. 'They might say you were flashing or something,' he said, securing me an adjournment when I answered my bail the next day (justice was a lot swifter in those days). By good chance I ran into my witness in Fleet Street a day or two later, a sub-editor on the *Sunday Telegraph* whom I did not know in person but had often seen around the office. 'I didn't know how to get in touch with you since you left the paper,' he said. 'I was so amazed at the way the police behaved that I thought of writing a letter to *The Times*.'

Subsequently, at Bow Street, where a decade earlier I had witnessed Mandy Rice-Davies, propelled to notoriety by the Profumo affair, cheekily waving to the crowds gathered for a glimpse of her and her coeval Christine Keeler, I now found myself sitting in the historic old dock once occupied by Oscar Wilde, Dr Crippen and William 'Lord Haw-Haw' Joyce.

The barman gave his account of events to the magistrate, alleging that I had sworn at him, which induced the magistrate to ask each of the two character witnesses I called whether I habitually used bad language: 'I should describe his use of words as well chosen,' said one, judiciously. During the lunchtime adjournment the barman and I were both invited, by way of a settlement, to be bound over to keep the peace, itself technically a conviction. I declined, and the magistrate finally dismissed the case against me but, complaining of my 'insolent demeanour' in the witness box and my noisy supporters in court, refused to grant me costs.

Alan Watkins promptly wrote to his friend Sir Elwyn Jones, the attorney general, urging him to take a look into this injustice. So the stipendiary magistrate at Bow Street, an extremely busy man who might hear dozens of cases in a day would, months later, have had to work his way back through the files to recall the details my little cause célèbre, and then write a letter explaining his decision to a senior law officer of the Crown. Nothing came of it, of course, but it was satisfying that a ridiculous case which should never have been brought, and which, in retrospect, anticipated the niggling regime of persecution by petty rules and regulations that was to disfigure the Blair and Brown administrations after 1997. Once the crash and the prosecution were out of the way, the way was clear for me to concentrate on my Big Idea.

Chapter 23

MORE than thirty Fleet Street colleagues and other well-wishers, mostly from the *Telegraph*, instantly contributed to my start-up costs when word went around that I was trying to set up a new newspaper, their generosity overriding their natural scepticism and the fact that at the time – the early 1970s - the country was in deepest recession.

I suggested that £25 per head would make an appropriate individual contribution towards the expense of forming a company, covering my office costs, researching the available new methods of production, and making a start on trying to raise serious money. Some gave more.

Fleet Street at the time was in an appalling state. A Royal Commission was sitting and as Royal Commissions do, in Harold Wilson's words, taking minutes and lasting years, to examine the industry's problems without much expectation within the trade that answers would be found.

What was apparent to everyone was that newspapers were nearly all losing money hand over fist, were stuck with an outdated technology and a recalcitrant non-editorial workforce (though journalists would soon catch the strike fever), and were on average dependent for seventy per cent of their income on advertising, which in a recession was obviously in decline.

The concept I first came up with was for a four days a week morning newspaper, on the argument that with the expansion of the Sunday papers there was still plenty left from over the weekend to read on Mondays, and that few commuters came into London on Saturdays. I wanted to focus on the London metropolitan area but had a plan to expand more widely later with a franchise scheme for locally based versions across the country. The paper would be printed on contract at one or more of the modern web-offset presses owned by printing companies in or close to the capital: its costs would therefore be shared proportionately with all the other customers for the services of these print houses. It followed that something on these lines could be established at a fraction of the cost of setting up or buying an existing 'conventional' newspaper. It could be run with a staff of perhaps sixty people and be profitable on a sale of 80,000 copies a day - a far, far lower circulation level than the existing Fleet Street range of 300,000 to 4 million-plus, while charging only one-third of the advertising rate of its competitors.

I had decided to call the prospective paper the *Globe*, after a Victorian daily that reached its apogee with a sensational scoop on the outcome of a secret deal made at the 1878 Congress of Berlin, which established, for a while, the political future of the Balkan nations: the scoop did not go unpunished, since it persuaded the British government of the day, when its prosecution of the *Globe's* editor failed, to enact the first Official Secrets Act.

Early on, I contacted two stockbrokers in the City recommended to me by friendly financial journalists, as a starting point in my search for backers. The first put the phone down on me and followed this up with an abusive letter railing against the print workers and, for good measure, journalists, asserting that only a madman would have anything whatever to do with Fleet Street, now or at any future date. The other at least granted me an audience but explained that he couldn't imagine anyone would be willing to back the notion of the *Globe*: nevertheless, having that day had a win on the horses and no doubt celebrated well over lunch, he generously gave me £200 from his winnings, while insisting that he preferred to remain anonymous for fear of destroying his reputation.

Meanwhile, I had cobbled together an outline of how I saw the

Globe. I had various models or inspirations in mind, including New York's Long Island Newsday and the newly-launched Le Quotidien de Paris, as well as the *International Herald Tribune*, squeezed out of its home town of New York and resettled in Paris. These were not all examples of the power of computerised printing technology to create new-model newspapers - for the most part they still employed the traditional hot-metal processes; however, all, in one way or another, were challenging existing media market ideas. The one that interested me most was the *Herald Tribune*, criticised by some as a 'second-hand newspaper' for its reliance on mainland American columnists and agency reporting, and aimed at American tourists and travelling businessmen in Europe. What intrigued me was that it was published from an editorial office in France and transformed into plastic moulds that were then, page by page, transmitted via a system formerly set up by the US air force, for whatever purpose, to a printing plant outside London from where the paper was printed and distributed in the UK.

I wanted to get away from 'old' Fleet Street. The hundreds of us who shared the warren of tiny rooms in the *Daily Telegraph* building, the walls and floors shuddering each evening as the huge rotary presses in the basement started to throb like the Titanic's engines working up to maximum revs, I found tremendously exciting and romantic, but it was a technology that had been around for the best part of a century, was madly expensive and for which a revolutionary replacement was already waiting in the wings.

Before the *Telegraph's* old presses rolled, every word of that day's newspaper would have been set in lead type on composing machines that differed from the QUERTY keyboard of the typewriter, thereby excluding, among others, women from joining the trade. The compositors became an exclusive, highly-paid almost entirely male elite constantly pushing up the price of their labour: I remember that in the bar of the Kings & Keys, the pub next door to the *Telegraph* frequented by a cross-section of the paper's employees, the only customer who could afford a new Alfa-Romeo car and a subscription to the stylish St George's Hill golf club, was a compositor. And alongside the compositors, other print workers, each with their own union and areas of demarcation were on the Fleet Street gravy train, jealously guarding their own corner.

At times of political tension, as in the slump of the seventies, the independence of newspapers began to be challenged by the print workers, who demanded changes to the editorial content of the papers (as in the case of the *Evening Standard*, not the only example, whose printers refused to allow a cartoon critical of trade unions to be published).

Delegations of British newspaper managers and trade unionists had paid visits to America to study the new technology - the Miami Herald was a favourite port of call - but the new ways were never copied by Fleet Street, whose long-running squabbles were developing into outright sabotage, echoing those of the Luddites, and might still be in full spate today but for Eddie Shah's launch of his *Today* newspaper in 1986 and, soon after that, Rupert Murdoch's 'moonlight flit' with his papers from Fleet Street to a new, secretly prepared ultra-modern plant in Wapping. But these momentous events wouldn't happen for another decade.

From first to last, the chief problem I faced was that of raising capital for the *Globe*. I wrote off letters to anyone I thought might be interested in backing a new paper, early on trying Michael Curtis, the admired former editor of the *News Chronicle* and at that time adviser to the ultra-wealthy Aga Khan. Here was a way, I thought, for Curtis to teach a lesson to a Fleet Street which hadn't allowed his old newspaper to survive, despite a circulation of around a million copies a day. But Curtis, or the Aga Khan, proved not to be interested.

I also tried the millionaire James Goldsmith, whom I had met once, before he was knighted, when he was rejoicing that a company he owned had bought the Marmite brand, my favourite accompaniment to dripping and toast. I knew his brother, Teddy, the environmentalist, a friend of my American chum, Wyche Fowler, quite well. Unlike Mr Curtis, who courteously but firmly penned a rejection letter, Goldenballs, as *Private Eye* magazine would soon nickname Goldsmith, at least invited me to discuss my ideas with him.

Our encounter proved a disappointment. A good-looking man in a slightly brutal way, with gimlet blue eyes and a smile that switched on and off quicker than a light bulb, he seemed less interested in my notion of launching a newspaper than in his own idea, which was for a news magazine on the lines of *Time* or *Newsweek*. He questioned me about the magazine market in West Germany (as it then still was) and Jean-Jacques Serban-Schreiber's *l'Express*: I knew little of either. At the end of our discussion he suggested we meet again, this time with his American adviser, Clay Felker, who was soon to found New York magazine. That meeting never transpired, apparently because any date I might offer – I was free, I felt, for the rest of my life – somehow never coincided with a free moment in Goldsmith's diary, though I notice that our desultory correspondence lasted for two years, long enough to keep my hopes of assistance from this direction tantalisingly alive. It finally became clear that he was determined – naturally enough - to fulfil not my ambition but his own, and then only briefly, with his founding of Now! magazine in 1975. (Now! lasted just three years, enriching its staff with generous pay-offs when it ceased publication, but costing Goldsmith £6 million.)

Meanwhile, I was forced to abandon my chosen title when a company distributing free local weekly newspapers in the north of England, each one preceded with the name of the towns where they were distributed followed by the word *Globe*, raised objections when they heard that we wished to use the title. I cannot imagine that a legal system that scandalously allowed the *Daily Express* group to launch a paper called the *Daily Star* while the venerable *Communist Morning Star*, also a daily publication, was still very much in business, would have halted a new Fleet Street paper called the *Globe*. But the reality was that I simply did not have the money to contest the case. So from then on, without letting it be known (for our circumstances might have improved in the meantime and enabled us to mount a challenge) we planned for a paper to be called the *Globe* but might have to be called 'a.m.'. (At least this new title gave me the idea of presenting the date an inch high on the front page in the style of a desk almanac: why do newspapers always make this one essential piece of information more difficult to read than anything else on the page?)

With advice pouring in from all around, a small group assembled to pursue the project. I was fortunate to secure the (voluntary) services of Dennis Hackett, a pugnacious Yorkshireman a couple of years older than myself, who had, I estimate, worked for at least half a dozen Fleet Street newspapers as reporter, sub-editor, designer, production man and executive, as well as editing two national magazines, *Queen* and *Nova*, with excursions into advertising and public relations along the way: it was Dennis who joined me for the encounter with Goldsmith. I'd first heard of him when, as a director of the *Mirror* group, he had fallen out with his then boss, Hugh Cudlipp, over the disastrous sale of the *Mirror* Group's newish daily, the *Sun*, to Rupert Murdoch - possibly the worst business decision in newspaper history, for under the Aussie the hitherto faltering *Sun* became Britain's largest-selling newspaper, its circulation always exceeding that of the *Mirror*.

When he left the *Mirror's* employ Dennis took with him both his company limousine and his chauffeur on temporary if unofficial loan, so as to impress future employers as he looked for another job. He was never a man to be overwhelmed or intimidated.

He brought with him the services of John Hill as putative art editor, whose experience covered the *Mirror Magazine*, *Nova*, and the *Mail* group, and John Kosh, from the advertising industry with bright ideas for a new-look newspaper. We also had the help and advice of Will Camp, novelist, public relations guru, and astute political fixer – it was Will who generously bore the costs of the legal squabble over the title of the *Globe*. I set up a publishing company, the board including Hackett, Camp, Richard Lamb, who had recently sold his business weekly, City Press (but held on tight to his capital gain), and designer Peter Campbell, later a mainstay of the *London Review of Books*, with myself as chairman. All pledged to resign when, or if, someone with real money were to come aboard and wished to appoint his own directors.

I had no idea where in the newspaper firmament the *Globe* would fit politically, nor did I much care since the word that buzzed through my brain was independence, though some mistook my coupling of 'radical' with independence as referring to politics, when I was thinking more of the paper's novel approach to production. Also, I had no wish to frighten the horses of finance by putting off potential investors and, if possible, I wished to keep the unions sweet. They, of course, were immensely more powerful in the 1970s than they are today and capable of damaging, even crushing an enterprise by non-cooperation and obstructionism. I knew, however, that in commercial printing companies the unions were less powerful, less militant and lower paid – but would their leaders resent the idea of a newspaper trying to 'escape' the hold they had over Fleet Street? Having written on the subject of trade unions for many years I knew most of their leaders and decided to discuss my plans openly with them. I wasn't surprised by the goodwill they expressed, tinged though it was by the same dispiriting, but perfectly understandable cynicism with which the *Globe* had been greeted by the money men; even so, I was a little sad to hear this from people whose members derived their livings from newspapers, but it was even more difficult to understand why they made it as difficult as possible for them to be run efficiently.

The two great rivals among the print unions were the compositors, organised by the National Typographical Society, and the print machine hands belonging to Natsopa, the National Society of Operative Printers and Assistants. Neither union had any intention of risking their members' money in the *Globe* – hardly surprising given the unfolding fiasco of the *Scottish Daily News*, where Tony Benn, then in his pomp as Industry Secretary, was in the mood to fling public money around to provide jobs for the staff of stricken companies, from motorbikes and shipyards to newspapers: I had no desire to become a temporary Bennite civil servant. He gave £1.2 million of taxpayers' money to a syndicate of workers made redundant when the *Scottish Daily Express* decamped to Manchester after coping with fifty strikes in its final year in Glasgow. A condition of the Benn grant was that the money had to be matched by £275,000 from the re-named *Daily News* workers' co-operative; the money was found, partly with the help of £100,000, it was said, from Robert Maxwell, but the *Daily News* (adopting the grovelling slogan 'Read the People's Paper and Keep 500 in Jobs') foundered in six months, swallowing up the donations of the Scottish public as well as the workers' redundancy money.

I was satisfied that I had the unions' imprimatur, though I kept quiet about a private undertaking from Richard Briginshaw, general secretary of Natsopa, that in the event of difficulties from any other union he would be willing to provide all the workers in all the trades necessary for the *Globe*: I certainly had no wish to precipitate an inter-union demarcation war that would prevent the enterprise ever getting off the ground and possibly closing down the rest of Fleet Street as well, but this gesture was never put to the test. Incidentally, there was no question of setting up a non-union newspaper because membership was still enforced by the closed shop in many industries, more so in printing than most other industries: Murdoch in 1986 finally succeeded in dumping the print unions when he moved his papers to Wapping, defying their sometimes violent demonstrations outside the gates by granting sole recognition rights, and all the jobs, to the Electricians' union, then in right wing hands, whose members could swiftly be trained to set the type on computers with QWERTY keyboards.

When we unveiled the *Globe* project, choosing the silly season of August 1974 to ensure publicity, I was overwhelmed by scores of applications from journalists, photographers and cartoonists from all over the country, and a few from the US, Africa, Australia, and even Korea, applying for jobs on the putative new paper. I wrote to these hopefuls pointing out that things were at a very early stage and promising I would get in touch with them when the happy day arrived that we had raised the half million pounds we would need to launch a project that had awakened a dream in the hearts of many newspapermen. At the same time, I felt guilty for raising their hopes while, privately, my own were sinking.

Still, there was fun to be had from the reactions of my friends and enemies to the idea of the *Globe*. 'Dream All About It!' was the headline on a piece in Punch magazine by an old friend, Alan Brien, who filled two pages with imaginings of what any newspaper he were to found would contain and how it would be staffed. It would not be the only paper, he said, with a gardening expert living in a bed-sit, a Tory industrial correspondent, a bankrupt racing tipster, a seasick travel writer, and a bachelor agony aunt - but the only one to inform its readers that this was the case.

There was generous encouragement from the *Sunday Times*, but that hardly counted, since their report was written by my dearest friend, Eric Jacobs. The same might have applied to Bill Grundy, but his press column in the *Spectator* maintained a proper scepticism. He quoted St Matthew's gospel, 'Oh thou of little faith, wherefore didst thou doubt?' wearily adding that 'a long study of the newspaper industry gets you that way'.

Yet another member of my circle, Auberon Waugh, in his *Private Eye* Diary, expressed his incredulity in a ragging way, suggesting that his own idea of launching a new *Dandy* or *Beano* comic, but with lavatorial jokes, was superior to my idea of yet another boring daily newspaper. What he called my 'footling scheme', was a shocking waste of talent, he wrote. 'Paterson, despite his rough upbringing... is one of the funniest men in London, with as pretty a line in puns as any I know.' How could I be cross?

Someone else pointed out that mine would be the only paper that could run a box in each issue headed 'In the *Globe* 150 Years Ago'. The *Guardian* flatteringly claimed that I had self-sacrificially resigned from the *New Statesman*, 'where it had been intended that [Paterson] should be groomed to follow Tony Howard as editor' – news, I'm sure, to both of us. The *Guardian* piece quoted me as saying, 'Fleet Street's problem is that the papers have become bureaucratic dinosaurs, loaded down with too many staff, vast distribution costs, too much duplication of news everyone saw on the telly last night, and an archaic printing technology', adding that my criticisms were 'largely justified'.

Eventually, I came to acknowledge to myself that my ambition to start a newspaper, conceived on that bright day on the beach of Savannah and pursued with some, but not quite enough energy and misplaced hope, was never going to happen. Even after I came to this realisation I hung on to the fiction that it was still going strong, partly because I was always running into acquaintances who asked how the *Globe* was going and, like the redundant businessman who pretends to go to work every day, but spends his time in the park, I found it hard to tell them that that it was not going, but gone.

Looking back, the moment I liked best, the prophetic moment as it proved, came near the outset of our adventure, in the media magazine *Campaign*. Over a long and detailed account of the project, alongside a half-page picture of me standing suicidally amidst the traffic in the middle of Fleet Street, was a bold headline in inch-high heavy black capital letters: DOES THE GLOBE HAVE AN EARTHLY?

NO IT DIDN'T! But it was fun trying. I felt no sense of frustration or bitterness. To borrow from Prospero, 'The great *Globe* dissolved like an insubstantial pageant, leaving not a rack behind'.

While all this was going on, I had become a full-time freelance journalist. Provided you earn sufficient money to keep a roof over your head and eat occasionally, there are advantages to be had from practising journalism as a freelance than as a wage slave in a staff job.

The essential attribute for a free-lance reporter with no regular retainer and on the look-out for work is patience. Sitting anxiously by the telephone hoping for a call that doesn't come may induce feelings of paranoia, best assuaged by leaving a telephone answering machine to take the strain, and indulging in plenty of displacement activity, like catching up on the films you haven't seen, and, not too often, frequenting Fleet Street pubs. And it helps to possess the right temperament for freelancing: I do not experience anxiety or depression.

Out on my own, I depended on a variety of sources of income, including the *Evening Standard*, the *Sunday Times*, and at one time or another, a range of magazines and Sunday supplements, as well as radio, TV and writing for foreign newspapers and magazines.

While not everybody can find a glamorous job as a foreign correspondent, it's surprising how often overseas travel can come your way as a freelance. Opportunities, known as 'freebies' often involved trips abroad with air tickets and accommodation paid for by commercial, charitable or diplomatic organisations. I had British Airways to thank for having travelled across the Atlantic by Concorde; I first went to the West Indies courtesy of, if I remember rightly, the International Labour Organisation; I stayed several weeks in Kenya, courtesy of the International Red Cross, and visited Japan several times, once paid for by the Japanese government.

Two memorable freebies came my way in 1975, the first introducing me to Moscow eleven years into the dreary reign of Leonid Brezhnev, when the Soviet Union, jeered an American scholar, was like 'Upper Volta with rockets', before it graduated into President Reagan's Evil Empire and disintegrated.

I flew to Moscow at the invitation of the Soviet trade union newspaper, *Trud*, the invitation arriving by means I have now forgotten. The city was down-at-heel, grim and cold. Phone calls to London entailed hours of waiting in one's hotel room for a line. Beefy female guardians manned a desk on each floor. The food was poor and meals didn't arrive until at least an hour after placing the order.

The high point of my visit was a function arranged by *Trud* at the House of Columns, a glittering club for aristocrats during the Czarist era, full of chandeliers and, as its name implies, white-painted columns. The occasion was billed as an 'oral newspaper', where the paper's editors and staff reported back to the readers. Since *Trud's* circulation was claimed to be seven million copies a day, and only 1,400 mostly elderly people were present, I surmised the event was a boondoggle for retired communist party officials and their wives.

When the interval arrived, the members of the editorial board and their guests went one way to a champagne and caviar reception, the readers meanwhile directed to something, in Orwellian terms, more equal in the catering line. In an opulently-furnished salon, I chatted to Russia's leading poet, Yevgeny Yevtushenko, tall, languid, handsome, and a fluent English speaker, wearing an electric-blue suit and a floppy-collared shirt that would not have shamed the wardrobe of a Keats or Byron.

Yevtushenko had already performed his turn for the *Trud* audience, after speeches from the chief architect of Moscow, who provoked ripples of sceptical laughter when he promised that all Moscovites would soon have a flat with a room for each member of the family and situated no more than thirty five minutes from their work. A cancer specialist followed, predicting that a cure for the disease was already on the horizon. The poet came next with a strange speech scolding officials and planners who spent precious foreign currency importing earth-moving equipment from abroad, and then left it to rust on the muddy banks of the Kamar River at the construction site of a new truck factory.

I wondered why on earth a poet was required to speechify about tractors and earth-moving machinery that would have come more appropriately from a junior minister of production? Unsurprisingly, his rebuke to officials and planners for their shortcomings received less applause than that earned by the architect and the doctor, although *Trud's* deputy editor, my translator, explained that Yevtushenko was expected to say something out of the ordinary: 'He can say things that don't appear in the paper's reports. We'll take it from him.' At home, I reflected, the poet laureate is obliged to write lines on royal births, engagements and deaths in exchange for a few bottles of port - not the same thing at all as the political role of a Soviet poet.

During my interval conversation with Yevtushenko, who had just spent three months in hospital with inflammation of the heart, he sounded less like a poet than a freelance journalist. 'I've written a 5,000 word article on détente and offered it to the *New York Times*,' he said, 'but they wanted to cut it to 700 words. Then I sent it to *Time* magazine, who said they would only run 2,000 words. How is that freedom?' However, a minute later his mood was transformed as he was presented with an executive briefcase by the paper's editor. 'A bribe, a bribe,' he shouted exuberantly, 'James Bond, secret agent!'

A couple of reporters from *Trud*, on my final day in Moscow, took me for a sight-seeing trip, inviting me en route to visit the 'foreigners' shop', only accessible to Russians who possessed foreign currency. In casual conversation I said that I liked caviar, but bought none. A few days later the pair accompanied me to the airport after a few too many farewell vodkas at my hotel, taking charge of my canvas bag, and ushering me straight through emigration.

On my return, I realised there was a price to pay for the VIP treatment I'd received at the airport. When I unpacked my bag I found, lying on its side, a one-litre plastic beer glass with an inch or so of caviar left in the bottom, and, nearby, the elastic band and piece of paper intended to confine the contents to the glass. Everything was smothered in the roe of the sturgeon, traces of which would stick to its insides for months. I sat on the floor, using the handle of my toothbrush to spoon out the small amount left in the glass, laughing slightly hysterically at the careless generosity of my erstwhile friends in Moscow.

If the caviar could be counted as a cultural embarrassment, several more awaited me on a visit to Japan. One occurred when I was invited to the geisha house of a nonagenarian Japanese newspaper proprietor in Kyoto, together with a handful of his editors and executives. On a bitterly cold night, we were warmed by a huge cast-iron, Russian stove fed with logs by two elderly geishas clad in gorgeous traditional costume who interrupted their singing, dancing, and badinage every now and then to attend to the stove: someone explained to me that geishas grow old alongside their patrons.

The dinner went on for a long time and the press baron, misinterpreting my discomfort at having to sit on the floor for such an extended period, interpreted my agonised look to mean that I would probably rather drink whisky than sake, ordering one of the geishas to bring me a bottle of Johnny Walker. This failed to reconcile me to sitting on my haunches, so after a while I rose to perch on one of two narrow shelves running along the wall behind me. Before I could settle down, one of the editors sprang up in alarm to disabuse me of the idea that this was a seat for sitting on but a repository for flowers and small china pots in remembrance of ancestors. Outside in the snow as I left, my ears were burning from embarrassment.

Later, in the atom bomb-victim city of Nagasaki, I was dining in the upstairs room of a tiny restaurant overlooking a beautiful creek filled with junks decorated with coloured lanterns. The setting was idyllic, the ambience superb, as a pretty waitress placed a tray of starters before me. Bread is not a staple of the Japanese diet, but there in front of me among the dainty dishes lay what appeared to be a perfect Hovis bread roll. I was astonished to see it, and the simian instinct of mankind made me tentatively extend an index finger to explore it. In the split second before I started back I had almost burnt off my fingerprint, for it was not a bread roll but an almost red-hot stone on which I was meant to barbecue the raw meat and fish contained in the other dishes. My injury was bandaged up, but the throbbing pain quite ruined the occasion for me, except for a remarkable tale told by one of my hosts at the dinner, a public relations man for the Mitsubishi corporation. He told me he had received an oddly nostalgic letter from an English prisoner of war who had been working as a forced labourer in the Nagasaki shipyard in 1945.

The PoW recalled a devastating raid on the shipyard by American fighter-bombers at the beginning of August, damage repairs resulting in the PoWs being confined to their prison in the city centre. On the morning of the 9th August the Englishman was assigned, alone, to work on repairing a slit trench near the outer wall. Attracted by the sound of engines, he looked up and was puzzled to see a parachute emerge from a US bomber while the aircraft flew serenely on, before a blinding flash blew him back into his trench. Unconscious for several minutes, when he emerged he was astounded to see the prison walls flattened and neighbouring buildings all around collapsed and in flames. Then he heard the pattering of hundreds of feet as the surviving workers from an adjacent factory, panting and gasping, some with charred skin hanging from their bodies, came running through the prison yard. The prisoners joined the stampede towards a nearby hill. During the night Japanese soldiers arrived, marching the foreign captives at rifle point back into the devastated city, putting them to work collecting some of the estimated forty thousand bodies of those who had died instantly in the explosion, heaping them on to wooden pyres where they were burned. Even after word arrived that the Japanese government had surrendered on 15th August and the war was over, the prisoners continued performing their grisly work.

Thirty years after his experience of prison life and harsh labour, climaxed by the horror of being at the epicentre of the explosion of an atomic bomb, this man could still feel a certain nostalgia for Nagasaki, to the extent that in his letter he expressed the hope that he might one day be able to revisit the scene. He had enjoyed good health ever since, had married and fathered children, all of whom were unaffected by their father's proximity to the radiation released by the bomb. I contacted him on my return home, but he wisely declined to become a focus of publicity at a time when the Cold War was in progress and people's fears of nuclear war were running high.

Chapter 24

I soon discovered the easiest and swiftest way to earn a little extra money, without resorting to crime, when I first joined the *New Statesman* in the 1960s. Our offices were in Great Turnstile on the edge of the legal ghetto of Lincoln's Inn Fields, ten minutes walk away from the Aldwych where the BBC's *World Service* occupied Bush House.

Here was a hive of radio producers constantly in need of contributors who could at the drop of a hat talk with authority, or at least with confidence, on a subject in the news. As the *Statesman* was nearby it received more than its share of the work: I noticed when I was on the *Spectator*, a cab ride away in Bloomsbury, that the number of calls I got from Bush House diminished.

TV was a different proposition: it might make your fame and fortune, but my encounters with the medium did not suggest this would be the outcome for me. The first time I ever went on television was in 1964, following my visit to China, then still a newsworthy experience because the Chinese had fallen out with the Russians and few westerners were allowed into the country. So my TV debut came on an early-evening BBC programme called Tonight, presented by Cliff Michelmore and produced by Donald Baverstock (known as Noddy because he was married to a daughter of Enid Blyton). It was also the show on which my old *Extel* colleague Alan Whicker was developing his brilliant TV career.

Before heading to the BBC studios in Lime Grove my head was filled with helpfully intended but, as it proved, useless advice from people at the *Telegraph* who themselves had never been anywhere near a TV studio. I swiftly concluded following my stumbling performance that appearing on TV was a particularly humiliating activity, leaving one in an agony of worry that one's friends and family would have witnessed the awful exhibition one made of oneself, balanced by a contrary fear that they hadn't watched it at all.

There was another TV programme I was involved in that outdid even the horror of Tonight. In the late 60s the country was experiencing a series of particularly damaging strikes by dockers, whose pay structures in those days were as complex as the pipe-work in the engine rooms of the merchant ships they were currently refusing to unload. I was called in to explain these complexities, the producer suggesting that I might summarise the multiple inputs that constituted the pay packet of a dockworker by writing some headings on a blackboard. As the proceedings began, the blackboard was placed close to me - except that, just as I listened to the first question addressed to me I realised that someone had moved it, and its easel, far away to the side of the studio, its contents too distant even with my 20/20 vision to make out. It was a disaster as I tried to recall what was on the blackboard, bamboozling the discussion panel and, no doubt, the viewers. When the show ended, I crept off in a taxi without, as one normally would, going into the green room for a drink and some self-congratulatory chat with the other participants.

For a while TV became an important part of my life, mostly with regular appearances on the long-running What the Papers Say made for ITV by Granada (and now on BBC), a useful form of outdoor relief for journalists, freelances and staffers alike. The series' all-time most frequent contributors, were Bernard Levin, Brian Inglis and Anthony Howard, but for a while I came high on the list of also-rans who appeared fairly often: i.e. once every month or six weeks. The best thing that could be said about Papers is that it was the quite like radio, in that it depended on a wonderful group of actors – unseen by the viewers - who would read the quotations chosen by the presenter in what was usually a supposedly witty commentary on the week's news.

One of the joys of visiting the Manchester studios of Granada TV was the array of Francis Bacon paintings on the walls, including, in my recollection, prime examples of his rage-filled 'screaming Popes' series. Amid all the takeovers, mergers and other vicissitudes that have transformed commercial television, I sometimes wonder what happened to these pictures, and whether they were the personal property of the Bernstein brothers, Sidney and Cecil, who founded Granada, or belonged to the company.

I met Sidney Bernstein several times, the first when I was doing interviews during a Labour Party conference in Blackpool for Granada's own regional coverage, working with Bill Grundy, whose status made him the Robin Day of the North. Bernstein was showing us some credit card-sized promotional giveaways for Granada, listing the best years for French wines. Grundy told him that, given the station's northern audience, a list of the finest beers might prove more useful.

Some years later, I had a most peculiar experience when Sidney, then in his mid-seventies and still chairman of the company, invited me to meet him at his offices in Granada's London base in Golden Square. I had no idea why he should wish to see me, as he poured me a large whisky, sent his secretary home, and chatted about this and that. Finally coming to the point, to my utter astonishment he declared that he wished to offer me a job – not to present a TV show, or to work in his public relations department, which might just have made a little sense, but nothing less than to oversee all aspects of the Granada brand. My duties would cover TV production, enabling me, he said, to scrap a series or a single programme if I believed it was on the wrong track or had outworn its appeal to the public, and to decide what new programmes to make. 'You can go on the set while the show is being made and call a halt, if you think it's a complete waste of time,' I remember his saying, as I sat there, completely bemused. I wondered what would happen if I were to give the order that Coronation Street, Granada's longest-running and the country's most popular soap, should be scrapped: it would be like the South declaring war on the North. But there was more to come, for not only was I apparently to be in dictatorial charge of the company's television interests, I would also supervise its network of motorway service areas, a much more sensible idea if only because of my fondness for fry-up breakfasts. I decided that poor Bernstein had taken complete leave of his senses, for however heavily my career in journalism had relied on self-confidence, I knew that the proposition he was putting to me was nonsensical: if anything, this was the boss of Granada offering me his own job. He suggested I should take a few days to think about his offer. I left the building alternately laughing to myself and fretting over the poor man's sanity. It may be that the men in white coats arrived the next morning to take him away, for I never heard another word about this bizarre episode, feeling, largely out of pity, quite unable to contact him to discover whom he must be confusing me with.

Radio soon became my chosen and familiar ground in broadcasting, not only in frequent visits to Bush House, but also to Radio Four's *Today* programme in the 1960s, when I would tumble out of bed at an unearthly hour to get to the studio in Broadcasting House before 7 a.m. There I would be grilled on the latest union pay claim or strike by John Timpson, who with his Norfolk accent seemed to have wandered off a gardening programme, or the clownish Jack Di Manio, whose selling point, in his languid public school accent, was to get the time persistently wrong in his time-checks.

One particular advantage in appearing on the early edition of *Today* in those days, unlike its modern version, was that interviews aired in the first were often repeated in the second, thus earning a double fee: that way, one never minded being rousted out of bed for the early shift.

Gradually, my appearances on the *Today* programme led to the producers of the World at One inviting me on to their lunchtime news-and-analysis show, and then, at teatime I would pop up on PM, followed occasionally by The World Tonight. Just once, I think, I was on all four in one 24-hour period, provoking Tony Howard to allege, hopefully in jest, that on each occasion I was tipsy, which I naturally put down to a serious mishearing of my fairly deep and, given my cigarette addiction, gravelly voice.

The money was not great – hardly more than £12 an appearance – but it was frequent and, unlike TV, it was not time consuming. My favourite presenter, or invigilator, on these current affairs programmes, apart from *Today's* charming and beautifully spoken Sue McGregor, was William Hardcastle, a former editor of the *Daily Mail* who often presented both World at One and PM. He had been popular at the *Mail* where the story is told that when he was sacked someone had the temerity at a lunch given by the paper's proprietor, Lord Rothermere, to question the decision. 'Well, I had a fat editor,' mused his lordship, 'so I thought it was time to have a thin one.' Unlike Di Manio's irritating misreadings of the clock, Hardcastle's errors were accidental and more endearing. My favourite was his sign-off from a piece pre-recorded in Manchester by the reporter, and now distinguished author, Simon Winchester - 'That was Simon Manchester in Winchester.' Another fond memory I have is of PM on a Friday afternoon with Hardcastle interrogating me for the final item of the final programme before the weekend he was clearly most anxious to embark upon. He put his closing question to me, yawned, stretched, unplugged his headphones and pushed back his chair without paying me the slightest further attention, while I stumbled through my answer and tried hard not to laugh.

I had the most tremendous stroke of luck when Alastair Osborne, editor of The World Tonight, invited me to take a more regular role as a reporter on his programme, paying me a monthly retainer. Osborne, a South African whose father had intended him to be an engineer, had been sent to school in England and then started work in a Glasgow shipyard. Physically, with his red hair and pale skin, he resembled his Scottish forebears, but close up his face was covered by a myriad of tiny indentations giving the impression of an ancient parchment, a condition attributable, I supposed, to exposure to the fierce African sun in childhood. He was a superb editor, ruling his staff of presenters, reporters and researchers with a light hand, and fending off occasional criticisms from the Radio 4 executives above him: he took the flak for going ahead, at a delicate time in the debate over nuclear disarmament when the apparatchiks wanted to suppress an interview I had obtained with the controversial CND activist and Catholic priest, Monsignor Bruce Kent (who later got married and quit the priesthood). In the 1970s and 80s the BBC often shied away from anything so vulgarly exhibitionist as a scoop, pleading with outsiders like me from Fleet Street to give any exclusive stories I came across to the newspapers before they were judged fit to be repeated on air.

One of Alastair's many great skills lay in his administration of a programme budget which, despite annual cuts, he stretched magically to ensure an ever-flowing supply of drink for the politicians and other notables arriving to be interviewed on The World Tonight, as well as meeting the cost of covering foreign stories and features; I sometimes thought he must have had a secret source of private wealth that allowed him to supplement the budget.

One memorable outing for which I had Alastair to thank was a journey to the Navaho Indian reservation in the American south-west, the reservation carved out of the states of Arizona, Utah, Colorado and New Mexico, and about the same size as Ireland. It has its own capital, Window Rock, named after a remarkable geological feature, a great sandstone cliff pillar through which, over the course of many centuries, the wind has blown a perfectly circular hole. The reservation had for long been governed by the Department of Indian Affairs in Washington, a relationship that provoked major tensions over the exploitation of substantial deposits of coal, uranium, gas and oil, believed by the tribe to have been sold off too cheaply to commercial interests. The DIA had been prepared to accept a royalty of $250,000 over 25 years for an oil and gas pipeline crossing the Navajo land, but after a democratic council was elected they secured $70 million.

In a bid to curb alcoholism, far and away the most serious social problem among the Navaho, the council had introduced prohibition, but was unable to prevent Indians - not yet known as Native Americans - flocking to bars in the small towns adjoining the reservation. At breakfast time in Window Rock, emerging from the town's one motel with my producer, David Powell, a reassuringly bulky and even-tempered man who made an agreeable travelling companion, it was necessary to step over dozens of recumbent Navaho men, lying unconscious from drink just where they had been dumped from the pick-up trucks which had collected them from the border town bars the night before.

The elected chief, Peter MacDonald (the name, he told me, conferred on him at a mission school around the time that 'Old MacDonald Had a Farm' became a popular song) had been a rocket scientist working on the Polaris missile for the Howard Hughes company in

California before he was chosen to govern his compatriots. He was therefore excited when NASA decided that one part of the reservation, overgrazed by the hundreds of thousands of sheep by which the Navaho assess their wealth, bore a resemblance to the arid surface of the Moon and was therefore ideal for the preparations of the Apollo 11 crew of Neil Armstrong, Buzz Aldrin, and Mike Collins.

Moon buggies weaving around the parched earth and rocks of the reservation, amid NASA technical trucks and accommodation caravans, were observed from a nearby bluff by a traditional Navaho shaman who promptly asked the chief what was going on. The situation was explained to him, whereupon he asked to be allowed to talk to the astronauts. In the Navaho language, he rehearsed the creation myth of the tribe, which held that their ancestors had once lived on the Moon, and requesting that the astronauts convey his greetings to any Navaho they might encounter still living up there. Armstrong promised to tuck the message into a corner of the spacecraft: in translation it read, 'These white men come in peace, and I urge our brothers on the Moon to show them every courtesy and kindness. But I warn them, on no account must they sign a treaty with white man.' A title for our radio documentary immediately wrote itself – Take a Message to the Moon.

A minor difficulty was to emerge, however, over the title of another of our American documentaries, this time on the so-called 'old China hands', whose careers were destroyed when they were accused of being 'the men who lost China'. The assault in the 1950s by the egregious Senator McCarthy on this group of foreign service officers with long experience of China was backed by the China Lobby, an influential group whose business interests in China had been destroyed by the arrival in power of the communists in 1948. The businessmen's ire was buttressed by the paternalistic sentiments of many Americans who regarded China as a kind of unofficial colony of the US, and the churches, who feared that their many years of missionary work was being undone by the godless communists.

We tracked down some of the China hands living in retirement two decades and more after their ordeal at the hands of McCarthy and his allies. All those I interviewed turned out to be gentle, highly educated individuals, any bitterness they felt over their treatment perhaps eased by the time I met them, as their names had by then finally been cleared by the Senate Foreign Relations Committee, which pronounced that their only crime had been to point out to their masters in Washington that in the struggle against the Japanese invaders the communists were more popular with the Chinese people and militarily more effective than the corrupt and incompetent nationalists under Chiang Kai-Shek: they had, in short, been 'persecuted because they were honest'.

Among them O. Edmund Clubb, was eventually reinstated, but ended his career in what must be one of the least coveted jobs in the State Department, that of US consul in Liverpool. We found Owen Lattimore living in retirement in Norfolk, he and his wife having quit the US after a gruelling eighteen months of government loyalty tests and endless committee hearings into his actions as principal US advisor to Generalissimo Chiang. At the height of the debate over who was to be blamed for 'losing' China, Lattimore was denounced as 'the top Soviet spy in America' – a title habitually overused by McCarthy – leading to his ejection from his post as consultant to the State Department and the ruin of his academic career. In England, he became the first professor of Chinese at Leeds University, spending twelve years in Yorkshire between 1963 and 1975. I can remember his nostalgia when he spoke of the China he had known in the 1920s, when he and his wife Eleanor lived in Beijing, then a must-see destination on the world tour for the Scott Fitzgerald generation of the rich and young. He told me how his chef would cook their American visitors a dish containing scores of roasted garlic cloves, which surprised them as a new and delicious taste that left no odour on their breath. However, after an energetic night spent dancing at the city's night clubs, every pore in their bodies exuded the same universal smell of garlic which is such a repugnant feature of any Chinese crowd to this day.

One of the things I most love about America is that it always produces individuals who passionately believe in lost causes. One of the most notable of these naysayers, until his death in 2008, aged eighty two, was the colourful Right wing journalist, magazine-owner, yachtsman and would-be politician, William F. Buckley, whom I went to see in New York to discuss his view that the actions of the old China hands had indeed been injurious to the interests of the United States. Buckley marched up and down his large office as he made his points, but I was distracted when I noticed something amiss about his appearance, pondering how I might tell him without causing too much embarrassment to either of us. I opted for the precedent reputedly set by Winston Churchill, who had responded in similar circumstances by remarking, 'Old birds don't fall out of their nests'. Some time later, I received a cutting from Buckley's column in the National Review, the magazine he owned, telling his readers that 'a young, Leftie reporter from the BBC' had 'had the effrontery to point out that my flies were undone'.

The China programme had the Biblical title, Without Honour, which caused no kind of stir until, many months later, someone in the BBC's current affairs department needed to look up a recording of the programme. It could not be found, but when it eventually come to light, it transpired that it was misfiled as Without Humour.

I momentarily thought of suing the Beeb for libel.

The World Tonight gave me my first experience of live interviewing on radio, after veteran presenter Douglas Stuart retired. It is a tense, nerve-shredding process, a combination of one's first wait in the corridor outside the headmaster's study for a beating, first invitation to a girl to dance, first job interview or discussion with a bank manager about an unauthorised overdraft. It's a kind of three-dimensional chess as you concentrate on what the interviewee is saying while thinking of your next question, and the one after that, sometimes reading a scribbled note or interpreting frantic signals from a producer through the glass dividing the studio from the rest of the suite, plus the constant awareness that the time available is strictly limited.

Sudden breaking news events were the most difficult, when the scripted introductions you'd hammered out were tossed aside, along with the previously agreed running order for the programme. On 4th May 1982, during the Falklands War, the news that the destroyer, HMS Sheffield had been struck by an Argentine Exocet missile arrived just as the programme was starting. A confusion of interviewees from the Navy, the Institute for Strategic Studies, and both sides of the House of Commons, joined me, one after another, in the studio, their names written in capital letters on a piece of paper held up to the glass screen.

The programme went by in a blur, but what helped me through was experience: only four months earlier I had been happily coasting along when a news flash arrived that an airliner with seventy four people aboard had crashed into the Potomac river in Washington DC, two miles from the White House. We had some marvellous young researchers, reporters, producers and trainees, men and women, on The World Tonight, including Harry Schneider, an expert on Germany, Dominic Lawson, son of Nigel and brother of Nigella, and later editor of the *Sunday Telegraph* and the *Spectator*; Tony Hall, who would later emerge as administrator of the Royal Opera House, as well as – continuing the artistic theme – a senior presenter, John Tusa, who after heading the BBC's *World Service*, would run the City of London's arts centre at the Barbican. Everyone on duty on the night of the Washington crash made sure that within minutes I was talking to eye-witnesses and aviation experts they had conjured up even while attempts were still going on to pull survivors out of the icebound river. Sixty nine passengers and crew on the plane perished, along with four unfortunate motorists who were driving over the 14th Street Bridge at the fateful moment.

One small responsibility, privilege even, was attached to working on The World Tonight. A minute or so before the end of the programme one would be handed the news headlines to read, and to avoid overrunning the allotted time one or two items would occasionally need to be deleted from the list. Being of a republican inclination at that time – I have since recanted, mainly at the prospect of a politician (imagine President Blair) as head of state – I would make a point of excising any reference to the Royal Family. Had these stories been important, I reasoned, they would have been not at the end, but the top of the running order.

As smooth-running a radio programme as it was, The World Tonight did have its disasters. Once, with Karolyn Shindler, an excellent producer I often worked with (our rare disputes were known in the office as Shinpats), we went to 10 Downing Street to interview Alan Walters, Mrs Thatcher's economic adviser.

Mr Walters was in his usual spiky form defending the PM's

economic views with vigour, whether or not they chimed with the views of then-Chancellor of the Exchequer, Nigel Lawson. When we emerged from Downing Street it was rush hour and taxis were unobtainable, so we took the underground back to Broadcasting House. Arriving, Karolyn switched on the BBC standard issue Swiss-made Uher tape recorder to play over a sample from the interview to Alastair, hoping he would make it the lead item on that night's programme. But the tape was blank. The subsequent inquest into this mishap found that the recording had been wiped, either by the electronic anti-terrorist counter-measures at Number 10, or it was all my fault for placing the heavy Uher, which I had chivalrously been carrying for Ms Shindler, on the floor of the underground train where the tape was corrupted by the motors beneath the carriage.

Chapter 25

IT might seem churlish for someone who earned his living from journalism for just short of sixty years between 1948 and 2007, to assert that by his own estimation his career actually came to an end nearly twenty years earlier when he became TV critic for the *Daily Mail*.

I had joined the *Mail* as industrial editor in 1985, just as the tragic, year-long miners' strike was collapsing – tragic because of the hardship it wreaked on the mining communities as Mrs Thatcher pressed home her advantage against the ineptitude of Arthur Scargill, until the coal industry was all-but destroyed.

Once the strike was over, I realised that Mrs Thatcher had shot the labour correspondents' fox, so that our job, having rivalled in status, even occasionally dominated that of the top dog political correspondents, would now diminish. In the meantime, leaving the excellent David Norris, my deputy at the *Mail* (who'd had a splendid reporter's war in the Falklands) to comb the domestic battlefield for the dead and wounded in the aftermath of the strike, I started to explore and expand the possibilities, finding reasons to go to the US, Japan, Russia, and even Australia on various assignments that could optimistically be construed as laying down a new and exciting pattern to enable industrial correspondents to wean themselves off purely labour relations matters.

On the last of these journeys, in August 1986, my task was to write about an economic recession in Australia, with particular emphasis on the criticisms expressed by a Down Under politician, that the Australian workforce was disinclined to work.

Unwisely letting slip a mild expletive in the course of a radio interview on my first night in Melbourne, I learned that accompanying the well-known Australian robustness of language is a surprising prudishness when they hear even the least offensive of swear words from the lips of those who appear on radio or TV. Basking in my immediate unwonted fame, I allowed myself to be goaded into repeating the offence on a breakfast TV show in Sydney: very odd, as my friends and family would attest, for I rarely swear. I was immediately snapped up for a week by the country's leading current affairs programme, Sixty Minutes, as a promising Pommie object of ridicule. First, I was filmed at a hotel drinking champagne and eating fois gras (at the programme's expense) as though I were a jumped-up envoy from the colonial power, before being marched off to debate the supposed Australian propensity for work avoidance. I started with the dockers, or wharfies, in Sydney, and over lunch with a man called Doyle who ran a fish restaurant on a promontory of the city's great bay: he affably informed me that Australians were not yet ready to accept criticism from representatives of nations who had yet to master the art of 'building a brick dunny', which he interpreted for me as an outside lavatory: I assured him that the British had long since acquired that skill.

I also interviewed a group of young women sunning themselves midweek on Bondi beach, asking them why they were not at work. Their spokesperson told me, 'We're chucking a sickie, thanks to our wonderful trade union negotiating so many days a year when, whether we're unwell or not, we're entitled to call in sick.' I followed that with an on-camera chat with a man wearing nothing but a pair of shorts and a bush hat as he idly surveyed quite the scruffiest beach I'd ever seen, informing me, as he stretched and yawned under the hot sun, that his job was to keep the beach clean. Everything I learned naturally went into my despatches to London, the time difference making it easy to spend my days filming and evenings writing for the *Mail*, and out of habit, a piece on a different subject for the *Spectator*.

Unlike the BBC documentary programmes I was accustomed to, the Sixty Minutes crew took a delight in including in their finished film a momentary lapse of memory on my part – I had been unable to recall the name of the Australian historian, Geoffrey Blainey, whose history of the dominion, Tyranny of Distance, I had read before I left London. My mouth hung open when I was asked for the name of the traitorous academic from whom I had received my strange ideas about Australia. Assuming from the director's obvious pleasure over this faux pas that he wished to play it rough, I regarded it as a challenge when the moment came for me to sum up my findings on Australian laziness, or 'bludging' in the local parlance, in a final interview. Against the background of the Sydney opera house sprawling like a giant concrete armadillo, I recalled for my Antipodean audience an old story about Noel Coward once being baited by the Sydney press, with an aggressive reporter demanding, 'You're supposed to be a comedian, Mr Coward – why don't you say something funny?' 'Certainly,' he responded – 'Aws-tralia!' And I was on the next plane out.

I thought that my world tour at the *Mail*'s expense was not going to be extended indefinitely, and nor was it. In the spring of 1987, the paper's TV critic, Herbert Kretzmer, a highly regarded and popular journalist, already famous as a song lyricist from his partnership with the French singer Charles Aznavour, gave up TV reviewing, presumably, we all thought, because he had, or was about to become rich from his work on the hit musical, Les Miserables (just as my old friend James Fenton was enriched by earning a share in the same show, the difference being that it was Kretzmer's lyrics that eventually made it to the stage).

Understandably, Kretzmer didn't hang around for long, obliging *Mail* editor David English to take emergency action to ensure the continuation of the daily column of TV criticism. He decided that the paper's specialist writers on various subjects should each produce nine hundred words of opinion on what viewers had watched the previous evening. When my turn came, there was one programme that obviously had to be reviewed, an ITV production of Evelyn Waugh's novel Scoop, a task enriched, perhaps, by my having briefly met the late (Lord) Vere Rothermere, chief of Asscociated Newspapers, founder of *The Mail on Sunday* and descendant of Lord Northcliffe, the pioneer of the modern popular newspaper and, it's said, Waugh's inspiration for Lord Copper, proprietor of the *Daily Beast* in Scoop.

Along with a dozen members of the *Mail's* editorial staff I had been invited to dinner in Rothermere's suite in the paper's old building off Fleet Street. Towards the end of the evening, I, along with the paper's hugely popular sports writer, the late Ian Wooldridge, simultaneously felt the need for a comfort break and were directed towards the facilities by the butler. Unfortunately, we lost our way before finding a small room equipped with a Belfast sink pitched a little too high on the wall to be of use to us, and a draining board on which was perched a large, beautiful silver-gilt bowl which we made use of. Before returning to the dining room we read the inscription on the bowl, discovering that it was the award for the Newspaper Boy of the Year – one of Lord Rothermere's favourite benefactions, according to Ian. We instantly swore an oath not to tell anyone the story for fear that it might find its way into *Private Eye* magazines' press column Street of Shame.

Waugh's 1938 satire on Fleet Street and war had long been a sacred text for journalists, an hilarious tale of confusion, mischance and incompetence in the press coverage of a small war in Africa, clearly a picture of Mussolini's annexation of Ethiopia in 1935 and 1936 which Waugh had covered for *The Times*. Its naïve hero, the young nature correspondent, William Boot of the *Daily Beast*, having been confused with a more eminent journalist of the same surname and sent off to the war with a mountain of equipment covering all possible eventualities, had long been identified as a portrait of Waugh's fellow scribbler in Abyssinia, William Deedes, destined to become a Cabinet minister and editor of the *Daily Telegraph*.

When I saw the programme I was aghast that Waugh's mordant humour had been transmuted into what I thought was a standard TV comedy send-up, despite the expenditure of £2.5 million on the project. It also taught me the first law of TV reviewing – the worse the programme, the better the review. This may be because the English language is far richer in negative terminology than for songs of praise. So given the choice, the critic confronted by two peak hour programmes will naturally devote most of his space to the inferior production, regardless of acquiring a reputation as a curmudgeon.

The upshot of my own 'Boot moment' was that David English invited me to lunch at the Savoy Grill and offered me the job of TV critic, together with a pay rise. After a pleasant hour or so of chat, as we prepared to leave I remembered something I had failed to mention earlier. Apparently thinking I was trying to improve on the offer he had made me, he looked distinctly tetchy. I told him I did not possess the basic tool for the job, a TV set (I'd watched Scoop in a small office at the *Mail*). A shiny new set was delivered to my flat next morning, but I wore that one out, along with several others, before I finished my long stint as a member of the TV chapter of the carp of critics.

It was not the job I would have chosen for myself, or even dreamed of having, but the price of industrial reporters was falling and that of TV critics on the rise. I consoled myself that it was still reporting of a kind and the range of subjects could hardly have been wider, but a solitary existence all the same, lacking the human contact and excitement I'd enjoyed all my working life.

There was an impression among the *Mail's* readers, and one's friends, that a TV critic sat up every evening drinking whisky and watching the programmes he, or she, had selected for review, before burning the midnight oil to compose a column ready for the following morning's paper. This is indeed how it happened in the early days of TV reviewing, with pioneers like the *Mail's* Peter Black and the *Guardian's* Nancy Banks-Smith enduring such a nocturnal existence.

By the time I started reviewing, however, programmes were shown in advance to the critics in one of several tiny viewing theatres in Soho, also used for the same purpose by film critics, or at the swanky Piccadilly premises of Bafta, the British Academy of Film and Television Arts, home of the Bafta awards.

This system was unable to cope with the sheer expanding number of TV programmes available for review, so we were obliged to visit the BBC or the London offices of the individual ITV companies and Channel Four to view their programmes. I quite liked sitting in some executive's office while his secretary padded to and fro with coffee and biscuits while I lounged in front of the TV set. At the Shepherds Bush headquarters of BBC television, by contrast, we would be ushered into bleak basement 'viewing rooms' by a commissionaire or a press officer and left to view the programmes we had asked to see. One day, I was in the usual state of solitary confinement watching a gangster drama when a comely girl from a women's magazine entered the room and expressed her disappointment, with a petulant tossing of curls, that she'd thought the facilities would be vacant. Assuming that I'd got the drift of the programme I was watching, which had only a few minutes remaining, and guessing that it was inevitably heading for a happy ending, I gallantly halted the tape at once and handed over the room to her. Later in the day I wrote and transmitted my review and, that evening, far too late to be sending corrections over for an item that had long gone to press, I caught the final moments I'd missed in the viewing room. To my horror, the story ended with the central character, whose gloriously tranquil future I had confidently forecast in my column, being blown to pieces. Curiously, I didn't receive a single letter of complaint, either from the programme's makers or a reader.

An absence of complaints was not, however, the response to my review, three years into my new role, of the four-part Gothic drama series, Gormenghast, based on the works of Mervyn Peake, which clearly didn't go down well with *Mail* readers, who wrote in large numbers to disagree with my enthusiastic verdict. I've no intention of offering an overview of the more than 7,000 TV programmes I must have reviewed, but the drama that sticks in my memory for its acting, production values and all-round brilliance was Gormenghast, adapted by Malcolm McKay from Peake's great bubbling stew of fantasy and make-believe, marvellously performed by, among others, Jonathan Rhys Meyers, Celia Imrie, Ian Richardson, John Sessions, June 'Dot Cotton' Brown, Christopher Lee, Zoe Wanamaker, Lynsey Baxter, Fiona Shaw, Stephen Fry, Martin Clunes, with a cameo by Spike Milligan as De'ath. The very names of the characters made one drool: Lord Sepulchrave and Lady Gertrude, the Earl and Countess of Groan; Dr Prunesquallor, Steerpike, Nannie Slagg, Rottcodd, Mollocks, Mule, Perch, Fluke, Shred, and The Fly. I used to rail in my columns against the showing of frequent repeats, particularly in the summer months, when I would imagine TV executives taking themselves off to the Riviera thinking to themselves, in the spirit of Kingsley Amis, 'Sod the viewers'. But I admit, if there's one repeat I'd opt for as a Desert Island choice, it would be Gormenghast.

Once video players became the norm, the TV companies (including the BBC) bombarded the critics with dozens of videos each week of shows that for years had been the standard – or sub-standard - fare of daytime television for the unemployed, the housebound and the elderly - cookery in all its forms, antiques fairs, travel, quizzes and so on – a diet that, with the decline of drama, has weirdly been transmuted into dominant peak-time viewing.

What was never in doubt was the sheer hard work involved in reviewing several TV programmes a day over a four-day period week after week (though I did manage in my spare time to write a biography, published in 1993, of the late politician George Brown). An hour of TV can take up to three hours to view, depending on the complexity of the content, and is very difficult to do without switching the tape backwards and forwards and taking notes. Wading through two or three programmes in succession, even if only one is worth watching, can be wearisome indeed: switching on the TV in one's leisure time was out of the question, and an ability to write swiftly turned out to be the greatest asset I possessed.

There's no doubt in my mind that the standard of TV deteriorated year by year during my time as a columnist on the subject. The biggest culprit was the arrival of 'reality', or as I prefer to call it, 'zoo' television, in all its forms, the worst example being Channel Four's Big Brother, arriving in 2000 to pollute the airwaves, followed by its 'celebrity' variations. Only once or twice did I ever watch this mindless and degrading spectacle of voyeurism, humiliation, bullying, exhibitionism and the ever-present but thankfully never fulfilled prospect of the inmates of the Big Brother house having sex with each other. I declined to review it, nor was there any need, as the tabloids eagerly opened their pages to the daily outpourings of the spiteful, sometimes violent, always tearful and self-regarding antics of a revolving seasonal population of misfits, show-offs, sociopathic unknowns and, as an occasional change, D-list celebrities.

I have always believed, in a romantic way, that the role of newspapers is to report the news honestly and fairly, to right wrongs and pursue wrongdoers, to campaign for good causes, chivvy our legislators to take notice of the public's needs and wishes, and celebrate society's unsung heroes – as we did prior to the Age of Meaningless Celebrity, since when the unsung, in a reversal of the Sermon on the Mount, instead of inheriting the earth were ousted to make way for the somewhat too well-known.

I have admired so many wonderful newspaper stories – to pick just one at random, the exposure of the thalidomide medical disaster in the 1970s by the *Sunday Times* - that generated a tremendous feeling of pride in being a journalist.

I would choose three more examples of absolutely outstanding stories that came into the same category, none of which I was involved with, but all unmistakeably newspaper stories rather than prime TV moments such as the assassination of President Kennedy, the Moon landing, and the 9/11 World Trade Center massacre.

On Sunday 10th June 1956, the *Observer* threw out the contents its readers would normally expect to see on a Sunday morning – news, book reviews, arts coverage, fashion, bridge, even lucrative columns of advertising - to devote the entire issue to just one story. This was the 'secret speech', smuggled out of Moscow three months after it was delivered by Nikita Khruschev to the 20th annual Congress of the Communist Party of the Soviet Union.

In the speech, Khruschev confessed to the millions of deaths caused by Joseph Stalin's monstrous famines, death squads and gulags. In judging its importance and the rightness of the *Observer's* decision to publish it in full, there's no doubt the Soviet audience contained many, including the man who was addressing them, who had themselves participated in these crimes as executioners or accessories. In a longer perspective, who can now doubt that the speech was the first blow to the foundations of the Soviet dictatorship, indicating a loss of nerve despite future successes in rocketry in the sixties and seventies, would inexorably lead to its collapse three decades later? I like the story that one of editor David Astor's executives warned him that the decision to consign the entire paper to the 24,000-word speech meant that were the Queen to die on the Saturday night before they went to press, 'she'll only get one line'. He went ahead anyway: a newspaper-owner's prerogative.

The second of these (to me) landmark stories took place many years after the others. It was the decision by Paul Dacre, English's successor as editor of the *Daily Mail*, exasperated by the inability of the police and the courts to bring five alleged suspects in the murder of black teenager Stephen Lawrence to justice, to present his front page as a Wanted poster denouncing the quintet by name as 'murderers' on 14th February 1997, declaring, 'The *Mail* accuses these men of killing. If we are wrong, let them sue us'. Other, perhaps jealous, editors complained of 'trial by media', or pointed out that Dacre was on personal terms with Stephen's father, as though this represented an untenable conflict of interest: would that more newspaper editors were personally acquainted with victims of injustice. I thought it was a magnificent gesture exposing the failure of the Metropolitan Police and the Crown Prosecution Service to deal with a deeply troubling murder, which remains unpunished to this day. I immediately wrote a note to Paul Dacre congratulating him – the first and only such letter I sent to any of editors I have worked for.

But the greatest in the trio of stories I have picked out as inspiring examples of the Press at its very best was the sensational barrage of charges levelled against the honesty, integrity and basic common sense of nearly half the members of the House of Commons, from all parties, in May 2009 by the *Daily Telegraph*, followed up each weekend by its Sunday partner. The story, running day after day for an unprecedented four weeks, turned Parliament upside down and led to the end of a number of political careers, including that of Michael Martin, the first Speaker to be driven from office since 1695. The *Telegraph* did not deal in the weasel word 'alleged', or its variants that Fleet Street traditionally bespatters over its stories to protect itself against libel actions and contempt of court. The facts and figures they deployed were unchallengeable, coming straight from a source close to the Fees Office of the Commons, the institution which vetted MPs' various forms of allowances and expenses to ensure they were 'wholly and exclusively' connected with the performance of their parliamentary duties.

The paper had unchallengeable evidence in its hands - a computer disk containing the intimate details of every MPs charges on the taxpayer, revealing an astonishing shopping spree on the public purse by many of our politicians, including the most highly-placed. Some of their claims (a few of which were turned down but had nevertheless been presented for payment) were risible – payment for the cleaning of a moat around a country house; a rug bought from a New York antiques market, plus customs and shipping charges; the purchase of tons of horse manure; the elimination of dry rot in an MP's house a hundred miles from her constituency; and almost universally, £400 a month for food with no receipts required or presented. Other claims were simply shameful – the Home Secretary's husband-cum-employee renting blue movies, or an Honourable Member trying to reclaim the cost of Remembrance Day poppies at a time when soldiers were coming home from Iraq and Afghanistan in coffins. There were also sheer swindles, such as charging taxpayers for flats for MPs' grown-up children to live in, claims for non-existent mortgages, and the 'flipping' of subsidised homes to make a profit while evading capital gains tax. The *Telegraph's* brilliant scoop – whether they paid an insider for the revelatory disk or not was irrelevant when set against the vital public interest – and the professional way they presented the mountain of astounding information they'd uncovered could not be faulted.

What particularly amused me was that twenty-six years before the expenses scandal broke, I had written a long piece for the *Telegraph* at the request of the then editor, Bill Deedes, on widespread fiddling of expenses by MPs. I revealed comparatively minor wrongdoing without naming names, and could only imply that much worse was going on. I was well aware, too, that the Commons also had the power to punish anyone thought to have brought the House into contempt. (When John Junor, editor of the *Sunday Express*, was summoned before the House for claiming that MPs were being allowed more petrol than the general public during rationing caused by the 1970s fuel crisis, onlookers recalled that the only sound to be heard as he stood at the bar of the House was the knocking of his knees.)

Reporters do, of course, commit their own crimes and misdemeanours. I was guilty very early in my career of a serious breach of trust which I feel uncomfortable about to this day. I had been sent to cover a multiple drowning tragedy, instructed by the news editor not to return to the office without securing photographs of the victims. At the home of one young man who had lost his life I borrowed a picture of the deceased from his parents' mantelpiece, assuring them that it would be returned. Unforgivably, I forgot to make sure it was sent back after it had been through the maw of the production process, and by the time the parents sent me a reminder, the photo had been lost.

I was also once called before the Press Council as a malefactor following a complaint by the Ministry of Defence for a story I wrote in the *Sunday Telegraph* describing the old Woolwich Arsenal, an armaments factory before the site was turned over to housing, as a hotbed of fraudulent practices. I itemised thefts of government property, including the building of a boat – for, of all things, a boy scout troop - from defence ministry materials smuggled piece by piece out of the complex. I also exposed the widespread custom among Arsenal workers of charging spurious overtime for work on 'the Big Gun', a weapon, if it ever existed, that was said to have been produced during the Crimean War.

I appeared in person before the Council (something that, in the early 1970s, had only recently been permitted), where I saw one friendly face on the judging panel, that of Sir Trevor Evans, an old friend from the *Daily Express*. Next to him was the schoolmasterish Sir Lynton Andrews, a former editor of the Yorkshire Post, and retired judge Lord Devlin. It was the presence of the judge, a man of acute intelligence who had once had the power to pass the death sentence, that worried me, though in the event he asked few questions about my case. In the end, the Council found against me on the strange grounds that I had interviewed too few people to stand up my story – unfair, I thought, for how many would be the right number?

Fortunately, it did not prove a hanging matter, and I faced no punishment other than the publication (tucked away in a tiny corner) of the Council's adjudication.

All this was long ago, and as I write this, I am plunged into a state of misery by the condition of the British press, local and national, an institution that has sustained me for so long. I have lived through a number of recessions when the press continued to prosper, trying - unsuccessfully, it must be said, as I described earlier in this book - to launch a new daily newspaper in the midst of the 1970s downturn: I believe the difficulties that confronted me sprang from a perception that irresponsible union power made any such investment unfeasible. Now, it would be the sustainability of the medium itself.

In the much greater financial crisis facing the press today, local newspapers all over the country have been forced to close down or merge with others as their advertising income dried up. Fleet Street, similarly damaged, tried to fend off disaster by culling hundreds of journalists and cutting the wages of the survivors, as well as economising on coverage of the wider spectrum of home and foreign news in favour of witless 'celebrity' stories to restore flagging circulations. Peculiarly, they flirted with the new force, the internet, even as they saw it undermining their own role as primary purveyors of news, by offering their expensive content free on the web, supplemented by blogs written by reporters once they'd completed their stories for the printed newspaper: in my day there were no blogs, and we simply adjourned to the pub to tell our confrères the story behind the story.

I now fear it can only be a matter of time before one or more national titles collapses, squeezed to death by a recession brought about by overspending, over-borrowing and mismanagement on the part of government and a wayward financial industry. It seemed that the only way the newspaper press could survive and once more prosper, as Rupert Murdoch has argued, is by finding ways of making money out of the internet, possibly by denying the great search engines, if they refuse to pay for it, the right to re-publish material the newspapers had gathered. It was Murdoch who rode to a conjectural rescue by charging for access to News International's websites, including the *The Times*, *News of the World*, *Sunday Times* and Wall Street Journal: there are no signs, as yet, that this strategy will work.

What I have tried to convey throughout this memoir – as well as describing an unusual childhood – is the truth of H.L Mencken's observation, that news reporting offers its practitioners more fun than any other calling. Becoming a reporter was far easier when I was young than it is today, and I could scarcely have dreamed when I met Alan Trengove at that dancing lesson in 1948, that he was opening the door to a life that has given me many friends, worldwide travel, encounters with the great and, not least, a huge amount of fun.

I have not climbed to the top of the journalistic tree, and the closest I've come to 'award winning' status is occasionally to have engaged in the throat-cutting exercise of serving on squabbling committees that hand out such awards. As a way of life, journalism was never going to make me rich, but in so many different ways, as H.L. Mencken wrote, and I have been lucky enough to discover for myself, a reporter's life bestows on its practitioners 'the life of kings'.

ENDIT